5.95

UNCOMMON KNOWLEDGE

Judy Lewis

POCKET BOOKS

New York   London   Toronto   Sydney   Tokyo   Singapore

POCKET BOOKS, a division of Simon & Schuster Inc.
1230 Avenue of the Americas, New York, NY 10020

Library of Congress Cataloging-in-Publication Data

Lewis, Judy, 1935–
   Uncommon knowledge / Judy Lewis.
     p. cm.
   Includes index.
   ISBN 0-671-70019-7
   1. Young, Loretta, 1913–   —Family. 2. Gable, Clark, 1901–1960—
Family. 3. Motion picture actors and actresses—United States—
Family relationships. 4. Lewis, Judy, 1935–   —Family.
5. Children of celebrities—United States—Biography. I. Title.
PN2287.Y6L48 1994
791.43′028′092273—dc20
  [B]   93-40262
                                       CIP

First Pocket Books hardcover printing May 1994

10 9 8 7 6 5 4 3 2 1

DESIGN: Stanley S. Drate and Patricia Marcinczuk/Folio Graphics Co. Inc.

For my daughter, Maria, and my son-in-law, Dan,
and my two grandsons, Michael Joseph and
Gregory Daniel, with much love

ACKNOWLEDGMENTS

Many friends have contributed to my life, and some specifically to the creation of this book. I want to thank them with love and appreciation:

Robert Pollack, who twenty-some-odd years ago suggested that I write about my life; Patricia Bosworth for being this book's godmother—without her intervention it wouldn't have been born; Bill Grose, my publisher, whose faith in my story and trust in my ability kept me going during the difficult times; Molly Allen, my editor, whose critical eye and insight helped bring this book to fruition.

For their time, memories, and candor: Margaret Ash, Rosemary Ashley, Gary Crosby, Joe Cohen, Mary Coney, Patricia and Don Bevan, Gretchen Foster, Jack Haley, Jr., Don Robinson, Danny Selznick, Joy Schary, Jill Schary, Jerry Lawrence, Robert E. Lee, Mary Anita Loos, John Newland, and Joseph Tinney.

For their emotional support: to two very dear lifelong friends who have requested anonymity and without whom I would not have been able to continue, I am forever grateful; James Sheldon, who was there when I was in need; Joy and Steven Kabak, whose friendship enriched me; Dee Dee O'Moore, who always encouraged me; Andre Willieme, whose enduring love has brightened and enriched my life and given me a happy ending.

Dr. John Vacarro for leading me to awareness; Susan Buchanan for telling me that I must, Joanna Poppink for showing me that I could, and Davida Bornstein for guiding me through the how.

CONTENTS

CONTENTS X

Later that night I told Joe, "I can't marry you. I don't know anything about myself. You know everything about yourself and I don't know anything about me."

We'd talked about this before and I had told Joe my suspicions about my mother being my real mother, and I had also told him I didn't know who my father was. . . .

Joe listened quietly until I finished and then he said, "You're wrong. I know everything about you."

"What do you mean? What do you know? I don't understand."

"It's common knowledge, Judy."

"What's common knowledge? What are you talking about?"

"Your father is Clark Gable."

Conversation between
Judy Lewis and Joe Tinney,
shortly before their marriage

FOREWORD

≈

I first began thinking seriously about writing this book more than twenty years ago. At that time my world was in chaos. My marriage was ending, and there were other obligations that had priority. So I set the project aside and went on with my life.

Thirteen years later I began to work on it again, but I found I couldn't tell my story without revealing that my parents were two famous movie stars, Loretta Young and Clark Gable. My mother had asked me to keep that a secret. But how could I? For that *is* my story. Because I wasn't willing to risk harming or offending anyone, I stopped once again.

It has taken me all this time to find the courage to write my story the way it must be written, without any lies or evasions. My life has been filled with hypocrisy and deception from the moment I was born.

This personal history is an emotional journey of remembered moments and documented facts. This is so much a story of secrets, of purposely hidden truths, that I have had to arrive at the reality of what actually happened from two directions: the first, the emotional reality, as I remember it; and the second, the facts as I subsequently learned them. Sometimes what I felt and experienced intensely became comprehensible only when viewed from the vantage point of distance. Sometimes my perceptions of reality were further clarified by my personal journals, by letters, or the recollections of other witnesses. And sometimes, when the memory seemed lost, home movies, photographs, and newspaper articles brought back forgotten moments and put them into clearer focus.

My parents were two of the biggest stars of their time. Today my mother still has a following from the days of her television shows, and my father's fame has lived on beyond his death. The situation in which they found themselves in 1935 would not have posed such a problem in the Hollywood of today. But their story was played out in a far more moralistic time and they dealt with what happened in the only way that they felt was open to them. Unfortunately, their decision was not without cost to their child.

UNCOMMON KNOWLEDGE

GONE WITH THE WIND

~

I was in my early fifties before I was officially introduced to my half-brother John Clark Gable. It was in late June 1986 at a special screening of *Gone with the Wind,* held to commemorate the fiftieth anniversary of the publication of Margaret Mitchell's best-selling novel.

I had been invited by Danny Selznick. "They're showing a rare three-strip Technicolor print at the Motion Picture Academy," Danny told me, his voice warm and friendly as always. "A lot of people will be there, including some who were connected with the film. Those few who are still alive," he added with a laugh. "I thought you might enjoy seeing it. And," he went on, "John Clark Gable will be there."

I accepted without hesitation. I had seen John only once, years before, when neither of us knew we were related. This time, only he would be innocent of that fact.

I was very happy that Danny had thought to include me in this special event, and I was really looking forward to being with him. Although he and I had grown up together, we now lived on opposite coasts and it had been a long time since we had seen each other.

In the Hollywood kingdom in which I was raised, Daniel Mayer Selznick was a crown prince. His mother, Irene Mayer Selznick, was the daughter of Louis B. Mayer, head of Metro Goldwyn Mayer and the king of the realm. Danny's father, David O. Selznick, owned his own studio, and had produced *Gone with the Wind*. His uncle, Myron Selznick, had been an agent for my mother, Loretta Young.

May 18, 1939. Danny Selznick's birthday parties were extravagant Hollywood productions worthy of a crown prince. This is Danny and me riding the merry-go-round at his third-birthday party at Summit Drive, Beverly Hills.

Danny and I are the same age, and when I was growing up he was my very good friend. I adored him. Many of my childhood memories of Danny are recorded in photographs and home movies. In one photograph, a little boy of four in short pants stands next to me; I'm dressed in a Dutch costume, complete with wooden shoes. The boy has a wide grin on his face; his tousled hair stands up in front in a cowlick. Like me, he has buck teeth, but mine are worse than his; they stick way out over my lower lip.

In another, taken when we were five or six, we are standing side by side on the sand holding fishing poles, our lines cast out into the Pacific surf. Behind us is the Selznick beach house on Ocean Front, a strip of beach in Santa Monica along the Pacific Coast Highway.

And then, of course, there were all the movies of the children's parties. My mother took them on the 16mm movie camera that she took with her everywhere, even to the studio while she was working on a film. The birthday parties for Danny and his older brother, Geoffrey, were extravagant Hollywood productions worthy of royalty. David O. Selznick brought his finest studio cameraman and all the best equipment and he organized the day's event with a producer's eye for detail.

Actually, the last time I had seen Danny was in a studio screening room. We had talked so many times about those birthday parties that he finally arranged a private screening for as many of us "Hollywood children" as he could round up. In that darkened room I watched the 1930s unfold before my eyes. The era of the movie mogul, men like Danny's father and grandfather, is long gone, but in the silence of that screening room it came to life again as the large expanse of green lawn began to flicker on the screen. The camera focused on the back of the Selznick home on Summit Drive, lingering on the ivy climbing up the trellis of the wide porch that ran the length of the grand Georgian home with its vast grounds shaded by beautiful trees.

Suddenly a door opened. Children came spilling out onto the lawn and surged toward the camera. As they ran, the camera panned to reveal a large swimming pool and pool house decorated with party tables, balloons, and toys. A clown was waiting to greet the children and hand out party favors, while nurses, maids, and butlers mingled with a scattering of parents.

As if on cue, everyone in the screening room suddenly began to talk excitedly. "Who's that little girl with the long pigtails?" someone asked.

"Barbara Warner," Danny replied. Those long dark braids were very much her trademark, and the sight of her brought a rush of memories. Barbara's father was Jack Warner; her mother Ann Page, an actress. She lived in the most magnificent mansion I'd ever seen, filled with paintings by Marc Chagall and Henri Matisse, and there were portraits of her parents, painted by Salvador Dali.

"Is Barbara still living in France?" someone asked. Then I remembered that she had been married to Claude Terrail, the owner of the famous Tour d'Argent restaurant in Paris.

"No, she remarried. She's living in Los Angeles now," Danny replied.

"How about that little thing over there?"

"That's Linda LeRoy. Didn't she have the biggest eyes!"

Linda's father was the director Mervyn LeRoy, and her mother was Harry Warner's daughter. Looking at that petite little girl on the screen, I thought of the beautiful and accomplished woman I had recently seen in a New York restaurant. Today Linda is the wife of Morton Janklow, the very successful literary agent.

"Who's the kid in the fur coat?" someone asked. "She's too young to have a fur coat."

I recognized the child at once. Melinda Markey. Joan Bennett and Gene Markey's daughter. I looked closely, remembering how much I had liked her mother. Both of the Bennett sisters, Joan and Constance, were stars, and great beauties, too. Joan, who had married a number of times, enjoyed being a mother and always paid attention to us children. She had fun at Melinda's parties, leading all the games, even joining in herself.

As I watched the pretty child in the short fur coat I laughed to myself. She *was* too young for a real fur coat, but then so was I when my mother dressed me in Melinda's borrowed fur ski parka, and all her other ski clothes, for our trip to Myron Selznick's lodge in the mountains of Lake Arrowhead.

It wasn't difficult for me to find myself among that crowd of children on the screen. I was on the fringes of it, where I always was. Those birthday parties frightened me. I was smaller than most of the children there, and very timid.

"There you are, Judy, in the pink smocked dress with the white pinafore," Danny announced. "You were always dressed so nicely. And you always looked so poised and self-possessed."

He was right. No one looking at me could know how frightened and shy I was unless they paid very close attention. By the age of four I had already learned to mask my feelings.

As I watched the film a little boy moved away from the center of the crowd and made his way toward me. As he approached, he reached out his hand to me.

"And there *you* are, Danny," I said, as I watched my young self take his hand. The little boy grinned as he drew me with him to join the rest of the party. I remembered how I had felt then. With him holding my hand I was no longer an outsider.

That warm and generous childhood gesture epitomized the Danny I knew then and know today. His is a loving and gentle nature. In a world from which I had felt alienated and separate, he had always tried to make me feel that I belonged. And just as he had included me then, he had done so now, for the special showing of *Gone with the Wind*.

Accompanied by my very dear friend, television director James Sheldon, I arrived at the Academy of Motion Picture Arts and Sciences building promptly at seven, in time for the press cocktail party preceding the film. As we arrived at the front door I heard Danny's voice behind us.

"Wait up, you two. We'll go in together."

He led the way into the spacious and elegant red-carpeted lobby, packed now with people. Photographers were everywhere, their flashbulbs going off in staccato bursts all over the room. A wave of cocktail chatter met us as we waded into the crowd and made our way toward the bar, placed inconveniently at the far end of the room. It was a human obstacle course; James ran interference, with me in tow.

As James and I were working our way through the crush, I spotted Frank Edwards, a photographer I knew and liked, and we stopped to talk. I asked him if any of the cast members was present, since surely he would know.

"Well, the only major star who's still alive is Olivia de Havilland," he replied, "and she's in Atlanta. There's a big celebration there to commemorate this event. But I understand John Clark Gable is here."

"So I've been told."

I didn't want to talk about my half-brother, so I quickly changed the subject. "Is Cammie King here, by any chance?" She had played Scarlett and Rhett's small daughter, Bonnie Blue.

"No. I don't think so," Frank told me.

"Too bad. She's an old friend of mine. We went to Marymount together." It appeared this was going to be a night of memories. As if to reinforce that thought, a pleasantly familiar voice came from behind me. I turned to see William Bakewell, an old family friend. We embraced and I introduced him to James.

"Do you know how long I've known this girl?" Bill said, putting his arm around my shoulder. "Since she was three years old. I even taught her to drive. What are you up to now? Still producing soaps in New York?"

"Not since 1983, when NBC canceled 'Texas,'" I replied. "I'm back here now for good. And I've gone back to school to get my degree in clinical psychology." It all came out in a rush, as if, should I not get it said, it wouldn't be a fact. I had only recently changed my career path and I was uncomfortable talking about it. Putting my present goal into words was new for me.

Bill looked surprised. "I had no idea you were interested in psychology."

"All my life," I replied, not without irony.

Danny Selznick appeared and drew me away. "Would you like to meet John Clark Gable?" he asked.

"Yes! I would, Danny. Very much." My curiosity got the better of me. "What's he like?"

Danny laughed. "I don't know. I only met him myself for the first time tonight. But I do think people related by blood should meet each other eventually, and this time is as good as any."

He already had my hand in his and was leading me toward a small group standing in a quiet corner away from the crowd.

As we got within earshot, Danny whispered over his shoulder, "Don't say anything, I don't think he knows."

Before I could reply we had reached our destination.

"John, I want you to meet an old and very dear friend of mine, Judy Lewis."

A young man of twenty-five turned and faced me. He had blue eyes and dark blond hair and looked exactly like his mother, Kay Gable. I could see very little of our father in his features. He held out his hand to me with a smile. His grip was warm and firm.

"Her mother, Loretta Young, made two pictures with your father," Danny went on. I studied John's face carefully. If he had any knowledge of our relationship I couldn't perceive it; his expression never changed. The name Loretta Young seemed to mean nothing to him. I meant nothing to him. I had often wondered if he had heard rumors of my existence. Had his mother ever told him about me? If she had, there was no indication of it now. He greeted me as he would any other stranger.

He was no stranger to me, however. At one time I had put his picture (given to me by my hairdresser, who also did his mother's hair) into a silver frame and kept it on my desk. I would sit and study the confident-looking young man in the picture and wonder what he was like. I wondered if he missed knowing his father as much as I did. Kay had been pregnant with John when Clark Gable died in 1960. Did John know that I existed and that we had in common a father whom neither of us had known?

Now that I was standing before my half-brother I couldn't say anything to him because of all the lies that had begun so many years before. Once again I had to keep the secret, as I had kept it all my life. I had to pretend that I was a stranger to him when we had the same blood flowing in our veins. I longed to reach out my hand and say "We have a great deal in common. We have the same father." But all I could do was stand there smiling politely while I shook his outstretched hand.

Danny introduced me to John's wife, Tracey, and to his half-sister, Joan Spreckels, and her date, but unwilling to miss this opportunity to get to know John, I concentrated all of my attention on him.

"I just read that you're a new father, John."

He broke into a big grin. "Yes, Kayley is a week old now. We named her for my mother." Kay had died a few years before.

If he found it odd that this total stranger should know about him, he gave no indication. He was probably accustomed, as was I, to having people know a lot about him. It wasn't unusual for the child of a celebrity.

"I understand that you race trucks, John." Over the years I had kept track of John's whereabouts and interests, both through mutual friends and from various items that appeared now and then in the press, but I was not prepared for the passionate enthusiasm that my question prompted.

His entire face lit up and became animated as he described the mechanic's shop and business he owned in San Diego. He told me proudly that he entered truck races all over the country. I remembered that our father had loved motorcycles and cars, that many of his close friends were mechanics, and I wondered whether this passion of John's was inherited or whether it was his way of trying to emulate the father he never knew.

"What about acting? Do you have any interest in being an actor?" I was curious to see if we shared any interests in common. How strong was the genetic thread between us?

"It's funny that you should ask that. I want to start taking acting lessons. I've been offered some parts but I don't want to do anything until I feel comfortable with my work."

As we stood talking, the lights began to dim in the lobby, signaling the end of the cocktail hour. I excused myself and rejoined James, Bill Bakewell, and his wife, Diane. The theater was filled almost to

capacity, but we found seats on the aisle in the middle, a perfect location.

As we settled into our seats I glanced to my left and saw that John and his group were seated at the opposite end of our row. He was in an aisle seat, as was I.

James reached over and took my hand in his. "Well, how did it go?"

"Now I know how everyone else felt when they were with me, knowing who my father was and having to keep it a secret. It's very unsettling. Here I am talking to my own half-brother, saying unimportant things, cocktail chitchat, when I really want to talk about our father. There's so much I want to ask him."

James smiled. "Do you think he had any idea who you were?"

"Not a clue. I was just some stranger, a friend of Danny's."

"What's he like?"

"He's darling. Very unaffected, easy to talk to and warm. Kay did a wonderful job raising him."

As Fay Kanin, vice-president of the Academy, welcomed the audience, I drifted back to my only meeting with Kay Gable. My mother and I had gone to mass at the Church of the Good Shepherd in Beverly Hills. At the end of the services we were coming down the aisle just as Kay and her son, John Clark, were leaving their pew. My mother and Kay, finding themselves standing eye to eye in the main aisle, stopped and shook hands.

Kay put her arm around John, who was then about five years old. "Loretta, this is my son, John Clark Gable." I was aware, even then, of the note of pride in her voice.

"And this is *my* daughter, Judy." My mother stood straight and tall, her gaze steady. The exchange was brief, but I remember it clearly because of the underlying tension between the two women, an almost primal display of their children that I couldn't fully comprehend at the time. It had seemed odd behavior for my mother, who didn't usually push me forward. I didn't have proof then that Clark Gable was my father; although I had been told that he was, until I heard it from my mother's lips I couldn't really believe it. But the keen sense of competition between the two mothers made me wonder then if what I had heard was indeed true.

Now I wonder what my father would have felt if he could have seen the mothers of his two children squaring off in front of their God.

"Tonight we have in the audience the family of Clark Gable." Fay Kanin's voice brought me out of my reverie with a jolt. My heart skipped a beat and I thought it would come through my chest wall. I squeezed James's hand so tightly that he winced, and I felt myself rising impulsively out of my seat.

"His son, John Clark Gable, is here with us this evening." It was then that I realized she wasn't talking about me; she was talking about my half-brother. I turned to my left and saw John rise from his seat and stand up.

The roar of applause began in the back of the theater and rolled forward in a huge wave. I sank against my seat and slipped back into anonymity, letting that sound of public acceptance and adulation wash over me. I felt as if I were engulfed in its turbulence, sinking in the depths of nothingness, of illegitimacy. While hundreds of hands clapped to honor my father's son, I sat drowning in a sense of my own loss and nonentitlement.

For one split-second I had almost claimed my heritage. For one split-second in this theater surrounded by friends and members of the motion picture community, I was part of my family and belonged to my father. For one split-second I was his flesh and blood, I was his daughter, and I was known and acknowledged with applause. But it was a split-second of fantasy and it was over in a flash.

The applause finally subsided and John sat down. As the lights dimmed in the theater, I was grateful for the darkness that hid the tears now streaming unchecked down my cheeks. I sat in the dark and waited to see my father, the father I'd never known.

I had met him once, he even kissed me, this man who now as Rhett Butler was before me on the screen, blown up to immense proportions, bigger than life. He had kissed me once and I didn't know then that he was my father. Now his movies are all I have of him. I look for me in his face. His eyes are my eyes; I have his dark circles. His ears are my ears. His hands are my hands. What kind of a father would he have been? What kind of man was he? And where had he been? Did he want to stay away, or did he feel he had no choice?

I like to pretend when he holds Scarlett in his arms and comforts her that he's holding me, telling me everything is all right, that he'll protect me and bring me home to a safe place.

I like to pretend that he was thinking of me when he played all his scenes with little Cammie King. After all, he knew I existed, he'd even held my infant self in his arms just as he held Cammie. Ironically, in 1939, when the movie was released, Cammie and I were

My father, Clark Gable, with his Gone with the Wind *daughter, Bonnie Blue, played by my friend Cammie King. I like to pretend that he was thinking of me when he was playing his scenes with her.*

the same age. And hadn't he told the Hollywood journalist Adela Rogers St. John, his very close friend, "The only time that I ever saw myself when I thought I had a right to be called a good actor was in the scene when Bonnie Blue died. It was the only thing that I did in my whole career that satisfied me."

When I see him there on the screen, smiling, I like to think that he thought of me and loved me from a distance during his lifetime. I'll never know for sure because he never told me. I'll never know how he felt about me, and so I don't know what to feel about him except a deep, deep sense of loss.

Because I have a child of my own, I wonder each time I look at my father's image on the screen how he could have walked away, leaving everything unspoken and unresolved. No matter how many practical reasons I can produce to answer this question, the feelings of sorrow and loss and abandonment never go away.

That night I could not rise from my seat in the theater to claim him for my own. I could not claim him when I was born, and I cannot now. His son can, his daughter cannot.

When as Rhett Butler he walks off into the fog, turning back toward Scarlett to say, "Frankly, my dear, I don't give a damn," I am left to wonder if my father, Clark Gable, ever gave a damn about me.

2 CALL OF THE WILD

As I sat in the darkness of that theater watching *Gone with the Wind*, I realized once again I was seeing a cinematic legend, a movie that has taken on mythical proportions. Viewed today, the actors, too, have become mythic: lost gods and goddesses from a golden era—all the more so because almost all of them are dead. Like the old South destroyed by the Civil War, Hollywood's golden era—the pre-television days of the twenties, thirties, and forties—has also gone with the wind.

Hollywood of the 1990s bears no resemblance to that of the early thirties, when my mother, beginning to scale the heights at the age of twenty, signed a seven-year contract with Twentieth Century Pictures, the studio headed by Darryl F. Zanuck. This was not my mother's first studio contract. She had begun her career at the age of four, working as an extra in "the flickers," as the silent movies were called in 1917; at fourteen she signed her first contract with First National Pictures, and later, unlike a number of silent film stars, she succeeded in breaking the "sound barrier" into talking pictures. By the 1920s she was playing leading-lady roles with some of Hollywood's most popular male stars.

When she was seventeen and filming *The Second-Floor Mystery*, she eloped with her costar, Grant Withers. At the time he was a bigger star than she was; like her, he had been in silent pictures and had weathered the changeover to talkies. Eight years her senior, he was divorced, the father of a five-year-old son, and had the reputation of being a heavy drinker.

January 27, 1930. My seventeen-year-old mother and her new husband, Grant Withers, with whom she eloped to Yuma, Arizona. Here they are upon their arrival at Los Angeles airport in their chartered plane.

UPI/BETTMANN

Over half a century later, in 1986, my mother talked about this teenage marriage with author Gregory Speck for Andy Warhol's magazine *Interview*. (In it, she refers to herself as being a year younger than she actually was, but that may have been from force of habit, for, like many actresses, she often tinkered with her age.)

> When I was sixteen and, I thought, a big hot movie star, I was doing a picture with a man I thought was gorgeous. His name was Grant Withers. I am, I have to admit, very susceptible to men. I like all men—good, bad, indifferent. I gravitate toward them and find them fascinating, although I don't understand one thing about them. I was reared in a home full of women, since my father was gone from the time I was four. The substitute father I was weaned on, without even knowing it, was God Himself. I said the prayer of Our Father every day, but mine wasn't around, so I had no "father." And my mother would tell me to talk to the Lord about my problems.
>
> Anyway, Grant and I eloped to Yuma, Arizona, when I was sixteen. . . . We were doing a picture together at the time. When we flew back to Los Angeles, the airfield was jammed with the press, and

I saw my stepfather standing there. He had a very serious, perturbed look on his face. I greeted him very gaily, and he gave me a furious look and said, "Your mother wants you to come home, Gretchen, right now!" . . . When we got there my mother looked at me with a hurt, astonished look and said, "Why? Why would you do a thing like this?"

I replied that I was not really married, since it hadn't taken place in a church. I stayed home, without Grant, for four days, and, between you and me, I was delighted to, because I really didn't want to be Grant Withers' wife. . . .

Her mother, Gladys Belzer, filed papers for an annulment of the marriage, claiming that my mother was "too young to assume the responsibilities of marriage." In Arizona the legal age for marriage was sixteen, so she had met the requirements in that state, but in California it was eighteen. However, Grandma dropped the proceedings when my mother defied her and moved into an apartment with her new husband.

Anyway, the marriage lasted for nine months. My mother didn't speak to me for two whole months, and it just made me sick. I went to see a Jesuit priest who used to come to our home every Thursday night as our free private psychiatrist. . . . He said something to me that rang a bell: I was playing at being married in my mind, for as a young actress it was difficult to know where movie acting stopped and the realities of life started. In your own life it's hard to know when to stop acting, because you get so wrapped up in it, so involved in the role.

Father Ward told me I had picked a profession in which my life was going to be very, very public. "Now, you know that rather than give a bad example to others, you should have a stone tied around your neck and be dropped to the bottom of the ocean, as Christ said," he lectured me.

"You have been married two months now, and already I have had two Catholic girls do the same thing, and they say to me that if Loretta Young can do it, and she's a Catholic, they can do it, too. Now, if you don't want to take on this burden, get out of the business right now."

I don't recall a light switching on for me at the time, but in retrospect I believe that was my turning point. In fact, I think it's one of the reasons I never wanted to play evil people in the movies.

When she gave this interview, my mother was seventy-three years old and looking back over her life. It is interesting that she spoke of her teenage marriage as a turning point for her—that when she was only seventeen, a priest whom she had admired and respected called her attention to the fact that she was a public figure and had the power to influence others by her actions; this made an indelible impression on her. Undoubtedly it influenced her behavior when, some years later, she found herself pregnant with me.

Taking Father Ward's advice to heart, as her career developed she chose her motion picture roles carefully, giving attention to their content. At some point fairly early on, she decided that she wouldn't do studio "drape art," the publicity photography that was part of the curriculum for contract actresses, because, as she later said, she felt it was immodest. And when she was at the height of her career, she risked suspensions from the studio and loss of pay because she refused to play roles depicting characters living in an immoral fashion, but this was some years after she agreed to make a movie with Spencer Tracy called *Man's Castle*, in 1933.

The two fell deeply in love, just like the characters they were portraying in the film—two unmarried lovers who live together in a depression shantytown on New York's East River. Ironically, much of the film's dialogue paralleled their true feelings for each other.

At the time, she was a divorced woman of twenty, living at home with her mother and sisters. Tracy, the father of two children, was separated from his wife. However, since the Tracys had been married in the Catholic Church, the Hollywood community was certain they would be reconciled.

A Broadway star, Tracy had been in Hollywood for three years when he and my mother began working together. He was an unhappy and moody Irishman, with a reputation for having a serious drinking problem. Many years later my mother told me, "Spence was a darling when he was sober. He was absolutely awful when he was drinking."

Although they continued to see each other after they finished the film, there was no way to avoid the pressures that society put on them. There was no divorce for Catholics in those days, and so there

My mother and Spencer Tracy fell in love, just like the characters they portrayed here in Man's Castle.
SPRINGER/BETTMANN

was no hope for my mother and Spencer's relationship. In the late summer of 1934, Spencer Tracy reconciled with his wife, and he remained married to her for the rest of his life. It is my belief that it was my mother who encouraged him to return to her.

More than personal morality assuredly went into this decision, for Hollywood in the thirties was in the midst of a censorship crisis that extended beyond the movies and into the lives of the stars. Today's open lifestyle, where every intimate detail of a celebrity's life is written and talked about, is a far cry from the moral climate of the Hollywood into which I was born. The "constricted 1930s" was the product of a succession of scandals, beginning in the '20s, that involved several well-known film stars—among them Roscoe "Fatty" Arbuckle, a famous three-hundred-pound comedian in whose hotel room a film extra and sometime call girl named Virginia Rappe was found dead; and director William Desmond Taylor, whose unsolved murder ended the careers of actresses Mabel Normand and Mary Miles Minter.

To counter all the negative publicity about Hollywood, labeled the "graveyard of virtue" by one national publication, a group of industry leaders formulated the Motion Picture Production Code between 1927 and 1930 to enforce self-censorship. They selected former Postmaster General Will H. Hays to represent the industry.

The code, which came to be known as the Hays Code, was adopted not out of a sense of industry morality—Hollywood had little of that—but as a means of self-preservation. It contained three general clauses: no picture shall "lower the moral standards of those who see it," portray other than "correct standards of life," or ridicule natural or human law. It was particularly stringent where sex was concerned, and it was this aspect of the Hays Code that spilled over into the private lives of the stars and influenced their actions.

In 1935, when my mother and my father met on Mount Baker in Washington State to film *Call of the Wild*, they were both internationally famous movie stars. My mother, who celebrated her twenty-second birthday on January 6, 1935, had been in films for eighteen years.

But despite all her successes, my young mother brought insecurities and the memory of painful losses with her to the top of Mount Baker. She had behind her a broken marriage that had been both impulsive and impractical. Grant Withers had failed to provide the emotional support she wanted. Instead, he spent her money and took care of himself, later branding her "The Steel Butterfly" in the bargain. (Many years later, long after he had left pictures, he was to die by his own hand.)

The next time she fell in love, it was with Spencer Tracy. But that love was forbidden by her church. Her need to be taken care of had still not been satisfied. She was lonely and emotionally vulnerable.

On February 1, 1935, less than a month after my mother turned twenty-two, my father had his thirty-fifth birthday. At the party given for the cast and crew of *Call of the Wild*, both of the film's stars had much to celebrate. My father was at the peak of his career. He had won great financial success at no small cost to himself—and to a great many other people as well, most of them women.

Unlike my mother, who worked only in films, Clark Gable—who grew up in the oil fields of Oklahoma with his wildcatter father, William Gable, and his stepmother, Jennie Dunlap—began his career on the stage. As a young man he went to Portland, Oregon, where he auditioned for the Astoria Players Stock Company in 1922. Thanks to the intercession of Franz Dorfler, a beautiful twenty-two-year-old ingenue, he joined the company, under the name of Billy Gable. The company dissolved, but the love affair between the two young actors did not; they planned to be married. While Franz was touring with another company, she urged "Billy" to get in touch with Broadway actress and teacher Josephine Dillon, who was starting a theater group in Portland.

As it turned out, Billy Gable didn't marry Franz. Instead, when Josephine Dillon went to Hollywood in the summer of 1924, he followed her and five months later they were married; he was twenty-four and she was forty. She paid all his bills and arranged for him to work as an extra in films while she coached him.

Clark Gable, the name he now used, went back to the theater and toured in plays, while Josephine stayed behind in Hollywood. In 1928 he made his Broadway debut in *Machinal* to good reviews; women flocked to see his performance.

He was separated from Josephine by the time he met Ria Langham, a divorced Texas heiress, eighteen years his senior, and the mother of two children. When Clark divorced Josephine and married Ria in 1930, there were those who commented that he "married up." While there is no doubt that he enjoyed the status that Ria's money and social position afforded him, it is equally clear that she enjoyed the cachet of being Mrs. Clark Gable.

Yet another important woman came into Clark Gable's life at this time: Minna Wallis, a well-connected Hollywood agent. But the happy connection with his agent was not to last. In 1934 he left

Minna to sign with another, larger agency. That he and Minna remained close friends all of their lives is, I would assume, a tribute to the magnitude of his charm and appeal. While Clark's status in Hollywood was not acquired instantly—and certainly he did much to earn it—there is no question that he had two wives and one devoted agent dedicated to his advancement.

And, of course, there were other women lavishing attention on him, among them Joan Crawford. She and my father had made two films together before they were teamed in *Possessed.* From the moment Joan first saw him, she was in active pursuit, even though she was married to Douglas Fairbanks, Jr. But until *Possessed* got under way the attraction wasn't mutual. And at this point, Crawford's marriage was ending so she was available. It began to be rumored that she and Gable were having an affair.

While the studio had never denied Clark Gable was married, it also simply never bothered to mention it. Now, because of the Gable-Crawford rumors, Ria was officially launched as Mrs. Clark Gable, with Louis B. Mayer's blessing. She and her children went on a high-profile publicity tour arranged by the studio. Mayer enjoyed playing a paternal role in the lives of his actors and actresses, and he also cared about the "family" of stars and the image his pictures portrayed of family life.

Happily for Mayer, Clark finished the picture *and* his affair with Joan Crawford simultaneously. Ria returned from New York and the couple appeared together in public. Everyone seemed satisfied.

But Clark Gable wasn't. Among other things, he wanted and demanded more money. To punish him, Louis B. Mayer loaned him out to Harry Cohn, president of Columbia Pictures, for what he considered an insignificant comedy called *It Happened One Night,* to be directed by Frank Capra.

The rest, as they say, was history. *It Happened One Night* opened at Radio City Music Hall on February 23, 1934, and was an overnight success. It was just what moviegoers were looking for—comic relief from the depression days of unemployment, soup lines, and homelessness. Clark Gable got an Academy Award nomination for Best Actor and the raise that he had requested.

By the time he arrived in Washington to begin filming *Call of the Wild*, Gable was earning $3,000 a week, an enormous salary for the time. Other areas of his life, however, left something to be desired. After two marriages to much older women, he was still searching for his soulmate. He had yet to find her, and he was restless.

When the cast and crew left the town of Bellingham in northern Washington to begin the sixty-mile journey to their destination, Mount Baker Lodge, no one was prepared for what lay ahead. Midway up the mountain, the entire company was stranded by the worst blizzard the area had sustained in twenty years. Snow plows were sent for so that the company of one hundred fifty people could proceed to the final location site, and once they arrived there was nothing to do but sit and wait out the weather.

What had originally been planned as a ten-day location schedule extended for months. Everyone's nerves were on edge, especially director William Wellman's. Not only was the weather delaying his film, but so was the behavior of his leading lady and leading man. For the first time in his career, Clark Gable was acting unprofessionally, arriving hours late and holding up shooting.

William Wellman was contending with more than blizzards: he had a burgeoning love affair on his hands, one that is reflected in the movies my mother made on location. I grew up watching my mother's home movies; photography was her hobby, even back in the thirties. Yet it was only recently that I saw the film she shot while she was making *Call of the Wild*. Perhaps she had her own reasons for not wanting me to see it.

Watching it, I was able to get an idea of what she was feeling while she was with Clark Gable on Mount Baker. The camera doesn't lie; it records thoughts and feelings via expressions, as well as intimate moments.

In one playful sequence she has sneaked up behind Gable and called his name. As he turns around, he smiles and sticks his tongue out at her. The camera comes in closer and closer until it frames his mugging face in a large close-up. In another sequence, he is hidden by a snow fence with only his head showing. The camera lingers for a long time and finally he blows a kiss in its direction. But there is a

My mother and father's romance began during the filming of Call of the Wild. Here they are shown as on-screen lovers.

telling sequence taken by someone else. My mother sits bundled in fur from head to toe, wearing dark glasses to protect her eyes from the glare of the snow. She is sitting facing Clark, her knees and legs enveloped by his. He, too, wears a fur coat, fur hat, and gloves. His long legs shelter hers between them as the two of them sit facing each other, deep in conversation and totally unaware of the camera's intrusion. Jack Oakie sits to one side, and as he looks up and sees the camera, he waves it away with an impatient brushing motion of his hand. The moment was too private to be invaded. The camera had recorded the fact that my mother had fallen in love with my father and that he was in love with her. It had recorded what the entire movie company already knew.

Many years later, in January 1990, my mother gave an interview to *Parade* magazine. The writer broached the inevitable subject of my birth and asked if Clark Gable was indeed my father. According to the journalist, my mother looked at him with a direct gaze and replied, "It was a rumor then, it's a rumor now. I guess it will always be a rumor. And that's the end of it."

In 1935 it wasn't that easy to dismiss. The rumor of their affair grew in strength and fury, setting off an avalanche that careened out of control, down the mountain into the outside world.

When the location filming was completed, what had started as a rumor was now a fact that could not be ignored. A child had been conceived. And that was *not*, as my mother suggested, the end of it; it was just the beginning.

William Wellman wasn't the only person angered by Clark Gable's behavior on Mount Baker. Ria Gable was one of the first to hear about the romance between her husband and his costar. This time it seemed it wasn't just a fling that could be dismissed, as she had dismissed so many before.

She found the perfect opportunity to show the world that the rumors were untrue. A week after her husband left Mount Baker and returned to finish the picture at the studio, the nominees for the 1934 Academy Awards were announced. *It Happened One Night* was nominated for the five most prestigious categories: Best Picture, Actor, Actress, Director, and Writer. One thousand people attended the dinner, Gable and Ria among them. *It Happened One Night* won all five categories, the first time in Hollywood's history that one picture had captured all the awards.

Best Actor Clark Gable had much reason to rejoice. Negotiations began immediately for a new contract at MGM, granting him full star treatment. But my mother had little to celebrate. She had discovered that she was pregnant; she knew the father was Clark Gable.

By the time my mother found out that she was pregnant with me, the Hays Code was solidly in place within the industry. Two years before, in 1933, the Legion of Decency, a Catholic film-reform society, had enlisted the Catholic bishops of America to help boycott unacceptable films (and, by implication, "immoral" actors). In 1934 the production code was rewritten by Father Daniel A. Lord, and a branch of the Hays office, the Production Code Administration, was set up in Hollywood under the supervision of Catholic newspaperman, Joseph I. Breen, to enforce and police the production of every film from beginning to end. Studio contracts now included a new clause, the "morality clause," which could be used to void agreements with actors and actresses who became involved in scandal.

An unmarried movie star, pregnant by a married man, was very definitely a scandal in the eyes of Hollywood, as well as in the eyes of the Catholic Church. My mother, a devout Catholic, was in trouble on both counts.

To complicate matters, she was already weeks late in reporting for her next picture. The shooting schedule on *Call of the Wild* had extended far beyond what had originally been anticipated, and she was committed to begin filming *The Crusades* at Paramount. She and Clark were still secretly seeing each other, although it was extremely difficult now that they were both back in Hollywood.

Clark Gable's next assignment was *Mutiny on the Bounty*. He would be away on location, this time on Catalina Island; it promised to be another long and tedious schedule. Clearly, he had to be told quickly.

But before anyone else learned the news, there was someone my mother had to confide in first. She was full of shame, and horrified at her condition. And she was beside herself with fear. If the fact of her pregnancy was to come out, it would ruin her career, and Gable's as well. There was only one person in the world whom she could turn to, one person who would understand and comfort and guide her in this crisis: her mother, Gladys Royal Belzer.

I can only imagine the feelings my mother had when she told my grandmother that she was pregnant and that the father of her expected child was a married man. Her guilt and remorse must have been overwhelming.

When my mother finally told me the truth about the circumstances of my birth I was in my early thirties, married, and the mother of a daughter myself. She told me that there were no recriminations from her mother. Whatever she might have expected, she learned quickly that her mother was her most steadfast and loyal ally.

Together the two women lost no time in making plans for the difficult days that lay ahead. The first thing on the agenda was to set up a meeting with Clark Gable. He had to be told that he was going to be a father. There was no mention or even a moment's consideration of an abortion. It never even entered the minds of my mother or my grandmother. The Church considers abortion to be murder; life begins at the moment of conception, and I was alive inside my mother.

Given the moral climate that pervaded Hollywood in the thirties, the three people who gathered in the living room of 10935 Sunset Boulevard that evening in early March 1935 must have been very frightened.

I will never know what my father felt when he was told of my existence. I only know what my mother told me, that he turned to my grandmother and said, "I thought she knew how to take care of herself. After all, she had been a married woman."

Although it was too early to form any concrete plans, all three agreed that night to total secrecy. No one must know anything until every possible detail could be worked out. Two careers were at stake, two lives would be drastically changed if any word of my mother's pregnancy got out. Her reputation had to be protected, her privacy ensured; no one must even suspect the truth of my existence, no matter what the cost.

According to my mother, despite his initial reaction my father was cooperative and deeply concerned about her predicament. He was eager and willing to do whatever he could to help. My grandmother promised she would let him know the arrangements once they had been made.

And so began the conspiracy of silence that was to have a most profound effect on all our lives.

3 GLADYS ROYAL, THE MATRIARCH

It was only natural that Loretta Young would turn to her mother, Gladys Royal Belzer, for help when she found herself pregnant. No matter what their previous disagreements had been, she knew that Gladys was the one person in her life who would know how to orchestrate this drama. Gladys had a will of iron that had enabled her to survive a great many disappointments. Whatever her private distress at her daughter's condition, she was too good a Catholic even to consider abortion. On the other hand, she was too much of a realist to do anything but handle the matter pragmatically, for Loretta's career had brought money and comfort to a family that had known hard times.

The relationship between mother and daughter was extremely complex and not without its contradictions, but the bond they shared with each other was nonetheless a strong one. I have no way of knowing what my grandmother felt when she learned the news, any more than I can know how my mother felt when my father's initial response to her condition was to express surprise that she hadn't known how to avoid pregnancy. But it's not hard to imagine their feelings, or to empathize with both women, so alone in their mutual dilemma.

The possibility of a threat to her daughter's career was a clear threat to Gladys, too, and one that she was more than ready to head off. Although Gladys's life was comfortable now that her daughter was a successful actress, it had not always been easy. A Californian by birth, she was the eldest daughter of two transplanted Southerners, Robert Tecumseh Royal, born in Mississippi, and Fanny Watkins, born in Missouri, and to the end of her days she retained their Southern accent as well as some of the more unfortunate prejudices associated with the old South. In the late 1880s, when Robert and Fanny Royal arrived in Los Angeles, California held the promise of a good life. It was a land of opportunity for real estate speculators, with business opportunities not available in the South, which was still recovering from the Civil War. It was a perfect place to settle down and raise a family, which is what the Royals proceeded to do.

Fanny gave birth to her first child, my grandmother Gladys, on

My maternal great-grandmother, Fanny Watkins, posing with her father.
AUTHOR'S COLLECTION

The Royal sisters: Gladys in between Carlene and Cherrie. My mother remarked when she first saw this photo among my grandmother's things, "See how they both lean on Mama."
AUTHOR'S COLLECTION

July 18, 1888, in a hotel of sorts that was in all probability a farm-house. It sat in the midst of fields that were shortly to become the paved streets of the downtown Los Angeles business district. Fanny Royal bore two more daughters, Carlene and Cherrie, before she died in her early twenties in 1893.

Ill-equipped to raise three young children by himself, Robert did the natural thing for a widower of his era: He left his children with a sister living in Kentucky and sometime later transferred them to Fanny's family, leaving them on the Watkins farm in Fosterville, Tennessee. It was Robert Royal who launched the family tradition of the absentee father. By the age of five my grandmother had lost not only her mother but her father as well.

My grandmother was quite closemouthed about herself and her family, as if there were things that she didn't want others to know. At different times in their lives, each of her sixteen grandchildren made efforts to elicit information, in the hope of being able to learn something about the life she had led as a child and young woman, before she became the "Grandma" we all loved. But she cloaked her past in mystery, and much of what I have learned has come in bits and pieces from my cousins and from my uncle and my aunts.

Nonetheless, I do remember Grandma telling me about her youth on the Watkins farm with her Uncle Al and Aunt Lottie. She had such deep feelings for the South that every time she talked about it she made the South come alive for me, and she carried the memory of it with her like a treasured possession. Grandma was a Southern lady—from the light accent she never lost to her gift for Southern cooking. She was in the habit of calling people, no matter what their age, "dear," which came out "deah." Hers was a Southern soul and she viewed the world through a Southerner's eyes.

No one in the family seems to know just how long she and her sisters lived with their aunt and uncle in Tennessee, for Grandma was always vague about time, but it's my understanding that a significant part of their childhood was spent there.

At some point much later, after Robert Royal had remarried, fathered a son, Peyton, and divorced, he reassembled his family and moved them to Denver, Colorado, and it was there in 1907 that

Gladys met and married John Earle Young. They were both nineteen at the time. John's mother, Laura, ran a boardinghouse, which in those days was considered one of the few respectable ways for a woman to earn a living. It is possible that John Earle Young was illegitimate. He got the name Young from his stepfather, whom his mother married when John was a small child.

Like Gladys, John Earle Young was extremely good-looking. John, "the catch of Denver," and Gladys, with her perfect legs, generous figure, and long dark hair, made quite a pair. In the only picture that I've ever seen of the two of them together, they stand, in street clothes, on a beach, a child playing in the sand beside them. Gladys holds a parasol, shielding her face from the rays of the sun. It seemed odd to me to see my grandmother standing beside her husband, for

"The catch of Denver," the very handsome John Earle Young—my disappearing grandfather.
AUTHOR'S COLLECTION

I only knew her as a woman alone, sufficient to herself, with no male in the picture. The Gladys in *that* picture didn't match the powerful matriarch I grew up with.

That youthful Gladys had already sustained quite a few setbacks. According to a story one of my aunts told me, on the night before her marriage, she found out just how much of a ladies' man John Earle was: A young woman who was a boarder in Laura Young's home arrived at Gladys's house and informed her that she was pregnant by John. When Gladys refused to believe her, her visitor baited Gladys with the disclosure that John had a wooden leg. "How could I know that if I hadn't slept with him?" she said triumphantly, assuming that Gladys possessed the same knowledge. Gladys, however, had not been told, and she had no way of knowing, being, like all "ladies" of her day, a virgin.

On her wedding night Gladys found herself staring in disbelief at her new husband's wooden leg, the result of a childhood accident,

My grandmother, Gladys Royal Young, in her youth.
AUTHOR'S COLLECTION

he informed her. John had mastered his handicap so well that no one could know unless they saw him undressed. Whatever her feelings, Gladys did not mention the visitor she had received the night before, nor did she acknowledge to herself what that encounter might mean for the future of her marriage.

A year after her marriage to John, on October 25, 1908, Gladys gave birth to Polly Ann Young. The little girl had dark hair and eyes and looked like her father; he gave her the nickname "Peter Rabbit."

An auditor with the Denver Rio Grande, and Western Railroad,

Gladys Royal Young with her infant daughter, Polly Ann.
AUTHOR'S COLLECTION

John had to travel constantly. In the first few years of his marriage, he was away from home a great deal. By the time Gladys was pregnant again she knew her husband had been unfaithful.

Deeply hurt by his faithlessness, Gladys needed someone to talk to. An Irish Catholic friend suggested a priest he knew and Gladys sought him out. Their rapport was instantaneous, and after a number of visits to the rectory Gladys decided to become a convert to the Catholic Church, for its teachings had given new meaning and purpose to her life. Gladys began her catechism lessons with her new priest friend and was so enthusiastic that John soon joined her and they were baptized together.

Just when Gladys was almost due to deliver her second child, John was relocated to Salt Lake City. Determined to travel with him, she said good-bye to her friends and her father confessor, and, with Polly Ann, set out with John for their new home in Utah.

The family had gotten as far as Salida, Colorado, when Gladys began to have labor pains. They checked into the first hotel they could find and it was there that Elizabeth Jane Young was born on July 11, 1910; as soon as Gladys could travel, she and John, with two-year-old Polly Ann and the newborn baby, continued on their journey.

John found a small house in Salt Lake City, and shortly thereafter his mother, Laura, joined the family. Far from resenting the arrival of her mother-in-law, Gladys was pleased that there would be someone to help her with the two children, since John was so seldom at home.

But Gladys was far from happy when she discovered that she was pregnant yet again. Elizabeth Jane, nicknamed "Bet" or "Betty Jane," was two; and Polly Ann, or "Pol," was four. When friends suggested that perhaps she shouldn't have the baby, Gladys replied that "God will provide," reflecting her firm belief in her new religion. And in later years she was to have reason to rejoice, for He rewarded her with the child she would come to call her "little money-maker."

On January 6, 1913, my mother was born, and she was named Gretchen. With yet another baby, Gladys's days and nights were filled with tending to her children, and as time went by, she became less and less satisfied with her life. To compound her dissatisfaction, she suspected that John was continuing to be unfaithful.

A year later, Gladys found herself pregnant once again, and on October 7, 1914, John Royal Young, nicknamed "Jackie," was born. At twenty-six, Gladys, who had been married for seven years, was the mother of four young children.

When baby Jackie was a year old, Gladys went to visit her sister, Cherrie, in Des Moines, taking Polly Ann and Betty Jane with her and leaving her two younger children in Laura Young's care. Once with her sister, Gladys confided her disappointment in her husband, how every time he was unfaithful some of her love for him died.

She told Cherrie that she wasn't even sure if she wanted to stay married, voicing her deepest fear—that should she ask for a divorce, John would take the children away from her. That thought terrified her. Yet how could she take care of herself and her family? She had no special skills. John had always handled everything.

Cherrie assured Gladys that she would help her get a job, that she

1913. This picture was most likely taken in Salt Lake City, judging by the age of my mother, the bald-headed baby being held by her older sister Polly Ann. Betty Jane stands giggling beside her.

COURTESY OF THE ACADEMY OF MOTION PICTURE ARTS AND SCIENCES

could stay with her as long as she wanted, that Polly Ann and Betty Jane would be taken care of while Gladys was working. Gladys's brother-in-law arranged an interview with the manager of a local department store and she was hired to sell women's gloves. (As a child and a teenager I was constantly being told by Grandma to be sure I had my gloves with me. They were the sign of a lady.)

While Gladys enjoyed her job and liked her independence, she still wasn't ready to abandon her marriage, and so she decided to go back to John and give their marriage one more try. But once back in Utah, Gladys realized that the separation from John, far from helping the marriage, had simply made their relationship more strained.

Her solution was to take another trip, a much longer one, to Los Angeles, and this time all four children went with her. She wasn't sure whether she would ever return to John, but she kept this to herself and simply told him that she was going to visit her sister Carlene and her husband, Ernest Traxler, who had a job at a silent-film studio. The silent films, now in their heyday, had become big business.

Carlene and Ernest lived with their two daughters, Carlene, three, and Valerie, one, in a large enough house on Eighth and Green streets in downtown Los Angeles so that Carlene could take in boarders to help supplement her husband's income.

After a train ride that took days, a weary Gladys and her four youngsters were welcomed into the Traxlers' home. It was like an oasis for Gladys. She had her sister for comfort, and her children had their cousins as playmates.

When John Young realized that his family wasn't coming back, he moved to Los Angeles and found a job as an accountant for a fashionable and elegant club, the Midwick Country Club, in what is now the city of Montebello. Upon his arrival the Young family moved to a small house on Selby Avenue in the heart of Hollywood. It was a perfect location. The Traxlers lived nearby, and Famous Players–Lasky Studio, where Ernest was a production manager and assistant director, was right across the street. (Later that year the sign outside the entrance gates to the studio was changed to read Paramount Pictures.)

About 1918, after my grandmother had moved to Los Angeles. Left to right: Gretchen Young, Polly Ann Young, Betty Jane Young, Carlene Traxler, and Jack Young. The infant in the carriage is Valerie Traxler.
COURTESY OF THE ACADEMY OF MOTION PICTURE ARTS AND SCIENCES

There was money to be made in silent films, and Ernest Traxler was in the perfect position to help out his in-laws, for it was the job of the assistant director to hire the extras for a day's shooting. He had already put his own three-year-old daughter, Carlene, to work, so why not the Young children, even little Gretchen and Jackie? One by one, they were added to the casting sheet at the studio and hired as often as possible; once they were all cast as nymphs in *Sirens of the Sea.*

The Young children enjoyed being in the movies, and it was certainly very convenient; the studio—the biggest, most glamorous playground any child could wish for—was just across the street. Each set provided a new and different world, with a different make-believe game. And to top it off, they got paid for getting dressed up and playing in front of the camera. Mama was always there and

A*bout 1918. The Young children and their cousin in* Sirens of the Sea, *on
location on Catalina Island. Front row, far left: Betty Jane Young; Jack Young,
center, back to camera; Carlene Traxler, holding her costume in her hand; far right,
Gretchen (Loretta) Young.*

sometimes even she got dressed up and entered into the game with
them.

Both Polly Ann and Betty Jane, who by now were attending a
nearby Catholic school, were happy that their father was living with
them again, especially Betty Jane, for she was a very affectionate
child and adored her father. It was she who told me the actual circumstances surrounding her father's departure, a memory so intense
that she could recall the details clearly sixty years later.

According to her account, Gladys found John with the maid, and
in her shock and anger she ordered him out of the house, telling him
that she never wanted to see him. "Then take your last look,
Gladys," he replied. "You never will again." Betty Jane remembered
that she came home from school that day to find her mother sitting

on the front porch. It was a hot day and she was wearing a black-and-white-striped dress, made of a soft, gauzy fabric. She held a matching umbrella to shade her eyes from the glaring California sun, and she was sitting so still and lost in thought that the little six-year-old's heart began to pound. When her father came out of the house and bent to kiss her mother, Betty Jane saw Gladys turn her face away. Both parents stood staring in icy silence, and finally Gladys told her tearful daughter to go inside.

Later that night Polly Ann and Betty Jane waited up for their father. When he finally returned he gave them both some hard candy, embraced them, and kissed them good-bye, saying that he was going on a long journey. They did not see him for thirty-two years, and when they did, he was lying in his coffin, the long journey over.

While Betty Jane holds some treasured memories of her father, her sister Loretta apparently does not. In 1990 she was asked by an interviewer if she was bitter about growing up without a father. "Bitter?" she answered. "That's too strong. I don't remember him at all, so my feelings were just zero. It must have affected me in some way, though. I think I married two people because I hoped they'd take care of me the way my father should have and didn't."

The years may have dimmed my mother's recollection of her father, but I know her feelings toward him weren't "zero," for she once described to me the only vivid memory she had of him.

She was only three when she saw her mother standing on a stepladder reaching into a kitchen cabinet for a jar. Her father firmly lifted her mother down off the ladder. Gretchen flew at him, hitting him with her fists and crying, "Stop hurting my mother." The truth was that he was helping her by getting the jar himself, but Gretchen only learned that years later, when her distrust of men was already firmly in place.

It seems unlikely that my mother's feelings about men came just from her father's defection. Undoubtedly, some message was conveyed by her mother, for no matter how occupied Gladys kept herself, with her children, her home, and her work, she was still unfulfilled in her marriage and resentful of her unfaithful husband.

Toward the end of her life, my grandmother told me that at one point in her marriage she made a nine-week novena. Every day for nine weeks she said prayers and went to mass, seeking guidance. She told me, "I prayed and told the Blessed Mother that I didn't want anything bad to happen to John, I just didn't want to go on living with him." As it turned out, she didn't have to.

In the days following John's departure, while the children waited in hopes of his return, Gladys came to realize what answered prayers could mean. When John Earle Young left he changed the dynamic of the Young family forever. Papa, the provider and protector, became the traitor, the deserter. He left behind a legacy of matriarchal anger and a distrust of men. And Mama, the caretaker, the nurturer, now took full charge.

From what she later said, I have the clear impression that my mother saw John's desertion as did her mother—a cowardly act that robbed the family of dignity. Her sisters, however, seem to have warmer recollections of their father. Jack remembers nothing at all about him. He knows only what he learned from his grandmother Laura, who made an effort to keep her son's memory alive for her grandson. It is my recollection that my grandfather's name was never mentioned. "Out of sight, out of mind," a familiar family saying, certainly applied to John Earle Young.

Gladys may have prayed for relief from an unhappy marriage, but she didn't pray for abandonment and poverty. After the initial shock wore off and she realized that her husband had truly disappeared for good, she faced some important decisions. She was twenty-nine when her husband left, and apart from her brief career working in a store, she had not been schooled in the business world. Now she found herself with no income other than what she could generate; she had only herself to depend on. With no money coming in to pay the rent, obviously the family could no longer continue to live in the house. They would have to move. Again, Gladys prevailed on her sister Carlene for assistance, and she and her four children moved back into the Traxler boardinghouse for a time. Now, at least, she and her children had a roof over their heads. Meanwhile, Ernest increased his efforts to hire the Youngs as extras in the movies.

The one thing Gladys knew how to do was run a home, so she

decided to open a boardinghouse, like her sister. After securing a loan from her parish priest, Gladys found a house on Ninth and Green streets, right next door to her sister's. It was spacious and well appointed and even had a ballroom, not unusual for homes of that era and neighborhood. There were also living quarters above the four-car garage, perfect for the children's nursery. Gladys preferred renting to families with children, both because they were less likely to be transient and because the children would be good company for her own.

The Royal sisters were very ingenious. They did their shopping jointly and shared the cost of whatever household help they needed. They bought in bulk quantity at a lower price and pooled their resources for communal use. Gladys went to Barker Brothers, one of the finest furniture stores in Los Angeles, where the manager gave her credit so that she could furnish her new boardinghouse, allowing her to pay in monthly installments. That company's investment in a young woman's first business venture was one of the best it ever made. Years later, when Gladys was a successful interior designer, she never forgot and sent lots of business its way.

Because work in the movies was unpredictable, Gladys concentrated on pleasing her boarders. Her every waking hour was spent cooking, shopping, and cleaning. Her children's welfare depended on her success, for the Young family was now very poor and their life extremely hard; there were even times when the children went to bed hungry. Betty Jane developed a form of malnutrition called St. Vitus dance, but it wasn't until Gretchen also acquired the same symptoms that Gladys took them to a doctor and discovered what was wrong.

Certainly there was no money for new clothes for any of the children. Fortunately, Gladys could sew beautifully and she redesigned her dresses or the hand-me-downs of her sister for the older girls. Gretchen grew up wearing revamped discards.

In 1917, a year after John left, Gretchen and her cousin Carlene were given jobs as extras in *The Primrose Ring*, starring Mae Murray, one of the biggest stars in silent pictures. My mother remembers: "They needed little fairies to fly around the ceiling. They had little harnesses and wings for our backs. The other kids hated it, but I really thought I was flying."

When Mae Murray, who was childless, saw little four-year-old Gretchen, she fell in love with her and wanted to adopt her. She asked Gladys if Gretchen could stay with her, and as an inducement she offered to take her cousin, Carlene Traxler, as a companion so Gretchen wouldn't be lonely.

At that point the offer seemed a godsend to Gladys, who was barely making ends meet. If Gretchen went to live with Mae Murray and her husband, it would mean one less mouth to feed at home; moreover, Gretchen would be given advantages she never could have living at home.

At "Mazie's" (the nickname the two girls gave Mae) Gretchen had her own room in a house on a lovely estate and was dressed in expensive clothes of her own, not the hand-me-downs from her sisters and cousins. In addition to receiving the private schooling that Gladys could never afford, Mae saw that Gretchen had ballet lessons, something that she had been begging for, and the constant attention of a German governess. My mother and her cousin lived the lives of the daughters of the wealthy, powerful, and successful.

After six months Mae and her husband decided to move back east. They wanted to take both girls with them, but Gladys was reluctant to put 3,000 miles between herself and her child, so young Gretchen's fantasy life came to an end. The two girls returned to their natural mothers, and to their previous lives of reduced means.

The abrupt separation from a life of luxury and the return to one of meager circumstances and communal living must have had an effect on Gretchen, young as she was. Many years later she said, "I was six when I knew I was going to be a movie star. Not an actress, a movie star." Her brief stay with Mae Murray had taught her what movie-star money and power could buy, and by the tender age of six she knew she wanted it and had made up her mind that she would one day have it. She was not an easy child to live with after her introduction to affluence, and later her sisters jokingly nicknamed her Gretch the Wretch, a name she probably earned.

My mother was not the only child that Gladys loaned out. Although her brother, Jackie, who was barely two when his father left home, later said that he didn't even remember what his father looked like, he knew that he missed him when he was gone. His world was encompassed by women and he needed his father, so much so that he wandered the neighborhood in search of him.

It was during his travels down the back alley that he discovered the Beautier family. Eunicio Beautier, once the county assessor for the city of Los Angeles, had died a few years before, and his widow, Maria Francisca Beautier, lived in a lovely home with her three children, Frank, Rose Cecilia, and Ida. Ida was married to Angus Lindley, who, like the Beautiers, was also wealthy.

In no time everyone in the household was delighted with the adorable youngster who had drifted into their backyard, and soon Jackie's visits were daily occurrences. Sometimes, at Ida Lindley's request, Gladys would let Jackie spend the night. Ida and Angus bought him a brass bed and put it into the small second bedroom in their suite of rooms.

Busy as she was, it soon became apparent to Gladys that her youngest child was seldom at home. Often she would send Ernest Traxler to look for Jackie and he would bring the youngster back in tears. Once when his mother asked him what he was doing at the big house, Jackie said, "I'm looking for my daddy."

His search was finally rewarded, for he began to think of Angus Lindley as his father. Certainly the Lindleys, who were childless, loved him as if he were their own. Jackie was soon calling Angus "Dad." Although he didn't call Ida "Mama"—Gladys was Mama—Ida became "Mama Bear" from Jackie's favorite story of Goldilocks.

When Ida and Angus Lindley first proposed that Jackie come to live with them, Gladys was very ambivalent. She knew that the Lindley family could give him everything that she could not: financial support, a good education, and a lifestyle that he would never know if he remained at home with her. As a boy his needs were different from those of the girls, she reasoned. She had allowed Gretchen to live with Mae Murray, so why not let Jackie live with a family that loved him and that he had already become attached to? He had found the father he was looking for, and, as his mother, she wasn't able to deny him.

There was never any mention of adoption. Jackie just moved into the Beautier house. It was, as he later described it, "like being away at boarding school." He had unlimited visiting privileges. Any time he wanted to go home to see his mother and his sisters he just walked up the alley.

When Gladys gave her permission for Jack to live with the Lindleys, she had thought that he would come back home at the end of a year. After several years passed, and Jack had completed the first grade at Our Lady of Guadalupe parochial school, he still showed no sign of wanting to leave the Lindleys.

In 1920, four years after John Earle Young disappeared, Gladys divorced him on grounds of desertion. In the summer of 1922, Laura Young, who had moved back to Utah, returned to Los Angeles. That same summer Mrs. Beautier and her three children traveled to Europe on vacation, leaving Angus Lindley behind to look after his law practice. Jackie Young stayed with him. With the Beautiers away and Laura Young nearby to help her with the children, Gladys felt the time was perfect to bring her son back under her own roof. At the time, Jackie had no idea that she didn't intend to let him go back to "Dad" Lindley. However, once Jackie was back at the boardinghouse Gladys announced to Angus Lindley that her son would now be living with her permanently.

At the beginning of the school year Jackie's first-grade teacher called, wanting to know if he was continuing his education and where he was living. Jackie had no doubts about the father and family that he had adopted. Gladys capitulated and Angus Lindley picked up the eight-year-old boy and took him back. Jack never lived in his mother's home again.

Later he changed his name legally to Lindley. He did it, he told me, "to please them after they'd raised me. They acted just like my parents. And they took great care . . . showered me with love and privileges that I couldn't possibly have had if I'd stayed home."

It must have been a bitter pill for Gladys. Her son was the third male in her life to leave her: first her father, then her husband, now her child. My grandmother lived in the shadow of abandonment, a legacy that began with my great-grandfather Robert Royal.

In 1923, when Jackie was nine, Gladys married George Uncus Belzer, one of her boarders. He was an unassuming, dependable man with a reliable job as a bank examiner, and Gladys felt that he would make a good stepfather for her girls: Polly Ann, now fifteen; Betty Jane, thirteen; and Gretchen, ten. My mother told me how the three of them decorated their mother's bed with flowers when she arrived home from her honeymoon. And she chose a card for the new bride and groom with the greeting "Many happy returns." Two years later, the girls' half-sister Georgiana was born.

With more stability and financial security in her life, Gladys enrolled Polly Ann, Betty Jane, and Gretchen in Ramona Convent, a Catholic boarding school in Alhambra, California. The two older girls then went on to Immaculate Heart School in Los Angeles, while Gretchen remained in the convent one more year to finish grammar school, which was to mark the end of her formal schooling.

With only one child at home, Gladys had more time to explore some of her own interests; she began to attend classes at Chouinard Art Institute, which was the beginning of her career as a decorator. Married to George Belzer, Gladys no longer had to depend on boarders to earn her living, and the family moved, leaving her sister Carlene and her son, Jackie, geographically behind. During the twelve years that Gladys and George Belzer were married the family moved quite often. Gladys would always look for a comfortable home in a respectable neighborhood, like Oxford Street, and Fifth Street in the Fairfax district. (I remember her advice years later: "Always look for the worst house in the best neighborhood.") It then became a challenge for her to see how she could improve it. Her revamped homes became her calling card, attracting clients.

In the meantime, her beautiful young teenage daughters Pol and Bet were attracting a lot of handsome young men in the film business. Both were now working steadily in movies. Betty Jane was under contract at Paramount under the new name of Sally Blane. No matter how much money the girls made, they kept only a third of

In front of the Oxford Street house. Left to right: Sally Blane, Loretta Young, Georgiana Belzer, Gladys Belzer, and Polly Ann Young. Sally and Polly Ann, already in pictures, are posing in the popular cheesecake fashion.
AUTHOR'S COLLECTION

their salary and gave the rest to Mama. She still ran the household with an iron hand; her word was law. Gladys was determined to make sure that her daughters had strong moral values and a deep religious faith, even though they worked in an industry that often promoted the opposite.

Gretchen, now in her early teens, watched her older sisters and bided her time, literally sitting by the telephone. She was rewarded one day when a call came in for Polly Ann from director Mervyn LeRoy, who wanted her for a film. Gretchen told him that her sister was on location and wouldn't be back for a week, then added, "Will I do?" LeRoy suggested she come by First National. He must have been very surprised when a fourteen-year-old arrived in his office, but he hired her anyway, as an extra in a film starring Colleen Moore.

Although Mervyn LeRoy was later to claim Loretta Young as his discovery, in truth it was Colleen Moore who discovered her. Colleen Moore had created a new style of screen beauty, the Flapper; straight hair, bangs, and a boyish figure. She wasn't beautiful, or even glamorous, but she was the studio's biggest star, and once Gretchen was on the set she said she watched Colleen like a hawk.

Colleen noticed the newcomer at once. "She was a beautiful child. She had huge gray eyes. She watched everything, studied everyone. She seemed to be all business, and I got the studio to make a test of her." The studio gave Gretchen a contract, put braces on her teeth, and changed her name to Loretta at Colleen Moore's suggestion (after her favorite doll, Laurita). Suddenly, Gladys had three film careers to manage, to say nothing of her own decorating career, which was beginning to flourish.

It is difficult to determine what role George Belzer played in the lives of his wife and her daughters. Georgiana was nine years old when her parents separated. I don't recall anyone ever talking about their life together. Like his predecessor, George was simply blotted out as Gladys's husband, although he remained "Georgie's father." The family called him "Mutt." My clearest memory of him is the smell of his cigar, not unpleasant, but perhaps a bit more pungent than his personality. I liked him. He was gentle in nature and always very kind to me.

He was a quiet man who remained in the background, probably what he had to do in his marriage. It would have taken an extraordinary man to hold his own, surrounded by so many strong, competitive women. In any case, his skills as an accountant were very helpful to his new family, and as his wife's and stepdaughters' careers began to escalate he also managed their business affairs, and continued to do so long after his marriage had ended.

But it was Gladys who ran the show.

By 1929 the family moved to a small house on Fifth Street in the Fairfax district, a middle-class neighborhood. By now Loretta was sixteen and in her own words "a big fat star." In 1928 alone she appeared in six films and was earning $250 a week, a great deal of money for a newcomer in that crucial year when the industry couldn't make up its mind between silent and sound movies.

The year 1929 marked the birth of the talkies and the end for many of the famous silent-picture stars who were unable to make the transition, among them my mother's mentor, Colleen Moore. Ironically, her protégée, Loretta Young, stayed on to become a Warner's leading lady, passing the "sound test" successfully.

Of the three Young sisters, it was my mother who had the will, determination, and fierce ambition to become a star. She said that she was never aware of any competition between herself and her sisters until Sally told her that she'd have given anything to have Loretta's role in *Suez*. According to my mother, Sally never wanted to be a big star; she was more interested in the people around her. My mother was not.

At the studios, the Young sisters may have had their own dressing rooms, makeup artists, hairdressers, and wardrobe women, but at home life was austere. The first one out of the house was the best dressed, for they still shared a communal wardrobe. Loretta slept in the maid's room. Polly Ann and Betty Jane shared a bedroom upstairs. Gladys and George shared the other bedroom, and Georgiana slept on a sleeping porch off her parents' bedroom.

Even though the girls were almost grown up, Gladys remained central to their lives, and was an exceedingly firm disciplinarian as well. Although George Belzer was sent to meet Loretta at the Los Angeles airport when she arrived from Arizona after eloping with Grant Withers, it was Gladys whom she went home to, and it was Gladys who initiated annulment proceedings that same day on the grounds that Loretta was only seventeen and didn't have her mother's consent for marriage. It was Gladys who sat on the set the next day while the two stars, Loretta and Grant, filmed their scenes, and it was Gladys who decided that marriage would interfere with her daughter's career and insisted that the couple live apart, saying, "Young love is all right on the screen, but it is different in real life. I want my daughter to wait until she is old enough to realize what marriage means."

George Belzer handled the press a week later after Grant Withers had countered the annulment proceedings with a legal action of his own, and the new bride and groom had disappeared and couldn't be located. But it was Gladys who dismissed the annulment proceedings, refusing to speak to her daughter for many months thereafter. It was to Gladys that Loretta returned fourteen months later when she filed for divorce, and it was Gladys who was her corroborating witness in court.

As Loretta's career began to rise, so did her salary. By the early thirties she was earning close to $1,000 a week, and she bought, and Grandma designed, a gracious colonial home on Sunset Boulevard in Bel Air, and the entire family moved in.

In 1934 George Belzer left Gladys Belzer's life, leaving nine-year-old Georgiana in his wife's custody. On March 24, 1934, Gladys told the press, "Although love does not exist, my feelings toward my husband are friendly and the divorce will be as amicable as we can make it. For two years we have lived under the same roof as brother and sister instead of man and wife."

This is the only explanation that I have ever found for the dissolution of my grandmother's second marriage, and that wasn't told to me directly; I had to search it out in the archives of a library. Discussions about what was really going on were studiously avoided in my family. Still, the failure of this relationship must have been a tremendous disappointment to my grandmother. George Belzer was the fourth male to leave her.

Like her mother, my mother, Loretta, also had her share of losses and disappointments, and at an early age. Her first husband, Grant Withers, failed to take care of her, just as her father had. The relationship with Spencer Tracy had come to naught. Then, in March 1935, Clark Gable, a man she loved deeply, and the father of her unborn child, stood in the living room of her Sunset Boulevard house and distanced himself from her predicament by saying, "I thought that she knew how to take care of herself."

My mother had come of age with a rude awakening. As in the past, everything was now left in my grandmother's hands.

4 THE HOUSE ON RINDGE STREET

When my mother first told me what my father had said on learning of her pregnancy, it struck me as a cold and heartless reaction, making my feelings about him more conflicted than ever. What had he meant when he said that? I wondered. Was he angry with her for being irresponsible? And what about his own responsibility? Was he in love with her, or was this just another affair with a leading lady? What was I to think about this man who fathered me, a man I never had the chance to know?

Then it occurred to me that with the passage of time my mother's perception of that moment had become colored by her own strong feelings of rejection, so that her version was somewhat distorted. What had my father really said, and what had he really meant? Was I letting my own anger at him for staying away from me all his life deflect the truth about who he really was? Was I merely reflecting my mother's and grandmother's feelings about the men in their lives and the losses they had endured, echoing a family theme that "men are no good"? If these are questions that will remain forever unanswered for me, at least I do know some pertinent facts about my father's actions during that period, for they have been documented in the press and in various biographies of his life.

Immediately after *Call of the Wild* was completed (and at the time my mother told him that she was pregnant), Clark Gable asked Ria for his freedom. Given this fact, I choose to believe that he was an honorable man and that his actions were proof of his loyalty and love for my mother.

Ria did the only thing she could do under the circumstances—she let him go. No doubt it was difficult for her in light of the rumors about her husband's affair with his leading lady. Gable moved into the Beverly Wilshire Hotel, while Ria remained in their home. If it seemed clear that the marriage had ended, there was as yet no discussion of divorce, and Ria believed Gable would come back to her; he never did.

Meantime, my mother, in the early stages of pregnancy, reported to Paramount for work on *The Crusades*, an extravagant medieval spectacle directed by Cecil Blount De Mille. (Years later, after I was a grown woman, my mother and I were browsing in a theatrical bookstore in New York City, and in one of those expensively packaged picture books on "early" Hollywood she found a full-page photograph of herself in the long blond wig and flowing medieval costume she wore in that picture. She showed me the photo and, in a voice so low and intimate that only I could hear, she said, "I was three months pregnant with you when I made *Crusades*.")

Now that he was no longer living with his wife, Clark Gable was free to see my mother, but she was so terrified by her condition and the ever-present press that she refused to see him in public. She told me that they were in constant communication by telephone, but even that was subject to an intricate code system devised in case someone might overhear or even be monitoring their calls.

When they did manage to see each other it was only for brief periods, under cover of darkness, and after many complicated maneuvers, backtracking in case they were being followed. Clued in to the romance, the Hollywood gossip columnists were keeping a very close eye on the two of them. They couldn't risk discovery. Both were consumed by paranoia, my mother much more so than my father.

Years later, when I asked my mother whether my father had tried to see her after he learned she was pregnant, she told me, "He kept calling and calling, wanting to see me, and I kept telling him to go away, go away. I was so terrified someone would see us together. All I could think of was keeping him away."

But he didn't go away. He was as determined in his way as she was in hers. Since my mother wouldn't come to him, my father decided he would go to her. Mary Loos, a young starlet in the cast of *The Crusades*, was on the set the day that Clark Gable made a surprise visit. She remembers the incident clearly. She told me that the sound stage suddenly got very quiet as word circulated that Clark Gable had just arrived. De Mille stopped the production and made a big fuss over him. De Mille loved to perform and adored any excuse for a show, and here was the perfect excuse: The biggest star in Hollywood, the recent winner of an Academy Award, was visiting the set where his former costar and reputed lover was working. It was a wonderful drama, and De Mille played it to the hilt.

Mary Loos remembers how surprised my mother was when she saw Gable. It was obvious that she hadn't expected him, and what was even more obvious to everyone there that day was the tremendous electricity between the two lovers.

No matter how careful my father and mother were, the gossip columnists still speculated that she was the cause of the breakup of Gable's marriage. While she was inwardly thrilled that he was no longer living with Ria, in her Catholic view he was still a married man. The longer he remained separated from Ria, the more my mother felt compromised and vulnerable; for the longer he remained separated, the more persistent the rumors became. She wanted the publicity to stop. There were things to be done, plans to be made, and nothing could be accomplished under the relentless glare of the media.

By June my mother's pregnancy was beginning to show. Something had to be done, and quickly. She and Grandma devised a plan, telling the studio they were going to take a trip to Europe. They thought that if she left town all the publicity would die down. It seemed the perfect excuse, not just for the studio but for the press as well. She had been postponing a European trip for some time, and now she could plead exhaustion from a rigorous shooting schedule. Once out of the country, she could have some time to think. If her calculations were correct, she was due in late October or early November.

My father, Clark Gable, as Fletcher Christian in Mutiny on the Bounty. *His expression clearly portrays his feelings about the role. (He didn't want to wear knickers and thought it wasn't manly.) It turned out to be one of the most important films of his career.*

AUTHOR'S COLLECTION

Clark had finished *Mutiny* and was beginning another picture, *China Seas* with Jean Harlow. My mother told him about her plans before she and Grandma left for New York.

If my mother thought that by leaving Hollywood she would leave the reporters and the scandal behind her, she was mistaken. On June 30 she arrived with Grandma at the *Ile de France* just minutes before the gangplank was pulled up, hoping to evade the reporters and slip on board unnoticed. But the press found her. She was wearing a loose two-piece suit and she quickly held her coat and purse in front of her and smiled for the ever-present cameras.

The press was waiting for her when she docked in London, too, and reporters followed her wherever she went. They even appeared at the Wimbledon tennis matches and linked her name romantically with her escort, tennis star Fred Perry. She was quoted as saying, "There isn't any love life for me now."

Some forty-eight years later, my mother and I were sitting in her living room going through a lot of old photographs that my grandmother had stashed away in a trunk. There were family pictures that I'd never seen before, pictures of all three sisters when they were very young, typical studio glamour shots. As we went through the photographs, I came across a small candid shot of a young woman sitting at a desk in a living room. The light coming from the window behind her backlit her dark hair. Her face was without makeup and her expression was wistful. It was, without a doubt, one of the most arresting photographs of my mother I'd ever seen. I pulled it out of the pile and asked, "When was this taken, Mom? It's one of the loveliest I've ever seen of you." She took the photograph and looked at it in silence for a long moment.

I was totally unprepared for the fierceness of her response.

"That was in my hotel suite in London. A reporter was interviewing me. I was five months pregnant with you and never more unhappy in my whole life."

I think it was the coldness and anger in her voice that surprised me the most. It was the first time that I actually felt the shock of how much my mother had not wanted the unborn me.

It was during the first week of August, while my mother and grandmother were away in Europe, that George Belzer was granted an uncontested divorce in Los Angeles. There was only a very small item about it in the newspaper. George left his marriage as he had come into it, quietly and with little fuss.

When my mother, accompanied by my grandmother, arrived back in Los Angeles, there were no reporters to greet her. No one knew that she had returned, and that was exactly what she wanted, for she was noticeably pregnant now, with little hope of hiding her condition. Instead of going back to her home on Sunset Boulevard, she and Grandma drove to a small house on Rindge Street in Venice. No one but the family knew of its existence. Over the preceding years Grandma and my mother had invested their earnings in real estate.

The Rindge Street house was one of Grandma's rental properties, at present vacant and a perfect refuge from the prying eyes of the press. No one would find my mother there. She could stay safely hidden until the time came for her to give birth.

But there were complications. A movie star cannot be hidden for very long. *Call of the Wild* and *The Crusades* had opened within a month of each other while she was gone, and now her public wanted her. Her studio wanted her, too. She was under contract, and her next picture, *Ramona,* was set to go. She was to play the title role and the production was being held up pending her return from Europe. There had been some changes while she was away. Darryl F. Zanuck and Joseph Schenck had merged Twentieth Century Pictures and the Fox Film Corporation into Twentieth Century Fox.

Grandma and my mother needed some professional help in handling what was quickly becoming a very complicated situation. They enlisted the assistance of the family physician, Dr. Walter Holleran, whom they knew would keep his patient's condition strictly confidential. The studio was notified that my mother was ill and needed to rest and that Holleran would be her primary physician. All this was arranged to protect her from the standard morals clause then written into every Hollywood contract. Dr. Holleran made frequent calls to check on my mother and monitor her pregnancy, and it was he who carefully fed censored information about her to the studio.

Once the studio heard from Dr. Holleran, it announced that *Ramona* would be delayed until midwinter because Loretta Young had a "serious illness." An announcement that she was exhausted from overwork had already been made; next the press was told that her physician had "advised the studio that her physical condition required respite from work." The nature of her illness was left to conjecture. And there was a great deal of that.

Meanwhile, Clark informed Loretta that he had instructed his lawyers to begin drawing up a formal separation agreement for himself and Ria. My mother, fearful of discovery, kept putting him off, refusing to see him.

The rumors that had begun on the mountain escalated, but now

*The beautiful movie star Young sisters, Loretta Young and
Sally Blane.*

the word *pregnant* was attached. There were other rumors, too, the
kind of odd stories that float around celebrities whenever details are
vague. There was speculation that she had been in an accident and
was scarred. And there was speculation that she had lost all her
money and was penniless. But the prevalent gossip was that she was
pregnant with Clark Gable's baby.

In the midst of all the rumors, Betty Jane Young, now known professionally as Sally Blane, married Norman Foster on October 8,
1935, at St. Paul the Apostle Church in Westwood. Due to her sister's
"illness," it was reported, her wedding would be simple, with a

small reception at the Sunset house after the ceremony. My mother did not attend. Her "illness" had attracted more attention than Sally's wedding; the star had stolen the bride's thunder.

Associated Press ran a headline stating: "Costly Illness, Films Delayed, Loretta Young Out for a Year Through Illness, Four Films Canceled." Now that my mother's name was again in the newspapers, Ria called the Sunset house daily, trying to talk to her, begging her to hold a press conference to silence all the gossip. Ria was not alone. Pressure was coming from everyone who knew my mother personally and professionally, urging her to make an appearance to show how false the stories were. Naturally it was impossible for her to do this.

Clark wanted to know how he could help her, what she wanted him to do. Many years later, when she told me about this period in her life, she said, "I didn't know what to do. I told him to leave town. I thought maybe if he was away all the gossip would stop." Clark left immediately on an extended trip to South America. But his absence from Hollywood didn't have the effect that my mother had hoped for. The pounding from press and friends continued in earnest until it was obvious that something drastic had to be done, and immediately.

My mother and grandmother decided to grant an interview to Dorothy Manners, a reporter who had been very friendly toward the family in the past. She had been calling constantly, asking for an exclusive interview, and she seemed very eager to clear my mother's name, voicing her anger at the rumors. Well known and respected, Dorothy Manners worked for *Photoplay* magazine, one of the most prestigious of the fan publications. She was the perfect choice for the deception that my mother and grandmother had planned.

Miss Manners was notified that my mother would be able to see her at her home on Sunset Boulevard. She was the only member of the press who would be granted an interview, but even she could stay for only twenty minutes, on doctor's orders.

On the appointed day my grandmother and my mother, who had moved back to Bel Air for the interview, set the stage with great care and attention to detail. My mother, now almost nine months pregnant, lay in bed covered by rose-satin eiderdown comforters so thick that nothing underneath could possibly be discerned. The only thing that showed was her face, all but buried amid thick pillows.

My grandmother hired a nurse, highly recommended as trustworthy, to stand beside the bed during the entire interview. Should the conversation take a turn that might be uncomfortable or compromising, she had been instructed to end the interview with the excuse that her patient was being overtaxed and needed rest.

The nurse rigged an intravenous bottle with the tube taped to my mother's arm dripping slowly into a pan hidden under the bed. A fire was lit in the fireplace, lending a warm glow to the large, comfortable room. At the appointed hour Dorothy Manners was led into the bedroom, where, with all the acting skill she possessed, my mother played the role of a gallant sick woman conserving her strength to face an eventual major operation.

In her *Photoplay* story, which was written in the fall of 1935 but appeared in the January 1936 issue, Dorothy Manners reported:

> This is the truth about Loretta Young's mysterious illness: Hard work, her great popularity that put her to the physical strain of making one picture immediately following another, capped by the climax of two strenuous roles in *Call of the Wild* and *The Crusades*, has aggravated an internal condition from which Loretta has suffered since maturity. It has weakened her, sapped her strength in the great loss of energy; and an eventual operation is the only remedy. In her present run-down condition she is not ready for that operation. She may not be for months, perhaps a year! But as her strength returns, she will be permitted by her physician to return to the studio for one picture right after the first of the year.

My mother must have had a captivated as well as a captive audience because Dorothy Manners believed every convoluted word she was told. "In fact, not-too-strenuous work is believed to be a good thing for her," Miss Manners wrote, adding that Loretta expected to report to work no later than February 1. Even though the story was filled with holes, Dorothy Manners was convinced. Her article was titled: "Fame, Fortune, and Fatigue: The Real Truth About the Mysterious Illness of Loretta Young."

Dorothy did remark on the fact that Loretta looked neither worn nor exhausted.

> She has been surprisingly lucky in not losing too much of her preciously acquired poundage put on during her vacation trip to Europe. She wore no makeup and the freckles across her nose looked cute and healthy.

Loretta was probably the healthiest and heaviest that she had ever been in her life. Yet Dorothy Manners did not see what was right in front of her: a pregnant woman.

I doubt if that grand a deception could be carried out in the reality-based nineties; indeed, there would be no necessity for it. Stars have children out of wedlock all the time and hold news conferences to announce the baby's birth. That my mother's masquerade was successful at all is simply another example of the power that a star's word held in the thirties, and the delusions of a Hollywood that saw only what it wanted to see, and protected its own.

While my mother sat out the last days of her pregnancy in hiding back in the Venice house, Clark, mobbed on his South American tour, went from city to city in a vain attempt to find some haven from the hysteria that his presence created. At last he gave up and flew to New York City, checking into the Waldorf Hotel for a much-needed rest.

Finally the time came for my mother to deliver her baby. Dr. Holleran was summoned to the house in Venice. The last stages of labor began in the morning hours. As Dr. Holleran stood over my mother, urging her to bear down hard, out on the street the milkman was making his early-morning deliveries. At 8612 Rindge Street the shades were all drawn. Inside the house the baby's head and shoulders were now cradled in Dr. Holleran's hands. As he gently guided the newborn into the world he whispered, "It's a girl." It was 8:15 on the morning of November 6, 1935.

At the moment the newborn baby girl was placed in her mother's arms, the milkman rang the doorbell. The baby had opened her mouth to utter her first cry of life just as the sound of the bell reverberated through the house. In that instant, my mother later told me, she quickly placed the palm of her hand over my mouth to stifle the cry, so fearful was she that I would be heard and her secret discovered.

Hours later, 3,000 miles away in New York City, as Clark Gable was getting dressed in his suite at the Waldorf to go out for the evening, his doorbell rang. He opened the door to a bellhop who handed him a Western Union telegram. He tore open the envelope and read the message:

> BEAUTIFUL BLUE-EYED, BLOND BABY GIRL
> BORN, 8:15 THIS MORNING.

It was unsigned. He walked into the bathroom, tore the telegram into tiny pieces, and flushed the evidence of his fatherhood down the toilet.

My mother told me many years later that she never knew who sent the telegram. She was shocked to learn of its existence when Gable told her about it; he had assumed she was the sender. If Grandma sent it, she never admitted it, so there is yet another piece of the puzzle that will remain missing, a mystery never to be solved, another question that will have no answer. Whoever sent the telegram valued a father's investment in his parenthood and his right to know of his child's birth. That seemingly outweighed any risk of discovery. For my father's sake, I'm grateful there was someone who celebrated his participation in my existence. I only wish that I knew who that person was.

I have no idea how long my mother stayed with me at the Rindge house before returning alone to her home in Bel Air. She surely had to recuperate from the rigors of childbirth and regain her strength. But, given the circumstances, I am sure it was an extremely short time. There was much too much controversy surrounding her whereabouts and her condition to warrant any lingering with a newborn baby.

On November 13, 1935, Dr. Holleran filed my birth certificate with the State of California Department of Public Health Vital Statistics. It disclosed the following information:

Place of Birth: *District #1907, County of Los Angeles.*
Rural Registration District: *Los Angeles, 8612 Rindge St.*
Full Name of Child: *Judith Young.*
Sex: *Female, Full Term.*
Date of birth: *November 6, 1935.*
Father: Full name: *Unknown.*
Mother: Full maiden name: *Margret* [sic] *Young.*
Residence: *Los Angeles, California.*
Color or race: *White.*
Age at last birthday: *22 yrs.*
Birthplace: *Salt Lake City, Utah.*
Trade, profession, or particular kind of work done, as housekeeper,
     typist, nurse, clerk, etc.: *Artist.*
Industry or business in which work was done, as own home, law-
     yer's office, silk mill, etc.: *Motion Picture.*
Date (month and year) last engaged in this work: *June 1935.*
Total time (years) spent in this work: *10 yrs.*

Many years later I questioned my mother about her choice of the name Margaret. (She had misspelled it when she filled out the certificate.) She said that it reminded her of her middle name, Michaela, the name she had chosen at her confirmation.

On November 18 my father returned to Los Angeles. For the benefit of the reporters awaiting his arrival at the airport, he confirmed that he was now formally separated from Ria. Shortly thereafter he called my mother and said that he wanted to see me. She lied to him and told him that I wasn't in Los Angeles, that I had been sent away, outside the city. She didn't tell him that I was only a few miles from him in Venice.

On November 30 my mother again appeared in public. Reporters photographed her wearing a stylish two-piece suit. This time she held her fur away from her body, draped over her arm, not clutched in front of her as her coat had been five months before. A stylish hat and a confident smile complemented her thin figure. The bold banner headline read: "Loretta Recovers." She no longer needed to hide in Venice; she could resume her life as if nothing had happened.

I, however, was left behind, in hiding in the house on Rindge Street. A nurse, with the exotic name of "Frenchy," had been hired to take care of me in my exile. My mother left me as abruptly as her father had left her. She disappeared in the very early weeks of my life, taking with her the only voice and touch and smell that were familiar, taking also a sense of safety, security, mother love, and nourishment, in her haste to counter all the gossip and return to her professional life.

She told me many years later that she visited me several times a week, and she justified her absence by explaining, "You were surrounded by people who doted on you. You were always being picked up and held. You had lots of attention."

That, I suspect, is a highly idealized view of what in reality was a lonely, alienated, and frightening existence for a newborn infant. I was not surrounded by people who doted on me, merely one caretaker, a stranger paid to be there with me. A doting family's visits couldn't be risked, if indeed there was any inclination on their part to do so. Too many people coming and going from the house would arouse suspicion.

I was clothed and fed and sheltered: the bare necessities. But I had already known and bonded with my mother's touch and smell in the short time that she was with me. I must have felt the loss of her, even at so early an age. Each time she visited, I must have rebonded, and each time she left I had to have mourned her loss. Her visits were probably at night, accompanied by furtiveness and fear, all of which probably heightened my infant anxiety. These are familiar feelings, ones that go a long way back, ones that I can feel even today when I am alone for long periods of time.

My birth was not celebrated, it was concealed. My existence in the world was a secret, and it was to be kept that way at all costs. I was even denied a visit from my father.

On December 27, 1935, I was baptized into the Roman Catholic faith at St. Paul the Apostle Church in Westwood by a young Paulist priest, John F. Fitzgerald, C.S.P. Father Fitzgerald joined the conspiracy of silence when he signed the false documentation of baptism.

My baptismal certificate reads:

This Certifies that *Mary Judith Clark* Child of *William Clark* and *Margaret Clark* born in Los Angeles, California, on the Sixth day of November 1935, was Baptized on the Twenty Seventh day of December 1935, According to the Rite of the Roman Catholic Church by the Rev. John F. Fitzgerald, C.S.P. The sponsors being Mr. *R. C. Troeger* and Mrs. *R. C. Troeger* as appears from the Baptismal Register of this Church.

A couple identified as the R. C. Troegers were somehow joined in the conspiracy as my sponsors, or godparents. Since Polly Ann and Carter Hermann are my godparents, perhaps they disguised themselves as the mysterious R. C. Troegers. To this day, the name and identities of the Troegers remain a mystery.

My father may have been listed as Unknown on my birth certificate, but he certainly wasn't listed that way on my baptismal certificate. My mother had used my father's first name as my last name. In choosing a name for my father she used a combination of Clark Gable's father's first name, William, and his own first name, Clark. In choosing a name for herself, she used my father's first name for her last name. In a symbolic way she married him spiritually, the only way left to her.

As Mary Judith Clark, the child of William and Margaret Clark, I was legitimate; we were a family. But it was a lie: we existed only on paper. There wasn't any Clark family, just Judith Young, illegitimate child of Loretta Young and Clark Gable. For the first twenty-three years of my life, this baptismal certificate was the only legal document available to me.

In January 1936 my mother went back to work. Twentieth Century Fox loaned her to MGM; she and my father would be working on the same lot, only a few sound stages away from each other. My father was starring in *San Francisco,* with Jeanette MacDonald, a singing star usually partnered with Nelson Eddy in operettas. In a curious twist of fate, my father's costar was Spencer Tracy. The two men, though highly competitive with each other, became fast friends. According to Howard Strickling, MGM's head publicity man and Gable's close friend, Tracy envied the adulation that Gable received as the "he-man," and Gable envied Tracy's acting ability, which had earned him the reputation of being an "actor's actor." He called them "friendly enemies." They loved joking around, and together they paid visits to my mother's set, teasing her unmercifully. She once told me how upset and uncomfortable their visits made her. Having both of the men she had loved so much teamed up and focused on her *must* have been a bit confusing.

On January 23, 1936, when I was almost three months old, my mother attended a big Hollywood gala. It was a very formal affair and everyone in the industry was there, including Clark Gable. Reporting on the event, Louella Parsons, one of Hollywood's most powerful reporters, noted that Clark Gable and Carole Lombard, the beautiful blond comedienne, danced together and looked very cozy. How my mother felt about that I have no way of knowing, but in recalling that evening she told me, "I looked at him across the room and suddenly felt very guilty that I had lied to him. After all, you were his child, too, and he had a right to see you. When I asked him if he would like to see you, he was angry with me and said, 'You mean to tell me she's been here in town all this time, and you haven't told me?' I admitted that—yes!—that was true. He said, 'Yes! of course I want to see her.'"

Very elaborate arrangements were worked out for my father to make the trip to the house in Venice. Both my mother and father had to be sure that no one was following them. The rumors of their affair and of "a secret child" had not quieted down, and there was still a great deal of speculation about my mother's disappearance and the true nature of her illness.

It was late one night when Clark Gable saw his daughter for the first time as my mother led him into my tiny room in the house on Rindge Street. "You were lying there asleep in a bureau drawer," she told me. "He reached into his pocket and pulled out a large wad of bills. He took four one-hundred-dollar bills and handed them to me, saying, 'The least you can do is buy her a decent bed.' That's the only time he ever gave me anything for you." I remember when she told me this her voice was very angry, and at the time the thought occurred to me that maybe she kept him away all my life as punishment for not giving her any money to support me.

She went on to tell me that she had instructed her lawyer, George

Breslin, to set up a bank account in my name and to notify my father of its existence should he wish to make a contribution.

If, in my mother's mind, money was the measure of my father's love for her and for me, she was keenly disappointed. No funds were ever deposited into that account, either at the time of my birth or at any other time thereafter. It was very clear, from the moment of my birth, that there would be no assistance from my father. In no way was I going to be a "little money-maker" for my mother.

When I asked my mother what my father's reactions were when he saw me, she was quick to answer, "Oh! He couldn't keep his hands off of you, he just kept holding you; he couldn't stop."

I am told my father visited me once more in the house on Rindge Street. I don't know exactly when that visit took place, nor do I know for certain how long my nurse, Frenchy, and I stayed there together in isolation. Initially my mother told me it was for a period of six months; the time periods varied ever so slightly whenever my mother discussed my early history, but there always seems to be a two-month time span that remains unaccounted for. Where I was then and who was with me remain a mystery.

One thing I do know for certain, however. My mother did finally send me out of town, to San Francisco. I was placed in a Catholic facility, St. Elizabeth's Infant Hospital, run by an order of nuns, the Daughters of Charity of St. Vincent de Paul, and I stayed there for five months. St. Elizabeth's was both an orphanage and a home for unwed mothers. Adoptions were handled by social-services agencies totally independent of St. Elizabeth's.

If it was my mother's intention during this time to put me up for adoption, she has never admitted it to me. I know the facts only as she told them, but facts sometimes hide another truth. How much of the plans for handling me were my mother's idea and how much my grandmother's I shall never know, but I've often wondered if it was Grandma who finally talked my mother into keeping me.

(In 1990 I made a concerted effort to find out if there was any official record of my stay at St. Elizabeth's. My letters went unanswered and my subsequent phone calls proved disconcerting. No one had any information nor was cooperation of any kind given toward my search. Finally, in frustration, I abandoned my efforts, resigning myself to the fact that I would never know for sure. There seemed to be no record of me at all.

Three years later, to my utter amazement, I received a letter in answer to my initial inquiry. I was told that all of the client files prior to 1945 were destroyed by fire and the only records available for the period prior to 1945 were a set of index cards with minimal information, usually just names and dates of stay.

Enclosed in the letter was a copy of an index card which read:

> YOUNG, Judith (adm to St. E's 7-3-36) for care CA-385 bn. 11-6-35 @ home in Los Angeles. Father: Unknown. Mother: Margaret Young 23 yrs—actress—white. Disch to: Maternal Grandmother of Los Angeles on 12-14-36.

Fifty-eight years after my birth, five of those missing first months of my life were finally found and put into place, leaving only the six months prior to my "adoption" in question.)

I was my mother's natural child, so she couldn't legally adopt me. Since she never explained any of this to me, it seems likely that she was acting out of panic and confusion and that she was unsure about what she wanted to do. The cover of an orphanage was an ingenious way to disguise the fact that I was her child.

St. Elizabeth's original building has been torn down. There is nothing left that I can see to help anchor those months of my life in my memory. They are virtually lost to my conscious mind. I know where I was, but I have no way of knowing what that experience was like. The satisfaction of at least viewing my earliest surroundings eludes me.

The first nineteen months of my life will remain a void. There are no photographs of me as a newborn infant. None were taken. There are no movies to record those first nineteen months, nothing to show what I looked like, what my surroundings were, and who was with me, caring for me. It is as if I didn't exist at all until I miraculously appeared, at nineteen months of age, in my mother's home on Sunset Boulevard and began my life as her adopted child.

If the facts of my everyday world in those nineteen months are lost forever, the impressions and feelings are not. Through the language of dreams I know something about that space in time when I lived in limbo, waiting. The places that I was hidden (there were probably several) were not silent and restful but full of discord. Noise was a constant. There were always doors, many doors, with people coming in and going out. Could this be my infant's view of St. Elizabeth's? Or perhaps this was what the Rindge house looked like from the depths of my dresser drawer, where I lay, as if in a coffin, surrounded by sides too high to see over. I'll never know.

And there are hallways, lots of them. Cubicles, like shops, all lined up and down a central mall, or is it a hallway? Could these be cribs with other abandoned babies, like myself, lying side by side? Just lying there, waiting to be changed, to be fed, to be held, to be loved, to be brought into a parent's home?

There are people, always a lot of people, milling around, but there is no reassuring mother's face to gaze into. She disappeared in the first days after my birth. She may appear at times during the following months, but there's no constancy. There is no father's face at all. If I become attached to someone, they, too, disappear and are lost. Anyone who comes soon leaves me as Frenchy did.

The only known entity is me. I am the only constant in an ever-changing world that is filled with loud voices and strange faces. All women's faces, no men. It is frightening to be here and I am anxious and uncomfortable. This is not a safe place, it is a loud and scary place.

I roll my head back and forth to lull myself into a hypnotic sleep. It is the only nurturing I can give myself. I can depend on no one to give it to me, for there are no consistent human arms to hold me and rock me, so I soothe my infant fears by my rocking. Few of my emotional needs are met, except perhaps the most rudimentary ones, as I wait to be adopted by my own mother.

5 THE SUNSET HOUSE

The world that I was born into was pure Hollywood. My mother and grandmother dealt with my life as they would with a movie script. I could be written out of the plot when I didn't enhance the story, and I could be written back in just as easily when it was convenient.

And so, at long last, my mother and grandmother decided that it was time for me to be officially brought into their world. My mother's sister Sally Blane Foster had given birth to a daughter, Gretchen, named for my mother, on June 7, 1936. And on November 28, 1936, Polly Ann Hermann had a son, James Carter Hermann III. With the birth of my cousins my mother had a perfect opportunity to lay the groundwork with the press for my arrival as an adopted child.

In April 1937, in New York on her way to Bermuda with my grandmother, my mother spoke with one reporter about her sisters and how happily married they were. She said she envied them their motherhood. And, in another interview, she talked about wanting a child of her own and how much she regretted that she didn't have one. The script had been prepared for the press, paving the way for the announcement that was to come.

Ironically, also in April 1937, my father was making "parental" headlines of his own. An Englishwoman named Violet Norton was indicted by the U.S. Post Office Department for writing extortion letters to Clark Gable, asking for support for her fifteen-year-old daughter, who, she claimed, was Gable's child. The trial lasted three

days and it was quickly established that Gable had not been issued a passport until 1930 and couldn't possibly have fathered a child in England. As final proof, his old sweetheart, Franz Dorfler, testified that he was with her at the time.

It must have angered my mother to see Gable's name linked to another woman as the father of her daughter when his real daughter was still hidden away. It's possible that this paternity suit prompted my mother to make her announcement when she did.

The reporter she chose to release the story was a personal friend of hers—Louella Parsons, a gossip columnist for the Hearst newspaper syndicate. Lolly was both respected and feared, and she loved a juicy story every bit as much as she loved the incredible power her

Gossip columnist Louella Parsons shaking hands with my father, Clark Gable, in 1947. Ten years earlier she had announced my "adoption" by my mother in her column.

THE BETTMANN ARCHIVE

position gave her. This news item was ripe with possibilities, given all the past speculation about Loretta Young's being pregnant. Even though nineteen months had passed since the gossip surrounding her love affair with Gable had peaked, my mother was taking a tremendous risk.

On June 10, 1937, Louella Parsons introduced me to the world:

> Loretta Young, film star, admitted to me today she is a mother—by adoption. Two little girls, Jane, age three, and Judy, twenty-three and

a half months, have been adopted by Loretta. As she confirmed the
news she laughed: "Yes, it is really true. They are such darlings, blond
and beautiful. I can't tell where I got the children. That is a secret I
hope I never have to reveal, and I want to forget as soon as possible
that they are not mine. For I feel that they really belong to me."

Louella's wording in her lead sentence suggests that she knew the
truth but was being discreet for my mother's sake. My mother later
told me that she remained forever grateful to Louella for her sensi-
tivity.

I don't know whose idea it was, my mother's or my grandmother's, to announce that she was adopting *two* little girls, but I have to
give those women credit; it was an original idea, and daring, considering that the other little girl never existed. There was only me, her
natural daughter, but to construct a smokescreen, five months had
been added on to my age.

The next day, June 11, 1937, the United Press news service picked
up the story and, adding to the confusion, announced that Loretta
Young had signed adoption papers for a three-year-old boy named
James and a twenty-three-month-old girl, Judy. UP reported she had
found the children at a Catholic orphanage the previous Christmas.

Three weeks later, on July 4, 1937, piling more lies on top of those
already existing, my mother gave another item to the press:

LORETTA YOUNG RELINQUISHES TOT TO MOTHER

> After allowing the tentative adoption, the mother found the sepa-
> ration too much to bear, and asked Miss Young to return the tot to
> her. The star agreed.

She didn't reveal in the article which little girl she was giving up,
saying that she must keep that in confidence, and bow to the natural
love of the mother. The article stated:

> The two little girls, June [sic], 3, and Judy, 23½ months, were taken
> by the star into her home last June 10.

Louella's "Jane" had now become "June," probably due to a newspaper misprint, and United Press's "James" was never mentioned
again.

The article finished by saying that Loretta had applied to adopt another baby girl (supposedly to replace the one that she gave back). And so, the benevolent actress suffers the trauma of having to give up one child, but she keeps the other for the happy ending. Fadeout. The End.

The public lost track of who was adopted and who wasn't. The motion picture community knew a smokescreen when it saw one, but no one challenged it and so fiction became fact. I became my own mother's adopted child. And the truth was buried.

I have often wondered why my mother didn't leave me in St. Elizabeth's to be adopted by some anonymous couple. It would have been so much easier than keeping me and building such an elaborate camouflage around my origins. Of course there never is any one reason for making important decisions in life. There must have been many, and none of them simple. As much as anything, I think she kept me because I was hers, and she was still very much in love with my father.

There was now gossip that he and Carole Lombard were seeing a lot of each other and had been for almost a year. In fact, according to all the biographies of his life, they became an "item" in the middle of 1936. While my mother was pushing my father away, Carole was pulling him closer, giving him gifts like the white jalopy decorated with red hearts and white doves, and accompanying him on his hunting and fishing trips. But no matter how painful this must have been for my mother, she had something Carole would never have. She had his child. I was my mother's link to my father. If she kept me, she kept her connection to him through me.

It's also possible that my grandmother was influential in her decision. Grandma may have loaned her children to others, but she always knew where they were and saw them as often as she wanted to. In the case of both Jackie and my mother, her decisions were based on the belief that her children could have advantages that she wasn't able to give them. In her mind the "loan" was for the good of the child.

If my mother had given me up for adoption, it would have meant that she could have had no contact with me; she would not know

Clark Gable with Carole Lombard in the 1930s. While my mother was pushing him away, Carole was pulling him closer.
UPI/BETTMANN

where I was. Unlike my grandmother, she had the means to provide handsomely for me. I think my grandmother would have talked her out of letting me go.

My father was still available to my mother, should she wish to pursue him. He was a baptized Catholic and had never been married in the Church, nor had she. They could have married each other in a Catholic ceremony.

I do remember little bits and pieces of the years that I lived with my mother in the Sunset house. There are movies of my small self interacting with my cousins and aunts, with my mother and grandmother, but watching them, it is as if I were seeing someone totally separate. The sight of the little girl on the screen, swinging on the garden swing suspended from a thick tree branch, seems remote and has no resonance in my memory. I know nothing about her, what her thoughts and feelings were. I can't reach her, for I had virtually lost most of the first years of my life.

Fortunately, there is one person who was a link to those early childhood years: my nurse, Eunice Margaret Berger, who came into my life when I was three years old, and with whom I have kept in touch over the years.

During those earliest years, Margaret was the closest thing I had

My beloved nurse Margaret Berger with me. I am dressed in my favorite Dutch costume—complete with wooden shoes.
AUTHOR'S COLLECTION

to a mother. She was my mother's age and, like her, tall and very pretty. My childhood memories of Margaret are of a soft warm lap, strong arms around me, and a shoulder to burrow into and nestle against. She thought of me as her own child; she was always there for me.

My love of books had its beginnings as I sat in Margaret's lap with my head resting against her shoulder, listening to her read all the Raggedy Ann–and–Andy series. I soon knew them by heart, but I pretended I didn't remember, just to hear her soothing voice and to rest against her body. Margaret gave shape and substance to my early childhood.

Our shared living space was a small sun porch, which Margaret described to me as having "ugly old green tile at the end where a couple of sinks for washing and doing up some laundry stood. There were lots of windows with lots of old venetian blinds. I would today consider it a very unattractive room. But there were two daybeds in there. I had one and you had the other. Yours was the one that was closest to the laundry tubs. It wasn't a very classy environment for such a beautiful child."

There was also a sitting room complete with a marble fireplace, and decorated, thanks to Grandma's fine taste, with French antiques, plus another small room occupied by Cristobel Crippin, my mother's secretary and personal maid. These three rooms made up the nursery suite.

I have almost no memory of my mother during the first five years of my life, but then that doesn't surprise me, for she was very rarely at home. She was busy working at the studio most of the time. I seldom saw her, and when I did, it was for very brief periods.

As Margaret recalls it: "She would check in quickly to see if everything was all right. She didn't let days go by without having a peek. It was a breeze-in and a breeze-out."

In 1985 Margaret invited me to her home in Vancouver, Washington, to spend Memorial Day with her and her husband, John Ash, so that we could get truly reacquainted. I was full of questions about our early time together, and Margaret patiently answered what she could. As she talked I began to get a picture of how we had spent

Christmas, 1989. Margaret with me on my third visit to her home in Washington state. It was on this trip that I learned all about my early childhood.
AUTHOR'S COLLECTION

our days and what we had meant to each other. For the first time as an adult, I was reexperiencing who my first real mother figure was, and I was learning about my early childhood.

Margaret didn't give information freely. It wasn't easy for her to discuss subjects that she felt were private and shouldn't be revealed to me by anyone other than my own mother. Margaret thought of herself not only as my caretaker but the caretaker of my mother's secret. She had a deep sense of responsibility toward both of us. I had to keep reassuring her that my mother had already told me who my father was, and that she wasn't betraying the sacred trust placed in her many years before.

The following year, when I returned to Vancouver for another visit with Margaret and her husband, I was released from these strictures. By then I had received my bachelor of arts degree, and was preparing to enter a master's program in clinical psychology. My new knowledge prompted even more questions about my early life, ones I needed answered. It was on this visit that I saw an issue of the *National Examiner* with a picture of my mother and father side by side under the bold headline: "Loretta Young and Clark Gable: Did the Movie Idols Have a Love Child?" An unauthorized biography of my mother had been published and I was the publicity bait to sell the book. Seeing the article seemed to be a turning point for Margaret. From then on she was less inhibited about her recollections, less fearful of betraying what she had regarded as "a great secret" that she had kept all those years. Now that she had proof that this secret was known not only to me but also to the general public, it released her from her private vow of silence, one she had honored to protect the reputation of her former employer, whom she had idolized.

Scanning the article, I couldn't help experiencing a great sense of vindication and victory, despite the feelings of shame and anger when I read about my ears as big as "an elephant." All my life I had been forced to excavate discreetly for any little shard of information about my life history, questioning people whom I knew withheld the facts and truth from me in deference to my mother's feelings.

I always felt grateful whenever any minute bit of new information was given to me, forgetting for the moment, in my victory, that what I was searching for was really my due, not a favor bestowed upon me by some benevolent person in the know. It was my birthright to know about my life and my heritage, my right to know what everyone else knew about me. I hated the fact that others, even total strangers, knew what I didn't.

It wasn't until 1989, on a third visit with Margaret, that I finally was told all that I needed to know about my early childhood. Margaret recalled that my mother had interviewed her at her sister Polly Ann Hermann's home in Beverly Hills. "It was neutral territory, so I wouldn't be overwhelmed by her environment. She looked me over and thought that I'd do a good job for her, for a salary that she said was all she could afford—eighty dollars a month."

That was less than Margaret had been making, but she accepted the position.

"There was no question you were an adopted child. There'd been a newspaper article about this wonderful actress that takes this child of twenty-three and a half months and adopts her. I believed what I was told and I thought it was wonderful. She seemed very pleased with me and it was quickly settled."

Margaret readily adapted to life in the colonial-style home in the hills of Bel Air. One of the very first instructions she received was to dress me in bonnets. My mother emphasized the importance of keeping my ears covered whenever I would

"Adopted" nineteen-month-old Judith Young, wearing a bonnet to hide the ears she inherited from her father, Clark Gable. AUTHOR'S COLLECTION

be seen by the public. Margaret was instructed to keep my blond curls well trained over my ears, not a difficult task. She was quite diligent and ever eager to please my mother. If the day was sunny and warm and there was no necessity for a bonnet, Margaret always carried a comb, so that should a breeze blow she could always fluff my curls forward over my ears. By the age of three, I had become vaguely aware that there must be something wrong with my ears, so much attention was given to keeping them covered. In a subtle and oblique way I began to think of myself as being deformed. As I grew older, instead of impatiently brushing away the hand that held the comb, as I was accustomed to doing, I would at times take the comb and place the errant locks over my ears myself.

About a month after Margaret arrived, my mother called and asked her to bring me to the studio for a visit. Margaret was very excited at the prospect of being inside a motion picture studio. Probably this summons from my mother was an attempt to initiate Margaret into the life of a motion picture actress, perhaps to impress her, perhaps to facilitate a closer relationship between the two women. My mother also may have wanted to include me in some small way in her studio life.

Margaret remembered that she dressed me meticulously, as my mother had instructed, in a navy blue velvet coat with a white-lace collar and matching bonnet. It was a brand-new outfit that the studio wardrobe department had made for me. Herman, the chauffeur, and only male occupant of the Sunset house, drove us in the sleek black town car through the large iron gates of Twentieth Century Fox Studios on Santa Monica Boulevard, where my mother was still a contract player.

In 1938 the lot, which today is Century City, extended from Santa Monica Boulevard to Pico Boulevard and consisted of miles upon miles of bare land. When buildings did appear a backward glance proved them a near mirage, for the houses had no backs, just boards holding up a cardboard exterior. All was facade, painted fronts to fool the camera.

The dressing rooms were bungalows, full one-bedroom apartments, most of them tucked in among the numerous sound stages. The wardrobe department and the commissary had colonial facades, everything painted a fresh white. Studio streets were broken up with patches of manicured green lawn and trees to soften the harsh lines of row upon row of concrete-walled stages. It was the prettiest studio lot that I can remember, probably because it was the first one that I knew.

My mother met us at the projection room and took us inside, for a screening of "the dailies," the film footage of the previous day's work. The studio executives and personnel involved with the picture took comfortable seats at the front of the small screening room. Margaret and I settled in the back row. She held me tightly on her lap. I was a very fearful child, frightened of lights and cameras and crowds of strange people. Margaret quickly learned to sense when I was afraid and she would hold me closely to her and soothe me with a calm, reassuring voice. She told me that she never had to discipline me in any way, and that I smiled most of the time. As she put it, "I never saw you show any negative emotion but fear. Otherwise, you were always everyone's darling, just everyone's darling, doing what you were told."

As the lights went out, the various takes of each scene that had been printed the day before appeared on the large screen. I was very frightened by the darkness of the projection room and by the enormous bright screen filled with my mother's larger-than-life image. She loomed over me, many, many times her real size, overpowering me, until I felt I became nothing, disappearing totally into the darkness around me. Somehow the screen had captured my mother and now projected her blown into this enormous overwhelming monster. Would it ever give her back? Where was my real mother? Had she disappeared forever? Had she ever been real? I was terrified.

I began to cry softly, my body trembling with fear; I turned my head away from the lighted screen and hid my face in Margaret's familiar shoulder. She held me close to her, whispering softly in my ear so that only I could hear her voice. "You're safe, everything is just fine, I've got you," she crooned as she gradually moved forward, a row at a time.

When the lights came on, photographers with their lighting equipment quickly surrounded my mother. We were now seated in the front row, behind the lights that blocked my mother from me. She reached out her hand for me, and Margaret handed me to her while the cameras kept clicking.

My mother stood me next to her on the couch, a protective arm around my waist. As the shutters of the cameras made their loud clicking noises, my tears still lingered along with the apprehension and doubt that I was feeling but didn't want to show. It was the first of many portrait sittings that I had with her, some planned and some afterthoughts—impromptu, as this one was.

Life in the Sunset house was quiet and serene for Margaret and me. We were surrounded by beautiful things acquired by my grandmother. Grandma's reputation had begun to grow among the Hollywood community, and she was by that time an established and successful interior designer. She loved beautiful things, and she invested in fine antiques as well as in California real estate. My mother followed her lead. Together they owned the Sunset house, the Fifth

1938. My very first formal studio photograph taken with my mother. I'm wearing a dark blue velvet coat and bonnet made for me by the Twentieth Century Fox wardrobe department.

I found this postcard of the Sunset house in an antiques store. This was my first home where I went to live with my mother.

AUTHOR'S COLLECTION

Street house, and numerous other income properties, as well as the Rindge Street house in which I was born.

Grandma had to have some place to store the furniture she was accumulating faster than she could sell it. What better plan than to buy a house, decorate it with elegant antiques, and lease it to just the right tenant? It had a double advantage; she was improving her property, and others, thrilled to be living in such pleasant surroundings, were building up her equity for her.

When I think of my grandmother now, one of the pictures that comes to my mind is of the two of us climbing over piles of furniture and boxes in one of her rented garages somewhere in the city, looking for a piece of furniture that she had stored there. How I used to love those outings. Her garages were always stacked to the ceiling with wonderful things: hand-painted headboards from India, an old wrought-iron birdcage that she had wired into a ceiling fixture, an old door that she had pickled and made into a coffee table. Treasures, wonderful treasures, could always be found in Grandma's garages. How she remembered where they were and what she had stored in them I'll never know, but she always did, without fail.

My first home on Sunset Boulevard was a two-story colonial-style mansion on a hill. The house, which looked like a miniature Tara, stood on a large plot of land, with a swimming pool and a large pool

E arly 1930s. My mother in the living room of the Sunset house with James Stewart.
COURTESY OF THE ACADEMY OF MOTION PICTURE ARTS AND SCIENCES

house on the other side of the steep driveway. Two flights of brick steps led up to it from the street.

The entrance hall was large, with a graceful staircase that wound upstairs. A beautiful crystal chandelier hung from the ceiling of the foyer, and on the wall was a mural with a garden theme: a Southern lady in a hoop skirt and garden hat, surrounded by four beautiful girls, also dressed in hoop skirts. Grandma had commissioned the mural, the work of a struggling young artist. He painted what he saw — my beautiful grandmother and her four equally beautiful daughters. All the rooms were spacious and decorated with French antiques. Sunset Boulevard was an eternity away from Grandma's house on Ninth and Green.

I remember that my favorite place was my grandmother's big, soft canopy bed. It is my clearest memory of the time that I lived in the Sunset house. Frequently, I would climb into the bed when Grandma was being served her early dinner on a tray and nestle in under the covers, sitting as close to her as I possibly could. Grandma got up very early and her days were hectic and tiring, so she usually went to bed before I did. She smelled like roses from her bath water and her skin was still warm from the almost scalding-hot baths that she preferred because she found they relaxed her. It was good to be there, so close to her, and often she fed me treats from her tray. Margaret always got upset because she said that I would ruin my dinner, but Grandma would coax her, saying, "Oh! Margaret, just this once won't hurt." Margaret told me that when she watched "the queen and the princess" (her names for us when we were in that big regal bed) she knew in her heart that my grandmother truly loved me, whether I was her blood or not.

My mother's youngest sister, Georgiana Belzer, lived with us. At fourteen she was tall and beautiful and looked much older. She had already made some screen tests for David O. Selznick (whose Selznick International Pictures was the top independent film company in town), including one for the role of one of the sisters in *Gone with the Wind*. My mother had tested for Melanie, a role she very much wanted.

I remember that Georgiana was at home most of the time. She hadn't liked going to school and so a tutor came daily to the house to give her lessons. One day, as Margaret was pushing me in the garden swing, she overheard Georgiana and a girlfriend whispering and giggling while they sat by the side of the pool, dangling their feet in the water. "Why are her ears so big?" Georgiana's friend said, loud enough so that Margaret knew she was referring to me.

Margaret heard Georgiana explode into fits of giggles as she leaned over and whispered in her companion's ear. "Clark Gable?" came the startled reply, and then the two teenagers broke into gales of laughter and jumped into the pool and swam away, suddenly aware that their conversation might have been overheard.

Margaret continued to push the swing, wondering to herself what Georgiana had told her friend and what Clark Gable had to do with

A *mid-1930s family portrait in the garden of the Sunset house. Left to right: Polly Ann Young, Sally Blane, Gladys Royal Belzer, and Loretta Young.*
AUTHOR'S COLLECTION

me. She promised herself that she would listen more attentively to the conversations around her, and it occurred to her that perhaps my mother's secretary, Cristobel, might be able to answer some questions. The two women, from similar working-class backgrounds, had become close friends fairly quickly. Margaret knew that Cristobel had been my mother's personal maid during her visit to England in the summer of 1935. Cristobel had told Margaret how thrilled she was when she had been asked to come back to California as my mother's secretary.

Jack Lindley with Georgiana Belzer.

Margaret was sure by now that there was some secret surrounding me, and she tried in many subtle ways to question Cristobel about my arrival into the household, but Cristobel always insisted that I was an adopted child and referred to the Louella Parsons newspaper article. If Cristobel knew something, she wasn't telling Margaret.

When Margaret introduced Clark Gable into the conversation, Cristobel talked about *Call of the Wild* and the fact that he and my mother had worked together, but that was all the information Margaret could extract. Cristobel made only one slip, accidentally remarking one evening that "Loretta was very fat" when she first met her in England.

One day all the pieces suddenly came together for Margaret. "It was like a revelation," she told me. "I looked at your face of peaches and cream, the curls, those big eyes, and then the smile. You always smiled at me. And the dimples. I said, I know what this is all about, this little girl isn't adopted, she belongs. She really belongs, she is Loretta's child. And all these little remarks about the ears, and then some talk about Clark Gable. He's got to be her father.

"So, in my heart I felt that I knew the truth. But for years I kept up the lie right along with everybody else because I was, as an employee, not revealing what I felt was a very private matter. It wasn't up to me to go out and tell everyone I knew, just in order to excite their imagination, that I had information, for I didn't. I didn't have any real confirmation."

One of the clearest early memories I have of my mother I discussed with Margaret as we sat together in front of the fire in her Washington home. I remember when I was four years old being very excited because I was going to spend some time with my mother. I didn't see much of her, and when I could have access to her it was a big event and I looked forward to it. It was always a special occasion going to her bedroom; usually the door was closed and that meant that she was sleeping and I must be very quiet.

Margaret remembered the occasion, too. She had dressed me in my favorite peach-silk smocked dress and brushed my hair until it shone. I didn't mind it when she yanked a little and it hurt because my mother liked me to look pretty. She tied peach-silk bows in my hair and even let me pick out my favorite white socks with little flowers embroidered on them. She kissed me and told me what a beautiful little girl I was and how happy my mother would be to see me.

The waiting seemed almost unbearable, but finally Margaret said that my mother was ready to see us. I couldn't hold back my anticipation and enthusiasm any longer and I ran ahead of Margaret down the hallway into my mother's room. Her bedroom was spacious, with rose-colored walls. There was a big marble fireplace, a soft couch with thick feather pillows, and an even softer, large bed. My favorite place to play was her bathroom, which had many mirrors and bathtub tile with pictures of water lilies.

I flung myself at my mother with all my four-year-old enthusiasm, holding my arms up to be embraced. After a quick kiss and embrace my mother put me down and turned away, leaving me standing in the middle of the room. She and Margaret were now deep in conversation, involved with each other, and I was forgotten.

I must have wondered if my mother wasn't happy to see me. I was happy to see her. Why didn't she want to play with me? Why was she talking to Margaret when she said that she wanted to be with me? I didn't understand. She'd forgotten that I was there. It scared me, being forgotten. Sometimes, when we were out together in a crowd, or at a public place, and especially if there were cameras, she would drop my hand and I would be left standing alone and forgotten until I found Margaret or she found me. But this time Margaret had forgotten me, too. Suddenly, I knew that I had to do something to let them know that I existed, that I was in the room. It was too scary just standing there in the middle of my mother's bedroom, ignored and forgotten. I walked over to the coffee table and shoved it with all the strength that I could find in my small body. I wanted to make a huge noise, I wanted them to pay attention to me. The coffee table tipped over and all the bric-a-brac on top of it slid off onto the floor with a crash. I had finally gotten my mother's attention.

Margaret remembered that incident very clearly, for it was in those moments that her suspicions about my mother were confirmed. She recalled, "I delighted in making you look very beautiful, freshly dressed, to have a little time in her room, a short time, just before she was served something to eat, or if she was going on a date. You were dressed up like a little doll, it was a showoff.

"We were in her room. You were always perfect. You were sweet and you were beautiful and you were good, always. You had never, never made one aggressive move of any kind. But, for some reason, you suddenly gave a push to the coffee table. You were trying to knock it over. Loretta looked at me and said, 'Margaret! Margaret! Why does this child act like this?'

"Where I got the input I don't know, but all I said was, 'I think it's because she knows that you aren't her real mother.' And Loretta looked startled and a little hostile. And she said, 'I'll have you know, Margaret, I suffered labor pains with her.'

"She never, ever told me anything about you ever being her own child. But she slipped up there, it came out in a burst: 'I'll have you know I suffered labor pains with her.'"

"So that confirmed it; I had at least those words direct from her mouth. I felt that I was the possessor of a great secret and I honored that secret; I never betrayed her. As far as I can remember, not until after you knew yourself and were voicing it yourself did I ever tell anyone the real facts."

In the fall of 1938, our pool house, which was furnished as a separate apartment and doubled as a guesthouse, had a new male occupant. Secluded and private, an ideal bachelor's pad, it had served as David Niven's first home when he came to Los Angeles in the early thirties. Initially Grandma moved him into Georgiana's room, and Georgie slept on a cot in her mother's room. He stayed long enough for the Young girls to introduce him to the motion picture business, and for him to star in films with my mother. The girls loved having this handsome young Englishman living right in their own backyard, ready to escort them around town.

But the girls and their mama were not as pleased with, nor did they trust, the new bachelor who was now living in the pool house. His name was William Buckner. He was thirty-one, stunningly handsome, a lawyer, and seemingly very wealthy. He traveled a great deal, putting together business deals, and he had impeccable family credentials. His uncle was Thomas A. Buckner, chairman of the board of the New York Life Insurance Company. William Buckner was more than a tenant, for he had fallen in love with my mother and was doing everything he possibly could do to marry her. If that meant getting close to her little daughter in order to get close to her, he was more than ready.

Margaret didn't trust him, but I liked him because he paid attention to me and gave me presents, one of which was a Dalmatian. The dog was too big to cuddle so he slept on the exterior porch outside our quarters. It was hot and confining there and the poor animal howled his displeasure and discomfort. He didn't last very long before being given away to a more appropriate home.

My mother was lonely. She wanted to get married, but up to that point none of her romances had worked out. Sally was concerned for her sister's happiness. She knew that my mother had been very much in love with Clark Gable, and Sally wanted her sister to find someone who could make her happy. But Sally didn't trust "Bucky" (my mother's nickname for him). There were some disconcerting rumors going around town about his business dealings and she was afraid that her sister was being taken advantage of by a ruthless con artist. However, since she had no proof of her suspicions, she kept her feelings to herself.

My mother announced her engagement to William Buckner at a large formal tent party on the lawn. She never had any discussion with me about her engagement, or the fact that I might be getting a new father. To be honest, I don't think it even entered her mind that I had any connection with her impending marriage at all. As Margaret recalls, "There was no input whatsoever to you. You were just there with me."

The family was not pleased, but they kept their reservations to themselves, all except Sally, who could no longer contain herself.

She had been told by a business friend that Buckner had been encouraging influential people in Hollywood to invest in some fraudulent Philippine bonds. He warned Sally that if this information was correct, "Bucky" could go to jail. He told Sally to warn her sister not to become involved, but it was too late for that. She had already loaned Buckner $10,000, and she kept it a secret, even from her mother.

When Sally told my mother to be cautious, a nasty argument ensued and the two sisters stopped speaking to each other. Meanwhile, presents were coming in daily from friends and acquaintances, and wedding plans were already under way. Bucky, in Europe on a business trip, was unavailable.

My mother, then in the midst of a complicated negotiation with Joseph Schenck of Twentieth Century Fox to renew her contract, was being pressured by everyone to agree to the studio's offers. Even the press began printing unfounded rumors, planted by the studio, that her option wasn't going to be picked up; that was the usual scare tactic employed when a star was acting defiant.

On December 1, 1938, when Bucky returned to New York City on the *Queen Mary*, he was greeted by federal agents and arrested. His luggage and belongings were seized, and letters and cables from his fiancée were discovered. He was charged with mail fraud in connection with Philippine Railway bonds, which had been under investigation by the Securities and Exchange Commission. After being questioned in the office of the United States attorney general, he was fingerprinted, booked, and jailed.

Loretta Young and William Buckner were instant front-page news across the country, and none of it was flattering. There were innuendos that she had been knowingly involved in the scandal. After posting bail Bucky requested permission to "visit friends in California." It was granted after he posted another $2,000 bond.

Bucky had been indicted by a federal grand jury in New York, and my mother was subpoenaed to testify in Hollywood, along with other celebrities whom Bucky had contacted about dubious investments, among them Joseph Schenck. My mother's family was heartbroken for her. It wasn't easy for her to maintain her dignity and

My mother and William Buckner attend Christmas Day mass at St. Paul the Apostle Church in Westwood. "Bucky" was given permission by the federal court in New York to make a "business trip" to California before his trial for mail fraud.
AP/WIDE WORLD PHOTOS

composure against the daily onslaught of media hype linking her to Buckner, who was now being openly accused of swindling a lot of influential film people.

As each day went by, some new information came out about her fiancé's past and his dubious business dealings. She learned that the previous year he had been charged with embezzlement and had resigned from the bar because he didn't have a credible line of defense.

As the hearings progressed it became obvious that my mother had been set up by her fiancé and his business associates. It appeared that Buckner began the romance to borrow money from her and then used her to meet a number of important Hollywood personalities. But, in fairness to him, in the process he also fell in love with her. Through it all, she remained loyal to Bucky. Sally heard from a friend that Joseph Schenck had paid Bucky to talk her sister into accepting the new contract at Fox at a lower salary than the one she had been demanding. When Sally told my mother, she went directly to Bucky and confronted him. He denied the story, so she then went to Joseph Schenck and asked him. Reluctantly he admitted that he had made a deal with Bucky and that money had actually exchanged hands.

My mother called the wedding off immediately and the engagement presents were returned. After the hearings in Hollywood were finished, Bucky returned to New York to stand trial.

Clark Gable and Carole Lombard, now a definite duo, were also getting their share of negative publicity. A *Photoplay* article titled "Hollywood's Unmarried Husbands and Wives" suggested that they had been living together while Clark was still legally married to Ria. Yielding to studio pressure, Clark announced that he was going to ask Ria for a divorce.

On January 22, 1939, Ria Gable announced that she was leaving for Las Vegas to start divorce proceedings. The next day Clark Gable officially went on the payroll of *Gone with the Wind*. Vivien Leigh, an unknown English actress, had won the role of Scarlett O'Hara, and Olivia de Havilland the role of Melanie; within a few months my mother had lost her fiancé and the role that she had so wanted.

When Joseph Schenck made his final offer—a five-year contract for $2 million—my mother turned it down. She had decided that she no longer wanted to be a contract star, that she wanted to try free-lancing; no amount of money could change her mind.

Her family called her a willful fool. The press said that she was a "lesson in greed." She had been earning $200,000 a year and now she was blackballed by the studios. After her first free-lance film— *Eternally Yours*, with David Niven as her costar—no more scripts came in. Word had gone out among the studio heads, and no one would hire her.

In the early months of 1939, however, there wasn't much time to worry about when her next film would come along, for she still had public appearances and publicity commitments to do for Fox. She might have been unemployable, but she certainly didn't appear that way to the world. Three of her films were released in quick sucession. *Kentucky* came out in January, followed by *Wife, Husband, and*

Friend. But it was *The Story of Alexander Graham Bell* that the studio went all out for. Darryl F. Zanuck, seeing a perfect opportunity to use all the Young girls' talent and beauty, cast Loretta Young, Sally Blane, Polly Ann Young, and Georgiana Belzer as sisters.

Georgiana was absolutely thrilled about acting in a film. She had always wanted to be a movie star, like her big sister Loretta. But my mother was not excited at all, and she said so, to everyone. When Georgie had been put under contract by David O. Selznick, Loretta told her that she had done nothing to earn the $50-a-week salary that she was receiving from the studio. She felt that her youngest sister had never had to experience the difficult times that she and her mother and sisters had known when they were so poor. She said Georgie had had it too easy, "she was getting the gravy." She felt that Georgie was working only because "her name happens to be Young," and she said so in private and publicly in print. There was great sibling rivalry among all the sisters, but since the others had married and were no longer living at home, it all seemed concentrated now between Loretta and Georgiana. *The Story of Alexander Graham Bell* turned out to be the last film that Georgiana would make.

For still shots, Zanuck ordered a formal photographic session with the four sisters. The studio was planning to use the pictures in a massive publicity campaign, and there seemed no better or more natural setting than the entry hall of the Sunset house. The graceful, curving white staircase and the crystal chandelier provided an ideal background for the period costumes that the girls wore in the film. The studio couldn't have built a more perfect set.

It was on the day of this photo session that my mother met Tom Lewis, the man she was to marry. He was in charge of producing the Screen Guild Theatre radio show for Young & Rubicam Advertising Agency, and had come to ask her to appear on the show. He left, assured of her cooperation, and promised to send her a script for her approval.

The extravagant studio celebration for the premiere of *Alexander Graham Bell* was held the last weekend in March, in San Francisco. Fox chartered a special train from Los Angeles to San Francisco for

Four beautiful sisters photographed on the staircase of the Sunset house for The Story of Alexander Graham Bell, *the only film in which they appeared together. Left to right: Polly Ann Young, Sally Blane, Georgiana Belzer, and Loretta Young.*

UPI/BETTMANN

the stars, and there was a parade through San Francisco, followed by a formal reception given by the mayor. Most of the Hollywood press corps planned to attend the weekend festivities.

Knowing that they could slip out of town unnoticed during this celebration, Clark Gable and Carole Lombard chose that weekend to elope to Kingman, Arizona, where they were married by the minister of the First Methodist Episcopal Church. When my mother arrived back in Los Angeles from her triumphant trip to San Francisco she was greeted by front-page headlines stating that the father of her child had just gotten married. Ria's divorce had been granted on March 5. Clark Gable had been a single man for only twenty-three days.

So many years have gone by since then that I'm sure if I were to ask my mother now what she felt at the time she probably wouldn't be able to recall what her true feelings were. Yet she had just been

deeply disappointed by a man whom she trusted and had planned
to marry. She no longer had her work, which had nurtured her emotionally and supported her financially in the past, and she didn't
know when she would ever work again. She had been very much
in love with Clark Gable, and in some deep part of herself there was
perhaps a glimmer of hope that one day they might marry. They had
a child together and that was an important bond.

Now there was no hope at all. Everything that my mother had
had was taken from her. She had lost everything. It must have been
an extremely painful time.

In the mid-1960s when she was visiting me in Greenwich, Connecticut, I remember asking her as we sat in the twilight of my living
room what had been her biggest regret.

"I think the biggest regret that I have in my life is that I didn't get
your father to marry me," she replied.

I knew that I was adopted by my mother and therefore I was her
daughter, but I had not yet begun to ask the inevitable questions
about who my real parents were. Margaret knew I would begin to
ask. Probably soon, since I was already four and aware that my cousins and friends all had mommies and daddies. What being an
adopted child really meant didn't have any meaning for me as yet; I
was still too young—but not too young to have a vague and nagging
feeling of somehow being different. That made me even more shy
and fearful and I would cling to Margaret, the one person in the
world with whom I felt safe and secure.

Margaret was concerned that I would hear what she had heard,
the whispering and giggling about Clark Gable and how I looked
like him. She knew it was probably inevitable that some child would
overhear a parent talking and say something to me. Children are
often brutally frank and cruel with one another. She wanted to be
prepared if I should come to her with questions, as eventually I
would. But she didn't know what to tell me, and she didn't want to
confuse me.

There was only one person who could help her with this dilemma, and that was my mother. In an unguarded moment, she had admitted to Margaret that I was her child. What Margaret still didn't know for sure was who my father was.

And so she waited for an opportune time. It seemed to come rather propitiously one evening. My mother wasn't feeling well and asked Margaret if she would draw her a hot bath and keep her company while she tried to relax. Normally, the times that the two women spent together were scheduled around my mother's workdays and social engagements. This time was different. While my mother lay in the bathtub, Margaret sat nearby and talked about where we had gone and what we had done that day. Finally she took a deep breath and dared to say, "If Judy ever asks me who her father is, or anything about her father, do you know anything about him? What should I say? What shall I say to her?"

My mother looked at Margaret and said, "You just tell her that her father is dead. And that's what he is. He is dead." Margaret knew by the tone of her voice that the conversation was at an end.

"She knew how to stop a conversation dead cold," Margaret told me. "She knew how to do that so you didn't ask any more questions and you didn't show any doubt, you just accepted what she said; whether you believed it or not, you acted like you believed it."

In a sense, my father *was* dead to my mother; he died when he married Carole Lombard. If she couldn't have him, I couldn't have him either. I, his child, was never to know for certain that he was my father while he was alive. She put an end to my father that evening in 1939, and she killed any possibility of our connection as father and daughter at the same time.

Sometime that same year another father, who had for all intents and purposes been dead, suddenly reappeared. John Earle Young showed up on his mother's doorstep in Los Angeles. Laura Young, who had not seen her son since he had disappeared, did not at first recognize him. He told a highly preposterous story to explain the abandonment of his family twenty-three years earlier, claiming amnesia as the result of a fall. Remembering nothing of his previous life, he had changed his name to John Earle and moved to Alhambra, where he married and had been fairly successful. But his wife had died in 1934 and now he was in need of financial help. Laura made him promise that he would keep his identity a secret and do nothing to embarrass Gladys or his children.

The story that I was told by my grandmother was that John Earle did contact his family indirectly, through my mother's parish priest at St. Paul the Apostle Church. After it was verified that John Earle was indeed John Young, Grandma called her children together. When she explained that their father needed help, she was met with some very angry protests. The loudest voice was my mother's, for she felt they owed their father nothing; he had abandoned the family and he wasn't going to get a cent. Grandma disagreed, saying calmly, "He is your father, and whether you like it or not, we're going to take care of him. You can afford it." Once again, she was the conscience of the family.

Tom Lewis finally submitted the script for the Screen Guild Theatre radio show. My mother found she liked it, and she was pleased to see she would be in good company. Her costars were Fred Astaire and Herbert Marshall. After she completed the show, another star, James Stewart, was waiting to congratulate her and take her out to dinner. They had been dating and she was in love again, but Jimmy hadn't yet proposed marriage.

Several months later Tom was promoted to vice-president and head of all radio production for Young & Rubicam. Agency president Chester "Chet" LaRoche, Tom's mentor, wanted him back in New York, but the sponsor, Gulf Oil Company, felt that he should finish the season in California. Although New York was now Tom's official headquarters, he divided his time equally between both coasts.

One day when Tom was having lunch in his regular booth at the Brown Derby restaurant, Roger Pryor, who had replaced George Murphy as master of ceremonies on the Screen Guild radio show, came over to his table. In the course of their conversation, Tom told him that he was on his way back to New York and might be gone for a long time. Shortly thereafter, Pryor's wife, actress Ann Sothern, called to invite him to dinner before he left. When she asked him if there was anyone he would like to have her include for him, he surprised himself by replying, "Would you ask Loretta Young?" That dinner party was the beginning of their romance. Once it started, Tom and Loretta saw each other every day and night for the next three weeks until Tom had to leave for New York.

At first I wasn't aware of Tom Lewis's importance in my life. The men who visited the Sunset house and dated my mother had little effect on me. There was no opportunity for me to become attached in any way because Margaret and I led our own lives in the nursery suite, separated from my mother's social life.

I was included in her life if the occasion was something that I might enjoy, like going to the circus. But a small child, and an adopted one at that, was a liability, not an asset, to a young, vital, and beautiful movie star. She was not preoccupied with motherhood; there would be time for that much later. At the moment her life consisted of her career and her romances. I was an incidental person in her life, one for whom she provided excellent care and whom she could enjoy when she felt like it.

I have seen home movies of me climbing up into Bucky's lap and hugging and kissing him, so I must have been attached to him in a vague way. When he abruptly disappeared from my mother's life he disappeared from mine as well, and I suspect that if at four I had formed any impression about men, it was that they left.

I do remember Georgie's father, Mutt. I liked him, for he was always kind and gentle to me, as he was to everyone. He, too, came and went very quietly, remaining on friendly terms with his ex-wife and her family. I had no conception of what a father was supposed to be or do. I didn't have one, and Georgie's was always leaving her.

The one thing I most remember about Mutt was his cigars. I knew he was in the house when I smelled his cigars and I'd follow the smell until I found him, usually in the den, where he did his accounting paper work. He was the business manager for my mother and grandmother. It was my favorite room, probably because it used to be his room before he and Grandma were divorced. I loved the large fireplace with the cozy, squishy leather sofa opposite it that I could flop down into. It would make a small squeaky noise as the seats settled back to their regular size. In the corner was a little bar that was a pass-through into the kitchen. The room was small, but to a four-year-old it seemed ample, yet cozy and warm. When my mother had guests, that was where I would meet them.

It was in the den that I first met Mr. Lewis. I can't recall anything in particular about that first meeting, but it seemed that thereafter he was always at the house, and, unlike Bucky, when he went away to New York on business he always came back. My mother was happier than I had seen her in a very long time. I somehow knew it had something to do with Mr. Lewis, which is what I was instructed to call him.

Margaret was aware that "this was a rapid and exciting romance." On occasion when Tom was away in New York, Margaret would be called on to help my mother write love letters to him. Margaret told me that when she tried to correct my mother's spelling mistakes (there were usually many), my mother would get impatient and say, "Oh, it doesn't matter! He'll know what I mean. It's the thought that counts." She was embarrassed when anyone called attention to her educational inadequacies, especially her spelling.

Now that my mother had no film commitments and was spending so much of her time with Tom, it was only natural that she would do more Screen Guild radio shows. She and Tom fell into a routine of attending early mass together on Sunday morning, having a quick breakfast in the car at a drive-in, and then going to the El Capitan Theatre in Hollywood for the dress rehearsal and subsequent live performance.

I attended my first radio show at that theater. It was very exciting, much more exciting for me than being on a film set. The theater seemed very large; it probably wasn't, just that I was small. I sat perched on a tall stool in order to see through the thick soundproof glass of the sponsor's booth. I sat in a corner, out of the way of the hustle and bustle of men and women coming and going through doorways. The booth was located high above everyone. I could see everything from where I sat, much as I imagined God must feel in heaven, looking down on the world below him.

When I looked down I could see the stage where my mother and all the other actors sat in their chairs. Microphones stood in front of each of the chairs. My mother seemed so far away from me. I could see her talking to someone next to her, but I couldn't hear what she was saying. I sat silently on my stool, aware of the reality onstage below me, but transported by the voices coming over the loudspeaker to an imaginary land where wondrous things were happening: the make-believe world of radio.

In his unpublished autobiography Tom Lewis recalled that my mother waited a week to accept his proposal of marriage. According to him, she delayed her acceptance until she had contacted her mother, who was on a buying trip in Mexico, to get her approval. If this is true, my mother must have wanted to make sure there would be no repetition of her first marriage. Her mother's approval was very important to her. She and Tom decided to keep their engagement private and to tell only their immediate families. However, I was not told anything about my mother's plans to marry Mr. Lewis, neither by my mother nor by anyone else. "As far as I know," Margaret recalled, "we were fortunate to have been invited to the wedding."

If I had had any childish doubts about the men who came and went in my mother's life, this time it seemed I no longer felt that way. I was hopeful, and at four there is a natural yearning and attraction toward a member of the opposite sex. It was a novelty to have a man constantly in the house, and I liked Tom. I even loved him, freely telling him so.

In his unpublished autobiography Tom described me as my mother's "beautiful blond young three-year-old ward," a characterization that sounds like something out of Charles Dickens. He went on to write that before their marriage he made my mother an offer. "I'd like to adopt Judy, and she could take my name."

My mother answered, "We'll talk about that later."

Later never came, and there was never any further discussion about it.

My mother never told Tom that I was her natural daughter or that Clark Gable was my father. She didn't tell him anything about me at all. He never knew for sure whose child I was. After Tom died, my half-brother Christopher told me that at one point Tom had thought I was Sally's illegitimate child.

My mother recalled the period in her life when she was blackballed by the studios as one of extreme unhappiness. She hated the fact that she wasn't working and she felt at the mercy of the patriarchal studio heads, who could get together over a game of poker and tell one another not to hire Loretta Young. She had been working constantly for most of her adult life, and to be idle must have been intolerable. She herself said, "I thought I'd go stark raving mad." She must have felt uncertain about her engagement, too, because she called it off in the early months of 1940. Although she and Tom had known each other for over a year before they became engaged, she told him that she needed more time.

Finally her agent, Myron Selznick, made an independent picture deal for her with Harry Cohn at Columbia. Her asking price was $75,000 a picture. Harry Cohn offered $50,000 and she accepted. The impasse had been broken; now other offers could come in. She was successfully free-lancing.

In April she told Tom that now she was sure that she wanted to marry him. They set the wedding date for July 31, 1940, after she finished her commitment to Columbia: *The Doctor Takes a Wife*, with Ray Milland. Everyone agreed to keep the wedding as simple and private as possible. Invitations were sent only to the immediate families and a few friends. The ceremony would take place in the small private chapel for the resident priest at St. Paul the Apostle Church.

Margaret's annual two-week vacation coincided with my mother's honeymoon. When Margaret heard about the upcoming marriage she went to my mother and suggested that, if it was acceptable to her, she would like to take me with her to her mother's house in

Vancouver, Washington, where she had planned to spend her holiday.

She said that her mother had already painted a small room all white so that it would be nice and fresh for me if I could come. Margaret remembered how I had clung to her when she returned from her vacation the previous year: "When I came back you just reached for me, I took you up in my arms, we sat down in a chair, you put your head against my shoulder, and you kept sighing. Holding you there, I knew how important I was to you."

She didn't want me to be separated from her again this year, especially at a time that my mother would be away for a month on her honeymoon. My mother was delighted with the arrangement and told Margaret, "I have perfect trust, Margaret. You take her."

According to Tom's autobiography, when my grandmother suggested that he and my mother live in the Sunset house after they were married, he immediately declined, saying, "It wouldn't work." Tom had just received an increase in salary and more responsibilities at Young & Rubicam, and it appeared that they would be living on two coasts for a while. He asked my mother to see if Grandma could find them a small house in Beverly Hills, something that would be their very own.

Their marriage was to bring other realignments. Tom held a meeting with my mother, Grandma, and George Belzer to assess Loretta's financial affairs and to plan a budget for their future life together. Tom felt that the budget should be based on his income, since "Loretta's career would diminish to blend into our life together." Or so he thought.

Up to this point, Loretta knew nothing about budgets; she had been accustomed to letting her mother handle her money for her. Gladys was a wonderfully creative interior decorator, but she didn't know much about budgets either, so the task of handling the business affairs for the family had fallen to George, and it was not a simple one. There were loans and mortgages on the houses that my mother or grandmother held title to. The furniture that Grandma had bought was stored in various garages around the city and in houses that were not yet finished. According to Tom, Loretta Young owed "the German war debt."

Grandma found a house for them on a corner lot in the 700 block of Camden Drive in Beverly Hills. It was a dream house right down to the white picket fence, entwined with red roses. Gladys hired an architect and together they began to renovate and make additions. In no time what began as a small country house was well on its way to becoming a not-so-small, elegant mini-estate.

What I remember most about my mother's wedding day are the thousands of people surrounding the church. I was terribly frightened by large crowds, but what I recall most was wanting to be near my mother and not being able to be. I was excluded. I've watched the home movies, made after the ceremony, when everyone is back at the house and gathered in the back driveway. I see myself rush up to her with a Teddy bear in my hand, but I'm picked up by one of my aunts instead. What else I can recount of that day I've learned from Margaret, from Tom's autobiography, and from the newspaper clippings reporting the event.

Tom described an incident that happened the day before the wedding. He and Grandma were driving to St. Paul's rectory when Gladys burst into uncontrolled weeping. When he asked what was wrong, she replied, "Please don't think this is because of you. I love you almost as much as Gretchen does, because she loves you. I'm happy that you two are marrying. You're the only man that can handle her, my little Muley. She's stubborn. She's my baby, Tom."

Tom reminded Gladys that Jack was younger than Gretchen and that Georgiana was her baby.

To that she replied, "Not in the same way. Everyone told me I shouldn't have Gretchen when I became pregnant with her and I did, and the Lord made her the one to bring me money. Always. Gretchen's been my little money-maker."

Whether or not this really happened, no one will know. Both Grandma and Tom are dead now. Somehow I can't visualize Grandma, as I remember her, breaking into uncontrollable sobs. She was always in control of her emotions, and crying was not one of her usual avenues of expression. I remember how embarrassed she would get at movies when I would laugh.

She'd turn to me and say, "Shush, dear! You're much too loud."

But my mother's wedding must have been a very emotional experience for her. With the exception of the time my mother spent with Mae Murray and with Grant Withers, she and Gladys had lived together for twenty-seven years. There is no doubt in my mind that there was a special bond between them, perhaps a stronger bond than Grandma had with her other children.

She *did* feel that God had blessed her with my mother. She had guided my mother's career, handled her money, and orchestrated her pregnancy and my subsequent "adoption." Now her baby was marrying Tom Lewis. She probably was glad, at the time, that there was finally a man strong enough to handle her "Muley." That she loved him, I would strongly doubt. There was never much love lost between my grandmother and her son-in-law that I could see.

July 31 was a bright, sunny, clear, glorious California day. My mother, Georgiana, who was her maid of honor, and my grandmother were the first to leave for the rectory. They were all going to dress at the priest's house before the ceremony. Irene, the studio designer and a friend, had designed my mother's wedding dress. She was waiting there, with her fitter, to help her into it. It was still several hours before the ceremony was scheduled to begin, but as their limousine drove up, people were already beginning to gather.

Tom was dressing at Polly Ann and Carter's home. His brother, Charles, had flown in from the east to be his best man. Tom's mother was too ill to make the long trip from her home in Troy, New York. As Carter was helping Tom get dressed, a call came from a policeman on duty outside the church. He reported that a large crowd had gathered and that he had to reroute traffic. He gave Tom directions for a route that would avoid the crowds and assured him that it would be kept clear for the wedding party and guests.

When Margaret and I arrived, the crowd had swelled into what seemed like thousands. Indeed, the press reported "nearly three thousand people." People were sitting on the rooftops of houses to get a better view of the church. There were no longer any streets or sidewalks or even front lawns for the surrounding homes, just a sea of people waiting for a glimpse of the bride. Four women fainted and had to be carried into the rectory to be revived.

Margaret held me close to her as we made our way toward the back door of the rectory. We were fairly protected from the crushing crowds that surrounded the front of the church, but we could hear the noise as we moved between the policemen who were guiding us. Margaret remembers: "We had a perch. It was like a gallery where you sit and look down."

Tom and his brother, Charles, wore formal tail coats, gray pin-striped pants, and ascots. Preceding my mother was Georgiana, wearing a long white dress of layered net with a wide pink-satin bow at the waist. A saucy flowered hat and veil sat low on her forehead and she carried a large bouquet of roses. She was beautiful.

But my mother was the most beautiful and radiant of all. She walked down the aisle on the arm of her brother, Jack. Her dress, of multilayered tulle, was in shades of pale blue lavender that changed in hue as water does when it becomes deeper. The dress was high-necked and long-sleeved with a draped bodice and a tight waist that flared out to a full, flowing long skirt. She wore her long dark hair neatly rolled under. Her hat was a straw pillbox, with a stiff net veil that framed her glowing face. In her hands she carried a large cascading spray of water lilies, the perfect accompaniment to her iridescent dress. Her eyes were filled with tears as she said her marriage vows.

It was a long nuptial mass said by Father Francis Quinan, who was a friend of the family's. At one point, Georgiana turned pale and almost fainted, but recovered. When the bride and groom reached the door of the church after the wedding they were greeted by a roar from the crowd that almost overwhelmed them. Flash-bulbs burst in front of their faces as the newsmen surrounded them on the steps of the church, a buffer from the crowd that pressed around their car. After posing for pictures the newlyweds moved through the narrow passage the policemen had made, to their waiting limousine, as fans showered them with rice.

The luncheon that Gladys gave for the wedding party and guests was an intimate and festive occasion. Margaret and I didn't attend.

July 31, 1940. Mr. and Mrs. Thomas Lewis on their wedding day.
UPI/BETTMANN

Later, the wedding party of four gathered in front of the fireplace in the nursery suite to have their formal pictures taken. This was the first time that day that I had been even remotely close to my mother, and I was excited by all the noise and ceremony. I wanted to be closer to her, to hold her hand, but Margaret kept me next to her instead. I followed my mother outside, clutching my Teddy bear, while a family member took home movies in the parking area.

Finally I was able to squeeze in next to my mother and Georgiana and hold her hand for a moment, as she stood next to Mr. Lewis. Then suddenly all the excitement was over, and Margaret and I were alone again in the nursery. The house was quiet. My mother and Mr. Lewis had left to drive to Palmdale to catch their plane to Mexico.

The next day Margaret and I left by the train to visit her family in Washington. The excitement of my train ride was such that I forgot that my mother was married and that she had gone away. I was with

Margaret and there was all that beautiful scenery to look at outside the train window.

Margaret's mother and father lived in a rural area. While their home wasn't a farm, it seemed like one to me, a wonderful adventure for a four-year-old. There were chickens that lived in their own little house. Margaret and I went every morning and collected the eggs right out of the nests. I remember tiptoeing into the hen house, trying not to scare them so they would not flutter their wings and scare me in turn.

Some days Margaret packed a picnic lunch and I would go wading in the creek with her much younger cousins. She had many of them around my age, and there were lots of dogs too that always followed us wherever we went. I hardly ever wore shoes and could dress in shorts and overalls. No bonnets covered my ears. I was happy. I was part of a great big family, Margaret's family.

When the two weeks were over and we returned to the Sunset house, a message was waiting for Margaret. Her best friend was leaving her job and she could have the position if she wanted it. The salary was $150 a month, almost double what my mother was paying her.

Margaret remembers her dilemma. "When I was offered a job of one hundred fifty dollars a month, that sounded fantastic to me. I didn't want to leave you, but I needed money to go on with my life. And here it was suddenly doubled."

My mother was still on her month-long honeymoon in Mexico, so Margaret had no alternative but to write her in hope that she would match the offer.

"She wrote back telling me of her wonderful husband and how she wished she could afford to keep me, but she just couldn't. And that she, of all people, could understand what it meant to make a living, so she didn't blame me."

Margaret left me before my mother came back from her honeymoon. My mother was away, and now Margaret, who had been there with me day and night for two years, was also gone from my life. I lost the one person in the world that I could always depend on.

I didn't understand that money was what took Margaret away from me, and that if my mother had given her a raise she wouldn't have left me. I didn't understand why she had to leave. She told me that it was best, that another little child needed her care, and now that my mother had a new husband and I had a new father, it was time for her to move on. I thought I had done something wrong, that maybe if I had been a better child she wouldn't have gone away.

Today Margaret makes a virtue of her leaving by saying, "So, you see, it worked out the way it should have. After my having full choice of how we lived and how I cared for you, if your mother took over I probably wouldn't have been able to take it. I probably would have been deeply hurt. It was all very exciting and new for you then. At least Tom was taking over as a father."

I remember absolutely nothing at all about the next three or four months. They are a total blank in my memory, as if the living of those months was so painful that I had selective amnesia. Instead of being excited, as Margaret suggests, I believe that I was considerably traumatized by the loss of everything that was familiar to me. And there were still more losses to come.

Grandma had been working long hours, desperately trying to finish the Camden house by the time my mother and Tom arrived home from their honeymoon. All her efforts were to no avail. The construction and the architectural additions were months from being completed. So she made a decision on her own, without telling her daughter and new son-in-law. She totally redecorated the Sunset house and she and Georgiana moved to a small house nearby. I had now lost almost all my family.

As Tom recalled in his autobiography, Grandma and I met them in the town car at the Glendale airport. Grandma broke the news and told them that Margaret had quit and the Camden house wasn't ready as they had anticipated. After a long silence my mother said that Margaret could be replaced, but where, she inquired, were they going to live if their home wasn't finished? Grandma told them she had prepared the Sunset house for them, adding that Tom would love it.

We stopped at the Camden house on the way. It appeared that almost no progress had been made in the renovation since they had left a month before. But the Sunset house was completely redone. Grandma's bedroom was now the master suite. Her large four-poster bed was still there, but there was a masculine desk on which Tom could do his paper work. The delicate French furniture had been exchanged for more substantial antique pieces, and my mother's bedroom had been transformed into a guest room. Only the nursery suite remained the same.

My mother did what she said she would do: she hired a new governess, Marcella Daisy Shankey, a Canadian. My mother told me to call her "Miss Shankey," putting us on a more formal footing. Miss Shankey had traveled and lived all over the world, caring for other people's children. She spoke several languages fluently and was very well educated. She was much older than Margaret, and not nearly as pretty. In fact, she was downright homely. She dyed her hair jet-black in an effort to conceal her age, and she chain-smoked, but that didn't bother my mother or Tom because they were both heavy smokers.

For the next several months my mother and her new husband traveled back and forth between New York and Los Angeles, and I saw little of them. I was left at home with my new governess. I missed Grandma and Georgiana and, of course, Margaret. It wasn't the same anymore.

When my mother was home she was busy with the plans for the Camden house. She spent long hours on the phone with Grandma, discussing the progress of the renovation. It was an uneasy collaboration, and Sally Foster told Tom many years later that Grandma cried herself to sleep almost every night over it. And still the house wasn't finished.

On Thanksgiving morning Tom had left the Sunset house and gone to his office. While there he decided that he was not going back to the Sunset house.

When my mother called to ask when he was coming home, he told her that his home was the Camden house, and that was where he was going. When she protested that there was nothing there, he said that *he* would be there that night and for every night thereafter. "I'll be there, too," she replied.

And so I moved again. It wasn't the first move in my very young life and, unfortunately, it certainly wasn't going to be the last.

6 THE CAMDEN HOUSE

Christmas morning in our new home on Camden Drive is still sharp in my memory. I was five years old and very excited and could hardly bear to stay in bed, as I'd been told to. After what seemed an eternity, my mother finally came into my room. She and my new father led me to the closed doors of the living room, and when she opened them I saw a glorious sight, the Christmas of my dreams.

Santa Claus had come in the night. The huge tree rose to the ceiling, filling an entire corner of the living room. Oversize red balls hung on every branch, and tinsel glittered and shimmered in the glow of the tiny colored lights. As I stood gazing at this sight in wide-eyed wonder, my new father bent down and reached underneath the presents at the base of the tree. Suddenly a music box began playing "Silent Night" and the tree began slowly to turn around, as if by magic.

Riches that my childhood imagination might have conjured up were actually there before my very eyes: new books to read and costumes to play dress-up in; a "diamond" crown for my head to make me a princess; ballet slippers to dance in; a new doll with her own trunk and wardrobe; and a dollhouse to decorate, just as my grandma did.

This was the best Christmas ever, even if Grandma and Georgie and Margaret weren't there, as they had always been before. I had a new father and suddenly we were a complete family, like other families.

The Camden house with the white picket fence I liked to swing on.
ANDRE R. WILLIEME

Later someone from the studio came over and took movies of us. My mother, my new father, and I played a make-believe game: I opened the front door for my mother and brought her into the living room to see the tree, and we pretended that it was the first time we'd seen it. Then my mother and new father hugged each other on the couch, and he lit two cigarettes and handed one to her. I could see they were very happy. They kissed each other a lot.

My new father and I played together on the floor of the den while my mother stood watching us. I never had a grown-up man to play with before. Sometimes some of my mother's male friends would spend a little time with me, but they never stayed very long. This was different.

My new father and I made up our own special game of seesaw. He lay on his back while I sat on his knees, holding tightly to both his hands. When he sat up, I leaned back, and back and forth we went, endlessly. I kept going faster and faster until the two of us were laughing so hard we couldn't catch our breath and we had to stop.

The man I used to call "Mr. Yewis" (because I couldn't pronounce my *l*'s correctly) was now my daddy. But that was a pretend game, too. I wasn't the child of this marriage—or of any marriage, in fact. Tom Lewis didn't know whose child I was because nobody ever told him. I'm not sure whether he ever asked.

It's easy to see, in retrospect, that, had my mother accepted Tom's offer to adopt me, he might have discovered that I was my mother's illegitimate child. My mother couldn't risk exposure—not now, when she finally had the Catholic husband and marriage that she wanted. So she kept me an orphan because it was much safer for her.

But ensuring her safety made my position even more precarious, for although Tom called me his daughter, I wasn't and we both knew it. Even at the age of five I knew he wasn't my father, and in my child's view of the world, I figured if my own father could let me be given away, then my new daddy could give me away, too. That's what parents could do with their children; they could give them away.

So it was very important that I make him love me. I had to win and keep his love because if he didn't love me I thought he had the power to send me back where I came from. After all, I was an adopted child. My mother took me from the orphanage and I always believed that she could give me back if I didn't behave, and now so could my new father. But I kept all these thoughts safely inside my head; they were too scary to talk about.

I told only one special person how truly frightened I was, some-one who would understand: the Blessed Virgin Mary, whose statue was on a shelf in my bedroom. I wanted so badly to be kept, not to be sent away, back to the orphanage. I felt safer when I climbed in my canopy bed, under its organdy ceiling. It reminded me of Grand-ma's big cozy bed and her nice sweet smell when I'd snuggle next to her.

I missed my grandmother deeply. She was very much a part of my new home, however, because evidence of her artistry in deco-rating was everywhere. Grandma had added skylights in the halls and the den so that the house was full of light. Almost every room had its own fireplace, even the small entrance hall, with its pale, sky-blue ceiling crisscrossed in a white lattice design and its mural of a medieval castle, with beautiful formal gardens, standing against a pale blue background. I liked to sit there, on the love seat, and imagine this was Sleeping Beauty's castle, and that I was the princess in one of the castle's turrets, waiting for my prince to wake me with his kiss, just like in the fairy stories that Miss Shankey read to me. The fireplace in the den was bright copper, with wonderful hand-carved and -painted figures standing on copper shelves above the mantel.

On the dining room walls an artist had painted a mural of a family, three figures in a country setting: a father coming home from a trip waving to his young wife and little girl, who were waving back. Even though they were wearing period costumes to fit the French decor, I knew that this was my new daddy coming home from his trips to New York to my mother and me.

My mother had a Virgin in her bedroom, too, a much bigger Madonna who lived among the trees in an oval painting on the wall. The ceiling of the room was the pale blue of a summer sky. In an iridescent blue niche, next to the pink-marble fireplace, Jesus hung on His cross, his tortured body illuminated by the lighted candle in the hanging wrought-iron vigil light. This was a sacred place, like church. I loved to reach up into the small brass cup by the door and push my fingers down into the wet sponge of holy water and make the sign of the cross, just as I'd been taught.

My mother's bathroom glittered like jewels. The bath was made of porphyry, a rock with bright crystals embedded on it. The only decoration on the glass door was the monogram of her new name, Loretta Young Lewis, in gold—*LYL* intertwined. This interweaving of her initials must have held great significance for her because it appeared on everything: her towels, sheets, blanket covers, stationery, matches, even the crystalware. I remember that interwoven monogram as her signature. It was probably indicative of the sense of fulfillment that came with her marriage.

I don't remember exactly when my name changed; there was nothing to mark the event. My mother simply told me I had a new last name. Instead of being Judith Young, I was Judith Young Lewis, part of the new Lewis family.

When I think about it now, it makes perfect sense. By giving me her husband's name, my mother could give me the appearance of legitimacy. No one had to know that I was an orphan, and she probably thought that people might forget all the rumors surrounding my birth, that everything would just go away.

Having two last names must have been very confusing to me and I'm sure I had a lot of questions, yet I don't remember asking any. However, my childhood friend Danny Selznick remembers my name change clearly. When he asked his mother why I had two last names, she told him that I was my mother's adopted daughter, but now that my mother had married Tom Lewis, he adopted me, so I had a new name. He remembers her saying, "She came into the world Judy Young."

Danny recently told me, "It always seemed very sweet to me, the idea that Loretta adopted you and that she then found a husband that thought you were so cute that he wanted to give you his own name. There's a fairy-tale quality to it." It was indeed a fairy tale, all make-believe. Danny was in his twenties when he learned the truth from his mother about my birth parents. When he asked his mother then why she hadn't told him before, she replied, "It was a secret, and you couldn't be trusted with it."

If Tom Lewis had thought that by marrying Loretta Young he could transform her into a simple wife and mother, he must have been disappointed. When my mother was offered the role of the famous ballerina Varsavina, in a film called *The Men in Her Life*, she didn't tell her new husband at first, since he was under the impression that she wanted to retire. She told her mother instead, letting her act as intermediary. Grandma made it very clear to Tom that he had married a woman whose whole life revolved around her work; he would be making a big mistake if he expected her to forgo her career.

For his part, Tom viewed his new mother-in-law as an obstacle to be sidestepped, and in the winter of 1940, on the advice of his friend Dr. Francis (Frank) Griffin, who was married to my mother's close

friend, Irene Dunne, he hired a tax attorney to advise him. He liq-
uidated property that he viewed as "hopeless" and invited Gladys
to take anything that was left of the furniture and houses.

Grandma had worked long and hard to protect her daughter's and
her own financial security the best way she knew how. She was not
at all happy about Tom's business decisions, whereas he viewed her
methods of handling money as a danger to his financial welfare.
There was no love lost between them.

My aunt Sally told me years later that Grandma and my mother
owned fifteen houses between them. Gladys had planned to give
each of her children a house when she died, but instead of requesting five houses, she walked away from the property she owned; all
she requested from Tom was a few small insurance policies, which
she cashed in. She traveled to Europe, where she stayed for a year,
investing in antiques. This separation would allow both sides to ad-
just.

Since my mother was to do her own dancing in *The Men in Her
Life,* it was decided that she would have to study ballet in New York.
Fortunately, Tom was still commuting for Young & Rubicam and
had sublet a large apartment on Park Avenue at The Marguery, an
elegant old building just a few blocks from Grand Central Station.
This was to become our home in the beginning months of 1941.

We traveled to New York on the *Super Chief.* It was my first cross-
country train ride and it took three days. Miss Shankey and I had
our own compartment, and my mother and father had theirs, right
next door. I loved climbing up the small ladder into the upper bunk
bed. I lay awake at night feeling the rocking of the train and hearing
the clicking of the wheels on the tracks, until they lulled me into a
deep, sound sleep. I was particularly intrigued with the potty that
pulled out from under the lower bunk, and how miraculously our
small daytime sitting room could be changed into a nighttime bedroom, almost as if by magic. I never saw the porter or the maids at
work; the change was a mysterious metamorphosis.

But when our train pulled into the station in New York City my
excitement and anticipation soon turned to fear. Miss Shankey and
I were summoned into my mother and father's compartment,

where we waited together until all the other passengers had gotten off the train. There was a mob scene in the station and the police were having a difficult time controlling the crowd. The press had learned about my mother's arrival, and so had hundreds of her fans. The blinds were drawn on the windows so no one could see in, but we also couldn't see out. Finally, a policeman knocked on our compartment door, the signal that we could go.

My mother took my hand and we followed the officer down the narrow train corridor. My mother and I were the first to reach the train steps, and as we did, pandemonium broke loose. The instant the crowd saw my mother the screaming began and it rose in volume as others saw us, hundreds of voices shouting and yelling as people tried to get a glimpse of the movie star.

"There she is!"

"Loretta, give me your autograph!"

"Over here! Over here!"

Hands reached up to grab us and bodies shoved and pushed forward. The mass of people moved, almost as one, coming toward us so fast that the police line could not hold them back. People were stumbling and falling and being trampled, and still no one stopped.

In an instant the officer had jumped up onto the train steps and pushed us back on the tiny inner platform, blocking our bodies with his own. "Go back to your compartment. Stay there until I come to get you," he yelled over the crowd as he struggled to pull the train steps back up inside, away from the flailing arms and legs just below us.

It took several more hours before we could safely get off the train and walk through the station to our car. The experience left an indelible mark. I've been terrified of crowds ever since.

Once we were settled into the apartment, my mother totally redesigned the drawing room into a dance studio, installing large rehearsal mirrors at one end, along with practice bars.

She began working long hours daily with the choreographer, her

1941. My mother "en pointe," realizing her childhood dream of being a ballerina, as she portrays the dancer Varsavina in The Men in Her Life. AUTHOR'S COLLECTION

dancing partner, and her double, who would be doing the major portions of her dance sequences. The work that my mother undertook was enormously demanding physically, and she lost her toenails in the process, but at long last she was a ballerina. Her childhood dream had come true.

I loved watching her dance. I thought she was the most graceful and delicate creature I had ever seen. I would sneak very quietly into the back of the rehearsal room and make myself as small as I possibly could so that I could sit and watch her work with the other dancers. Sometimes they were so concentrated on what they were doing that I could stay in my chair for a long time without their knowing I was there. If I was discovered, however, I was sent out of the room.

While my mother was concentrating on her dancing, my new father was concentrating on his job as vice-president of radio at Young & Rubicam. Although his schedule was busy, Tom managed to find some time for me, and since he loved to walk, we took brisk outings together in Central Park. I particularly loved the zoo, with its smelly monkey house and large outdoor cages, so much bigger and more impressive than Griffith Park Zoo in California. My new father and I were getting to know each other well.

One night I awoke to see Tom standing at my open bedroom door, the light from the hall behind him. He was in evening clothes and he looked very handsome. "Wake up, Juddy." "Juddy" was his new nickname for me. "I want to show you something." He leaned down and, picking me up in his arms, he carried me over to the window that overlooked an inner courtyard of our building.

I looked out. I could see the lights from the other apartment windows shining on the ground, which had become a blanket of white. The black night was filled with soft white flakes blowing and drifting in a downward shower, covering what, a few hours before, was green lawn and bushes with a crystal-pure glaze that shimmered in the reflected light from the windows. Tom just stood there, holding me in his arms as we watched the snow falling so silently on that winter night.

"This is your first snowfall, Juddy." His voice was quiet and soft and I could tell that he felt deeply about what he was showing me. It was important to him, and therefore, it was an important "first" occasion for me. I had seen snow on the ground when my mother and Margaret and I had spent a weekend at Myron Selznick's lodge at Lake Arrowhead, but I had never seen anything like this falling from the sky.

"Isn't it beautiful," he said. It was a statement, not a question. It *was* beautiful, but what was more beautiful to me at that very moment was that I was in the arms of my daddy and he loved me. There was no longer any question about it—he wasn't going to send me away.

By spring, my mother had finished her rigorous training, and film-ing was to begin on the picture in Hollywood. It was time for the family to go back home.

By late summer, *The Men in Her Life* was finished and my mother and father went on a long second honeymoon trip to Hawaii. We said good-bye on board the Dollar Line ship. I posed, smiling for the reporters, but I was very unhappy. I was crying as I stood on the dock, holding Miss Shankey's hand and waving while the ship pulled out to sea, heading for San Francisco and then on to Hono-lulu. Ironically, on the last weekend of their trip, my mother and Tom were the honored guests of Admiral Kidd aboard the battleship USS *Arizona,* which a few months later was to sink to the bottom of the ocean, all hands aboard, when the Japanese bombed Pearl Har-bor on Sunday, December 7, 1941.

When that day came, the United States was suddenly at war. I remember the black curtains that lined all the windows in the house. My cousin Gretchen and I would close them to make the living room dark and play "bomb shelter" under the piano. Some of my friends didn't have to pretend underneath a piano. They had real bomb shelters in their backyards. The heavy steel door rising out of a meticulously manicured lawn was the secret passageway that led to a hidden world belowground. Down the dark stairs we would go to a large room deep beneath the earth where there were bunks to sleep on and sleeping bags to curl up in. There was lots of food to eat, and lanterns and candles to light when the heavy door was closed. There were stacks of books to read and piles of games to play. I envied my friends' wonderful underworld playhouses, much nicer than mine aboveground.

As part of the war effort, Miss Shankey incorporated knitting into my French, reading, and arithmetic lessons. She took me with her to her sewing and knitting bees, where I sat with a group of her ac-quaintances, quietly knitting colored yarn into large squares. When there was a big pile of squares, Miss Shankey took them home with her and sewed them into an afghan for the Red Cross. The women in her knitting circle were the nurses and governesses of my friends, and they all had families in Europe. Most of what they talked about I didn't understand, but I knew that when the click-click-click of the needles got louder and faster, something bad was happening overseas.

Daddy came home one day in May 1942 wearing a beige uniform instead of one of his impeccable dark-colored three-piece suits. A hat with a hard brim and some insignia replaced the familiar felt one, and on his shoulders he wore some kind of gold pin. Miss Shankey called him "Major Lewis." He had taken a leave of absence from Young & Rubicam and had been commissioned in the United States Army. His new job required that he commute to Washington, D.C., to help create a plan for a global-communications operations called the Armed Forces Radio Service. He was now away from home much more than before.

In his absence, my mother played her role in the war effort, too. I remember riding with Miss Shankey in the town car to Union Station to see my mother off on a four-week war bond tour. She looked very beautiful in her elegant Irene suit with a corsage of Victory stamps and tiny American flags pinned on her lapel. Ironically, it was my real father, Clark Gable, who had asked her to make the tour. He was then head of the actors' division of the Hollywood Victory Committee. (His wife, Carole Lombard, had died in a plane crash returning from the very first war-bond tour on January 16, 1942.)

Despite the war raging in Europe and the Pacific, the Hollywood children's birthday parties went on as always. In true Hollywood style, they were grand productions in equally grand mansions. How I hated those parties. I was never comfortable around the children of my mother's friends. In truth, none of us saw one another except at those birthday parties. It was the mothers who put together the party lists, not the children. Everything was planned and ordered ahead of time by the mothers, and then the nurses and governesses ran the actual party. If any parents were there, it was generally only to socialize with one another.

I often complained that I didn't want to go and that I didn't really know anybody there. The truth of the matter was that I was painfully shy. My mother ignored my feeble pleas to be excused. "Do as you're told, Judy. You'll have a good time, you'll see." Then she would caution me. "Remember, when you're in public you're a reflection of me." But I didn't have a good time; I simply endured the experience.

The children's group grew as my mother's career grew. Now that she was married, her circle of associates had expanded to include her husband's business and personal friends. In Hollywood the power structure was reinforced by socializing. Relationships became intense during filming, and when a film was completed everyone went on to the next project. Some friendships lasted, some didn't, but what never changed was the pecking order.

Just as there was a pecking order for the adults, so there was one for the children. The children of the heads of studios seemed to have

At a 1930s party, Gretchen Foster, Susan Kohner—the birthday girl—and I smile obligingly for the camera. These Hollywood kids' birthday parties were not curtailed by World War II.
AUTHOR'S COLLECTION

a sixth sense about the power that their parents wielded. Although we were much too young and innocent to be aware of the political intricacies of our parents' world, we absorbed some of it by osmosis.

At seven I was already keenly aware of which children should not be allowed to see my shyness. Music Corporation of America founder Jules Stein's youngest daughter, Susan, was one child with whom I tried extra hard to seem confident, although inside I wasn't at all. Something about her frightened me. I felt Susan could sense the lame duck in a crowd—in this case, me—and that could be dangerous. I felt far more comfortable with her older sister, Jean. The one friend I felt very safe with was Danny Selznick. If Danny was there everything would be all right.

Looking back, I realize I was always afraid. Because I was adopted, I felt like an outsider everywhere. I thought the other children could see through me, that they could see I was different and therefore not acceptable. I was an orphan child in the Hollywood kingdom, unworthy to play with the naturally born elite.

One birthday party stands out sharply from all the others. It was held at Barbara Warner's home, the grandest of them all. Her father, Jack, owned a studio, and their estate stood high on a hill hidden behind tall iron gates off Benedict Canyon, on Angelo Drive. The long driveway to the house wound past a nine-hole golf course and ended in a cobblestone courtyard with a central fountain. In front of the majestic home, as far as the eye could see, were formal gardens, a perfect replica of those at Versailles.

Barbara's party was a swimming party. I had never seen a pool like hers. It was enormous. On the bottom of the pool were mosaic-tile marine animals—sea horses, whales, and sea serpents. As the water rippled over their sleek tile bodies, they appeared to be alive, moving and undulating. At the deep end the diving board raised and lowered hydraulically, and a high aluminum slide promised swift tumbles into the cool water. The party tables for lunch were set up in the large pool house, and there was a real soda fountain where we all chose what ice cream sodas we would have.

But then came the part I feared the most: the movie. The passage of years hadn't lessened my unease about movies. I lagged behind the rest of the crowd and waited until everyone went inside to the living room. Then I found a bench outside and sat down all alone. When Miss Shankey came out after a few moments and sat next to me, I was glad to see her. It was scary, being there all by myself.

"It's a Walt Disney film, Judy," she told me. "A cartoon. I think you'll like it." I didn't want her to leave me, so I followed her inside and snuggled down in the deep cushions of the long couch in the back of the room. She held my hand tightly in hers to reassure me.

Suddenly, the floor at one end of the large living room began to rise like an enormous monster. It lifted higher and higher until at last it stopped its hydraulic climb, inches from the ceiling. A huge motion picture screen now stood where before there was only a carpeted floor.

The lights went out and the theme music for Walt Disney's *Dumbo* began. When the other children started laughing at the baby elephant trying to walk and tripping over his long, flapping ears, something began to stir inside me. Why was everyone laughing? It wasn't funny. Echoes of "Cover her ears" rang distantly in my memory: the voices of my grandmother, aunts, and mother all repeating the same litany—"Cover her ears."

I hated the mean female elephants in the circus. They whispered behind their trunks and turned their backs on Dumbo, and when he eagerly tried to join their circle they crowded him out with their big bodies. He was an outsider. He was different. It struck a familiar chord. I cried when Dumbo cried, hanging his head in shame as he hid behind his big flaplike ears. I cried the hardest when Dumbo's mother was locked up for protecting her baby.

As I was leaving the party, two little girls stood nearby, whispering, "Dumbo! Look, it's Dumbo!" Even though they were holding their white-gloved hands up to cover their mouths, I could still hear them. I turned around to see where they were looking. Where was Dumbo? I didn't see any baby elephant. I looked back at them. They were looking directly at me. They started to giggle. "There's Dumbo!"

Where? I wondered. *I don't see him.*

They giggled even louder and continued to stare at me. "Look at Judy. Look at Judy's ears. They're big, just like Dumbo's. Judy's got elephant ears."

They were singsonging and laughing so loudly now that others were beginning to turn around. Soon everyone would be looking at me. I hated them and I hated my ears. I wanted to disappear.

I ran over to Miss Shankey. Grabbing the bonnet out of her hands, I shoved it on my head as quickly as I could.

"You don't have to wear it if you don't want to, Judy." She knew how I hated bonnets. Instead, I tied the strings under my chin myself and grabbed her hand, pulling her toward the front door and escape.

When I got home I ran right into my mother's room and burst into tears. "I'm never going to another birthday party again. You can't make me."

My mother looked surprised. "What happened, Judy? Why are you crying?" she asked.

It all came tumbling out. "Some girls called me Dumbo. I hate my big ears, I don't want to look like an elephant, I wish I didn't have them." And I covered my ears with my hands to hide them from her sight. She put her arms around me as I cried uncontrollably. "It's all right, Judy. It'll be all right. We'll fix them."

I didn't know what having my ears "fixed" meant. All I knew was that there was something wrong with me. My mother and everyone around me wanted to hide them. I was different. I was deformed in some way, and it had to do with my ears. Whatever it was, I was born with them, and as far as I knew they were stuck on me forever.

Shortly thereafter, I noticed a neat pile of children's books on the table in the den: fairy stories and some new Oz books, a whole collection of my favorite authors. When I asked my mother who the books were for, she said, "They're all for you, Judy. You can read them while you're in the hospital."

"What's a hospital?" I wanted to know.

"It's a place where you're going to stay for a little while. You'll go to sleep, and when you wake up your ears will be fixed," my mother told me.

"Are you going with me?" It didn't sound to me like someplace I'd like to visit by myself.

"Yes, Judy. I'll be right there with you all the time." That made it sound a little less scary. As long as my mother was with me, a hospital didn't sound like too bad a place. And maybe she wouldn't go away all the time and I could have her all to myself. I was excited about the possibilities of this new adventure.

The first thing I remember when I woke up after the operation was that my entire head was wrapped tightly in bandages. At first I didn't know where I was. It felt as if my head was gripped in a tight vise. I reached up and tried to tear off whatever it was that was putting so much pressure on my skull. All of a sudden I felt a searing red-hot pain. My skull felt as if it had been sliced into a million pieces by sharp razor blades. I screamed, tearing at the tight bandages that were wrapped around my head, covering my ears and pressing against my forehead. I wanted to rip them away, to get rid of this unbearable pain. The slightest movement of my head intensified the agony inside my skull.

Hands from nowhere held mine tightly, and no matter how hard I struggled I couldn't free them. Several voices spoke to me, but I couldn't hear them through the waves of pain that were engulfing me. My arm was being pulled away from my head and I felt a sharp stick. Then nothing, just the blackness of unconsciousness.

I awoke with the pain again, and before I could raise my hand, my arm was stuck with a needle. No matter how I begged and pleaded and cried "No more sticks!" to the nurse, whom I saw only as a glimpse of starched white, the shots still came, followed by unconsciousness. There was no day or night, no sense of time or place; I drifted in and out of consciousness throughout my hospital stay in the Queen of the Angels Hospital, sobbing and sleeping, adrift in time.

Then, one day, I heard my mother's voice floating through the fog around me. It was a soft, gentle sound. She was whispering quietly to the nurse. They thought I was still asleep. I lay still, not moving, my eyes closed tightly, faking sleep.

It felt good hearing their conversation. I liked the idea that I could hear them and they didn't know it. This would be my secret: The only control that I had now was my will to stay awake when everyone around me wanted to put me back to sleep, back into unconsciousness.

I lay with my eyes closed, listening to the soft voices whispering beside my bed. It didn't matter what they were saying. I didn't care what they were talking about. I cared only that my mother was there in the room with me. That was the only thing that mattered, that she was there beside my bed. I wanted to listen to her voice and enjoy having her all to myself for as long as I could stand it before the pain returned. If I let her know I was awake, I would get another needle, and I wanted to delay that as long as possible.

She had been by my side during the whole ordeal of the operation and was there every time I awoke. Or at least that was how it seemed to me. I was afraid if I went to sleep I might wake up and find she was gone. I wasn't used to that kind of concentrated attention from her, and I didn't want her to go away. It comforted me to lie there and hear her voice. She wasn't traveling anywhere and she wasn't away at the studio, filming a picture. She hadn't left me. She was right there with me now, in my hospital room. Just as I had wished, I had her love and attention, and I didn't want to miss a minute of it. I lay ever so silently, letting the waves of pain and nausea and the pounding in my head sweep me away until I could stand it no longer and began to cry.

Even when I came home the pain was not gone. "It hurts," I would cry, and my mother would put her arms around me gently, holding me close to her.

"I know it does, but you wanted your ears fixed. It won't hurt like this forever. I promise you."

Inside, I cried out to her: *I didn't want to hurt like this. You didn't tell me it would hurt like this. You just told me you'd fix it.*

But I couldn't tell her how angry I was that I was in such pain. I was afraid she wouldn't love me. And it was true—I *had* told her that I hated my ears and I wished I didn't have them. So I kept my thoughts to myself and clutched the crucifix on my rosary beads for comfort, trying with all my strength not to cry.

I later learned that Dr. Ginsberg, my surgeon, had told my mother that an operation of this nature was extremely painful and that there was no way that it could be performed without causing intense discomfort. He suggested that since I was very young to undergo such a procedure, perhaps it should wait until I was older, when I could more readily understand what an operation meant in terms of pain and discomfort. But she insisted that now was the right time; she didn't want any delays, and she assured him that I wanted the operation.

My ears were large and had stood out, flat, away from my skull. There was no natural bend. Dr. Ginsberg had to reshape them and bend them back to lie flat. It was a delicate and intricate procedure. Because my mother didn't want me to suffer any pain, she had asked him to administer as much morphine as my tiny system could tolerate, and he had complied.

The surgeon's work was extensive; he actually reformed my ears. Yet when the bandages were removed for the first time and I looked at myself in the mirror I was disappointed. I don't know what I had expected, but my ears hadn't changed in size; they were still large. True, they no longer flew away from the side of my head, like Dumbo's. Now they lay folded back, flatter, against my skull, with shape and form. The surgeon's knife had severed the one outstanding feature that could easily and instantly identify me as my father's child. I no longer had Clark Gable's ears.

My head was wrapped tightly in bandages for what seemed to me forever. The healing process was slow and very tedious. I made weekly visits to Dr. Ginsberg's office, and they were far from pleasant. In those days there were no dissolving stitches. Newly formed skin had grown over many of the stitches and they had to be removed manually in numerous delicate and painful mini-surgeries.

I sat in the doctor's chair and gritted my teeth, with tears rolling down my cheeks. I pleaded with my mother not to send me to the doctor, that I couldn't stand the pain and that I didn't want to go.

She was patient, but unyielding. "You have to go, Judy. The doctor has to examine you."

"It hurts when he does that," I'd wail.

"I know, but it has to be done. So why don't you think of St. Theresa, and follow her example? When there was something she had to do that she didn't like, she offered it up to the baby Jesus, for days off her purgatory." St. Theresa was my mother's favorite saint, and I always liked hearing stories about her.

The next time that I had to see Dr. Ginsberg I silently prayed to the baby Jesus to help me with my pain. I marked another day off my suffering in purgatory for my sins. If I was just like St. Theresa, whom my mother loved, then she would love me, too.

Miss Shankey, "Dearie" as I now called her, was very sympathetic to me but tolerated no complaining. She was a devout Christian Scientist and ignored illness of any kind. Pain was absolutely and totally unacceptable to her. She was loving and kind with me, but when it came time for any of my hurts, she became instantly stoically detached.

"Buck up, ducky," she'd say in her proper English way.

My tears dried up with those words and I would try to straighten my back like a brave soldier and struggle to stop my lower lip from quivering as quickly as possible. She wouldn't love me if I wasn't brave. It was very important that I be the good, brave girl that she expected me to be.

"One must suffer to be beautiful," Dearie would whisper to me in French as she stood beside me in the doctor's office, holding my hand tightly in hers. I struggled even harder to keep from crying, while he probed my skin. Somehow, her words gave me comfort; they had a lyrical quality to them. It became a private kind of mantra, just between the two of us, spoken in a language that no outsiders could understand, our secret communication.

And, after all, I had wanted the operation; I wanted to be beautiful. That's what my mommy and daddy told everyone. "Judy really wanted the operation. It probably would have been wiser to wait until she was a little older, but she wanted it now."

I remember the embarrassment my ears caused me, and the atten-

tion that had been paid to covering them for as long as I could recall. But at seven I was much too young to understand the real meaning and consequences of plastic surgery.

I may have wanted my ears fixed, but my mother wanted it even more. The surgery erased my connection with my father. My ears were his trademark. As long as they remained unaltered, there was little doubt about whose child I was. His most salient feature was genetically stamped on me, his daughter. The sooner this could be changed, the sooner my mother could rest more securely in her marriage.

I believed that the operation was my choice, but it was really my mother's. With my eager and willing cooperation, all physical association with my father was erased. She kept her secret, and I innocently enabled her to do it. There was no guarantee that I would have wanted the operation if I had waited until I was older, as the surgeon had recommended.

My ears weren't my only genetic imprint. I also had prominent buck teeth, just as my mother had had. Instead of waiting until my second teeth came in, my mother took me to an orthodontist, who put braces on my baby teeth, correcting my very noticeable overbite. The procedure had to be repeated once again when my second teeth came in crooked. Years later, when I looked at my childhood pictures, I was relieved that my buck teeth had been straightened, for they weren't very becoming, but I was also struck by the fact that they identified me as my mother's daughter. She still wore her retainer, the last remnant of her teenage braces. I bore both my parents' genetic "marks of Cain," and both had been "fixed."

My days as an only child came to an end two years later, on August 1, 1944. I clearly remember the night that my mother went to the hospital in labor with my brother. I thought she was dying.

My mother and father had been at a dinner party to celebrate their fourth wedding anniversary. I was awakened from a deep sleep by the sounds of voices in the front hallway. I couldn't hear what they were saying, but they sounded rushed and excited. As I climbed out of bed and tiptoed to the door, I heard footsteps running down the hall toward my mother's room.

I stayed in the shadows of the darkened room, fearful that I would be discovered if someone opened the door. I couldn't make much sense out of what was taking place, but I knew it had to do with my mother.

I heard my father's voice. He sounded upset. Then there was a woman's voice; it was calmer, but I couldn't tell if it was my mother's or not. It sounded as if there were other people, but I couldn't identify any of the voices. I heard a great deal of activity and footsteps scurrying back and forth between the entrance hall and my mother's room. Finally I heard the front door close and the house was silent again.

Where had everyone gone? Where was my mother? I knew that I was going to have a baby sister or a brother pretty soon. Maybe all this activity had something to do with the new baby.

Then I had a terrible thought. *What if she dies? What if she dies and I never see her again?* I was terrified. I began to cry and I couldn't stop. The more I cried, the more convinced I became that she was dying. My imagination was on a rampage and I was inconsolable.

I ran back into my room and knelt by the side of the bed and began to pray. "Dear Blessed Virgin, please don't let my mother die. I'll do anything you want me to do, only please don't let my mother die."

Miss Shankey found me the following morning, asleep on the floor beside my bed. I had spent the better part of the night praying and weeping. She knelt down beside me. "Judy, wake up. Your father just phoned from the hospital. You have a baby brother, Christopher Paul. He was born very early this morning. And your mother's fine."

I didn't tell anyone about my sleepless night of prayer and bargaining, but I silently thanked the Blessed Virgin for bringing my mother back from the dead. When I finally saw her again, when she finally came home after what seemed like weeks, she wasn't alone. She arrived with something wrapped up in a blanket in her arms.

Everybody was making such a big fuss. Why? It was only a baby, an ugly bald one at that. He was always drooling. Why was everyone paying so much attention to this squalling thing? I wanted her to take him back where she got him. I couldn't tell her that because she seemed so happy to have him, so I pretended that I was pleased that I had a baby brother. It wasn't easy.

The small guesthouse outside by the pool had been redecorated into a nursery. Now, if I wanted to spend any extended time with my mother and father, I had to share it with the intruder who was lodged there with his nurse.

I lay on the daybed beside my father while we watched my mother bathe this newcomer. It was a long, drawn-out, loving ritual, and I envied him. All eyes in the room were riveted on this tiny baby. When the adoration scene had finished and Christopher was bathed and diapered, Mommy held him up to the sky, gazing lovingly at him. I thought of the picture of the Madonna that hung in my classroom at Marymount School. Then she carefully handed him to Daddy, who sat in a big chair and rocked him back and forth, cooing to him. I felt I had disappeared. I no longer existed in that nursery.

The baby's nurse, Betty Smith, stood poised, ever ready in the background. She was petite, with flame-red hair in tight braids criss-crossed on top of her head. She always wore a stiffly starched white uniform, white stockings, and white shoes. Daddy told me that she had trained at Children's Hospital in New York. He made it sound very impressive, as if that was something special. But she seemed very cold to me. She was always alert and ready to give instruction at the slightest hesitation on my mother's part. I thought moms knew what to do with babies, but Miss Smith didn't seem to think so.

Finally my curiosity got the better of my reluctance even to touch the baby. What was so intriguing about him? I wondered. He was lying on a blanket on the diving board, taking his sunbath. With Miss Smith hovering nearby, I managed to bend down for a closer look at my rival. As I did, a stream of warm liquid hit my face. I jumped back in shock, not fully realizing what had happened. Miss Smith hurried over and covered his penis with a diaper. She began to laugh as she applied baby oil and wrapped the offending thing inside the folds of cloth.

I was humiliated; my baby brother had just peed on me. Embarrassed and full of shame, I hurried to the comfort and familiarity of my room. There I escaped into my own private world of make-believe, where new baby brothers couldn't read my mind and retaliate with weapons that I didn't possess.

My private inner world was a lavish fairy tale, peopled with everything and everyone I had encountered in the stories I had read. I lived there more than in the outer world of reality. It was safer. I was the queen or princess (I could always choose) of the realm, and my many subjects adored me. My castle gates were the gates to the play yard on the other side of the pool. My playhouse was my castle and no intruders could enter my kingdom. My loyal knights, dressed all in white, would shoot them down on sight.

Some days I'd climb the high wall that surrounded my castle and walk along the edge, surveying the land that I governed so wisely and so well. From this lofty position on my battlement I could look across the alleyway into the backyards of Beverly Hills, all under my rule, and all paying homage to me.

Two backyards away was the castle of my fantasy prince, Richard Romanek. Richard was about a year older than I was, and he and his older sister, Dorothy, went to public school. I imagined that he would lift me onto the back of his white horse and together we would ride into the woods, which was really his backyard. We sat together among the branches of his large tree, and the ripe avocados that fell into our outstretched hands were the fruit of love.

My castle roof was always warm from the sun, a perfect place to lie on my back, gazing up into the apricot tree and the clear blue sky beyond. The world inside my castle was as varied and rich as the one outside. My ladies- and gentlemen-in-waiting all had rooms of their own in my toy box. My entire court ate together at the red table with matching chairs, in contrast to my real-life meals in the breakfast room with Dearie. What were special occasions with my mother and father in the dining room were everyday occurrences in my kingdom.

When I played the queen, I had a princess, my Di-Dee doll. I fed her a bottle and she wet into her diaper from a little hole with a rubber stopper in her bottom. I gave her a bath and rubbed her body all over with oil and baby powder. I read to her and rocked her in my rocker. I placed her in her cradle and hid, waiting for her to come alive as I knew she would. I wanted a live baby just like my mother had. Then maybe I wouldn't feel so lonely.

Twelve months later my mother gave birth to Peter Charles. My kingdom was invaded and all the trusty knights of my realm couldn't keep the enemy from my castle gate. Christopher Paul and Peter Charles had intruded and my castle was destroyed.

"We've outgrown this house," my parents said. So we moved to a much larger house on Carolwood Drive in Holmby Hills. My playhouse moved with us, but it was no longer mine. Now it belonged to Christopher and Peter.

"You're too old for a playhouse, Judy," my mother said, and so their toys were put into my toy box, and the red table and chairs sat outside in the play yard until the sun cracked the wood and they had to be given away. My beautiful castle was now a storeroom for tricycles and boys' toys. No one went inside it anymore. I was no longer a princess. Two princes now reigned supreme in my parents' eyes.

7 THE CAROLWOOD HOUSE

The first Christmas with my mother and new father in the Camden house may have been the one of my dreams, but Christmas five years later, in our new home on Carolwood Drive, was quite the opposite. It marked the beginning of four confusing and far from happy years for me.

I remember waking up very early that day. I felt safe, high above the ground in the top bunk of my two-tiered pale blue bed. The witch that sometimes hid behind the heating grate, or underneath the bottom bunk ready to grab my feet as I got out of bed, or even behind the closet door when it was left half open, wasn't anywhere to be seen that morning. It was Christmas, my favorite day of the year, a perfect day.

In my mind I went over the items that I had carefully written on my Christmas list and played a game with myself of "guess which ones I'll get." The double holster with two shining metal cap pistols was one of my "really wants." It would look neat with new cowboy boots, another "really want." My cousin Gretchen and I went every Saturday to the Hitching Post Theater in Beverly Hills, where all morning we'd sit and watch Hopalong Cassidy, Roy Rogers, and Gene Autrey movies. Afterward, while we waited for my mother's chauffeur to come and get us, the boys from Gretchen's school would gather around us. Unlike me, Gretchen went to a coeducational school and was very popular. As a student at Marymount, an all-girls Catholic school, I didn't know any boys, so I was always happy to be included in her group.

A *winding driveway and tall foliage hide the Carolwood house from view.*
ANDRE R. WILLIEME

The boys loved to lay long rolls of red caps out flat on the ground and stomp on them with the heels of their cowboy boots. The loud noise frightened me but I didn't cover my ears. I wanted to be brave.

No, I decided, *I probably won't get the holster with the cap pistols. Mom doesn't like the noise they make either. But I'll probably get some Albert Payson Terhune books and maybe some more glass animals to add to my collection, and maybe even new spurs to go on my English riding boots. I know I won't get my own horse. Mom told me that I can have riding lessons, but I can't have my own horse.* I put it on my list anyway, and wrote "please, please, please" next to it, just in case.

The usual Christmas-morning ritual was to wait until my mother or father came to get me before I went downstairs, but this morning I couldn't wait.

"They'll never know if I sneak downstairs now, before anybody is awake," I told myself. "I've just got to see the tree and all those presents." The more I thought about it, the more excited I became. "Everyone is still asleep, the house is quiet. I could sneak downstairs for just one quick look and sneak back upstairs and no one would know."

"What if someone heard you?" said my cautious side.

"Who's going to be up at this hour? It's too early. Come on. Let's go."

"But that's being disobedient. You're supposed to obey your parents."

"They'll never know."

My inner argument settled, I climbed down the ladder. The hallway was dark, the door to Christopher and Peter's room was closed. So was the one to their bathroom. The rooms were right next to mine and both were locked from within. On both doors handwritten signs read: QUIET, DO NOT DISTURB. BABY SLEEPING. The boys' nurse, Betty Smith, had posted them. My mom and dad seemed to love her. I hated her and she hated me in return. She put up notes all over the house, even on my bedroom door. I couldn't practice the piano in the living room when Peter was taking his nap in the side rose garden. I couldn't listen to my radio in the afternoon after school because it was time for the boys' naps and the sound would disturb them. And I couldn't go in and out of the nursery whenever I wanted to. There were certain designated visiting hours, usually in the late afternoon, before my brothers had their bath and their dinner. I was expected to stay in my room until it was my time to visit.

Miss Smith had my baby brothers on very regimented routines and kept me separated from them as much as possible. Whether this was the result of orders given to her or just her own personal whim I don't know, but neither my mother nor my father seemed to notice that I wasn't invited to participate in my brothers' lives. In fact, with the arrival of my brothers I felt that nobody seemed to notice me at all.

I tiptoed quietly down the hall past Miss Shankey's room, past the sitting room, past the linen room with the sink for washing Mom's hair and the professional hair dryer she always sat under, and past Miss Shankey's office, where she so often sat, puffing on the ever-present cigarette that dangled from her lips while she autographed pictures of my mother for fans. She was not only my governess now, but my mother's secretary as well.

This new house (originally built as a wedding present by the Mexican movie star Gilbert Roland for his wife, actress Constance Bennett) was much bigger than the Camden house. There were so many more rooms, thirty-six of them I counted once. In the back hallway of the servants' wing a laundry chute, lined in tin, went down into the cellar, where the machines and washtubs were. There was a dumbwaiter to move food and dishes from the main kitchen to the second-floor kitchen just by yanking down hard on a pulley. In the den there was a movie screen. It didn't come out of the floor, like at Barbara Warner's house. Instead, the walls slid apart and it just appeared. There was even a projection room, with tall stools to sit on so you could watch the movie through the peephole.

As I made my way slowly past the suite of rooms where my mother and father slept and down the curving staircase to the front entry I could almost hear my heartbeats in the silence of the sleeping house. Only a few more steps and I'd be in the front room, where last night the Christmas tree stood unadorned in front of the big bay window.

As I rounded the corner I saw the tree, decorated now with all kinds of multicolored tin ornaments, and mounds of presents that seemed to spread out all over the room. In one corner I saw something large. It was a dressing table, just like the one my mother had in her dressing room, only smaller—the most beautiful dressing table I'd ever seen. It was kidney-shaped with a mirrored top and the most beautiful full pale blue lace and net skirt falling straight down to the floor. A small stool, covered in the same blue net, sat in front of it.

I moved closer to get a better look at this vision. There was writing on the three-panel mirror standing on top of the dressing table. On the left side was written, in pale blue lettering, GOOD MORNING, DEAR LORD. And on the right side was GOOD NIGHT, DEAR LORD. PRETTY IS AS PRETTY DOES was written on the middle one. There was a card lying on the mirrored top of the table:

> Dear Judy,
> Merry Christmas.
> With Love, from Mom and Dad

Suddenly, a loud and frightening voice exploded behind me, breaking the silence of the early morning and scaring me. "What are you doing down here?"

I was so surprised that I jumped instinctively and the card fell from my hands as I turned around.

"Answer me. What are you doing down here?" A few feet away from me, my father was standing like a statue, his arms by his sides. I will never forget seeing the initials *THAL* embroidered in red on the blue-silk cuff of his pajama sleeve, and the feeling of fright I had looking at him. He was very angry. I opened my mouth to speak but no words came out. Hot tears of shame and humiliation began stinging my eyes. I wanted to disappear, but all I could do was stand there, caught.

"Well, say something. Don't just stand there with your mouth hanging open. Why aren't you in your room, where you belong? You were told to stay there until we came to get you."

I wanted to explain that I just couldn't wait to see the tree, but still no words came.

"You're a very naughty girl, Judy." He moved closer and was now standing in front of me. He bent down and, with a look of disgust, picked up the card and placed it back on the dressing table. "You've ruined your mother's Christmas. She wanted to surprise you. She went to a lot of trouble having this dressing table made for you at the studio, and she wanted to surprise you on Christmas morning."

"I'm sorry, Daddy." Finally the words came out, along with the flood of tears that had been welling up and could no longer be held back. I was terrified that he would tell her what I had done. I didn't want to disappoint her. I didn't want to ruin her Christmas. "Please don't tell Mom. I'm sorry, Dad. Please don't tell Mom," I pleaded through my tears.

He said nothing, just stood there looking at me. I couldn't tell what he was thinking. He turned his back and walked out of the room.

I hurried back to my bedroom and climbed into bed, waiting to be called downstairs to begin Christmas morning. But my Christmas had already begun, and it was no longer my favorite day.

It was my mother who came and got me and took me downstairs before we went to Christmas mass. "There's something very special that I want you to see," she said as she led me by the hand down the stairs. She was smiling and excited. I felt miserable, and it was all I could do to keep from crying. I couldn't let her know anything about this morning; I had to put on a good act for her. I couldn't disappoint her. I didn't know whether I could be convincing enough.

My father followed closely behind. His expression told me nothing. Would he expose me? I didn't know.

"Well, what do you think?" My mother was standing in the middle of the room now, her eyes on me expectantly. I looked at the dressing table and pretended, as best I could, to be surprised.

"Oh, Mom! It's beautiful! It's the most beautiful thing I've ever seen."

And it was, but I didn't sound very convincing to myself. I sounded like a liar. My stomach was in a hard knot and I felt awful. I didn't have to look behind me; I could feel my father's eyes boring into the back of my head. I was waiting any second for his voice to say "You're such a liar. You've ruined your mother's surprise."

Filled with shame, I went over to her and hugged her as tightly as I could. "Thank you, Mom. I love you."

"I love you, too." And she hugged me back. "Aren't you going to read the card?" she asked. "It's from your father, too." I walked over to him. I couldn't look at him. "Thank you, Daddy."

"You're welcome, Judy," he replied, his voice distant and cold.

After church we gathered around the tree and began opening all our presents. Christopher, sixteen months old and barely able to walk, was into everything. Peter was only five months old, still too young to understand what was happening.

As a sedate ten-year-old I opened each present as it was handed to me and carefully recorded on a note pad what I had received and who had given it to me. Then I put it back in the box and placed the box on top of the dressing table. In the past this had been the only part of Christmas that I didn't like because it reminded me of all the thank-you notes I would have to write. But this year I was grateful

for the task; it kept me busy, distracted from the early-morning upset with my father.

He hadn't spoken to me since I had thanked him for the dressing table. I might have fooled my mother with my act, but he knew how dishonest I was. His silence showed his disapproval. But this wasn't a new experience for me. He no longer called me Juddy as he used to before my brothers were born. He played with his sons, picking them up and putting them on his shoulders for rides, but we no longer played our games together or took our long walks. In fact, we did nothing together anymore.

The fact that I had gotten everything that I had asked for on my Christmas list—except the horse, of course—just added to my feelings of guilt. I was really surprised by the cap pistols and holster, and with each gift I felt more and more unworthy and more and more ashamed.

Suddenly there was a loud crash, followed by the sound of shattering glass. I spun around and saw that the three-way mirror that a moment before had been sitting on top of the dressing table was now in a million little pieces on the living room floor. The last present that I had put on top of the pile had been placed in such a way that the boxes pushed against the mirror, sending everything crashing to the ground.

There was a split-second of dead silence as I stood staring at the destruction. Then piercing screams filled the room. Peter and Christopher, frightened by the unexpected noise, were both yelling at the top of their baby lungs.

My mother rushed to Peter, picking him up instantly, and began patting him gently. "Shh! That's all right. It's just a noise. Shh!" she cooed as she rocked the crying infant in her arms.

My father scooped up Christopher and began walking back and forth, talking to him as he walked the length of the room.

1945. That first unhappy Christmas in the Carolwood house. Left to right: my brother Christopher, me trying very hard to look happy, my mother in her Christmas finery with infant Peter on her lap.
AUTHOR'S COLLECTION

I felt as if I were in pieces, like the shattered glass I saw all around me. After I cleaned it up I went straight up the back stairs from the kitchen to my bedroom, where I closed the door and lay down on my bed. Finally the tears came in a flood, the tears that I'd held back all day long. I put my head down into my pillow and sobbed until I couldn't cry anymore.

Later, my mother came into my room and sat down on the bed beside me. "Don't worry about the mirror, Judy. I'll have another one made at the studio, just like the one that broke." She was smiling at me.

"I'm sorry, Mom." I started to cry again. She put her arm around me.

"It wasn't your fault, it just fell over, that's all. We'll get another one." What she couldn't know was that that wasn't what I was sorry about. I was sorry that I was such a bad girl and a disappointment to her and that I had ruined her surprise.

That night I had my recurring nightmare. Someone was chasing me; I was going to be caught. And every time I turned around I couldn't see who it was. When I awoke I didn't go back to sleep again, fearful of repeating the dream, as I often did.

When the war ended, my father went back to work at Young & Rubicam as vice-president of West Coast operations. A year later he resigned, and then, unlike my mother, he was at home most of the time. He called himself a businessman, but he wasn't like any of the other fathers I knew who went to an office every day and had a title like lawyer or doctor. My father was not only home almost all the time, but he didn't appear to work. I was told he "sat on boards," whatever that meant. Although I didn't understand what my father did, I didn't ask for any explanations. My mother worked in movies and my father stayed home. That's just the way it was in my family now.

My mother's career continued to flourish during the war years, and after the war she made one picture after another, almost non-stop. She was gone a great deal, either at the studio or on location. I saw very little of her, and even on those occasions when she was home she was rarely accessible. Much of her leisure time was devoted to the care and feeding of her career, which had been entrusted to her personal publicist, Helen Ferguson.

I don't know exactly when Helen entered my mother's life, but I connect her with my new father, since she seemed to arrive around the same time he did. She was small and wiry with dark hair, and she possessed a kind of silent Medea-like intensity. She was obsessive in her attachment to my mother. They went everywhere together and she directed interviews and my mother's professional life with a passion and dedication that left no room for anyone or anything else. She doted on my mother, who in turn depended on her and trusted her implicitly with her private as well as her public life.

Even when I was a small child I noticed that whenever Helen Ferguson entered the room my mother seemed to change spontaneously into the public person, the movie star. Helen's arrival generally heralded an interview or a photographic session, but whatever it was, I was instantly banished. So from the age of six on, I came to associate Helen with my dismissal, and I came to dislike her intensely for it. I felt invisible around her and I silently blamed her for keeping my mother inaccessible. As time went on, whenever I saw Helen, I didn't wait to be told to leave (or to "get lost," as my mother often put it), I just did it automatically.

As a child it was easier for me to blame Helen than my mother. I couldn't admit then what I probably felt but couldn't articulate. It was simpler to accept my mother's explanation that she didn't want me to be exploited than it was to admit that she didn't want me to exist publicly, for as I grew older I was beginning to resemble her more and more. While I was not aware of this at the time, I did feel that something about me was wrong.

When we did spend time together, it was usually in her dressing room. I'd settle myself in the chaise longue and watch as she applied her makeup in preparation for some social engagement. I was in-

A *rare family gathering in the garden of the Carolwood house. Left to right: Gladys Belzer; Norman Foster; Polly Ann Hermann; Carter Hermann; Sally Foster with her back to the camera; Loretta Young Lewis; Tom Lewis; Georgiana Montalban, and Ricardo Montalban.*

trigued with the thick mascara that she melted over a candle flame and applied carefully, lash by lash. I loved the smell in her closets. The clothes still held the scent of her perfume, sweet, like flowers. I tend to associate my mother with her clothes. She dressed in beautiful outfits, perfect down to the smallest detail. She could spend hours in a fitting room, standing on a small platform slowly turning while the seamstress measured the length of her skirt, or pinned a dart here, a seam there. Sometimes she took me with her when she went to the studio fittings. I sat quietly on a chair watching the ritual while dress after dress was put on, fitted, and carefully taken off. It bored me, but my mother never seemed bored. She loved it; she was tireless and never happier than when she was fitting and "talking clothes." When she was gone for a long stretch of time and I missed

her, I would sit in the chaise in her dressing room, among her clothes, and I wouldn't feel so lonely.

I learned how to delay my need to talk to her until I had private access to her. Then I would wait to see what kind of mood she was in and I'd try to mirror her. I'd try to fit what I thought she might want me to be; that way I knew that I'd have her attention. It was almost like playing a role with her; she wrote the script and I played my part the way she cast it. I became very adept at this make-believe game. After a while I could adapt to her mood almost instinctively and I moved into her emotional world with no effort at all, often sacrificing mine for hers.

I remember the frustration I felt when the time was limited, as was often the case, or when her attention was diverted from me to something else, so that she wasn't mine anymore. When I did have her attention I tried to gauge her mood to make sure she was emotionally available. If it seemed she was not, I would wait for a more opportune moment rather than risk a rebuff or dismissal, both of which were unbearable to me.

Looking back, all these many years later, I can see I was much like a starving child, coming away only half-filled from those interludes with my mother. I was starved for attention, for affection, for recognition, and for love.

I don't remember the exact moment that I began to sense there was something not right about my adoption. I always felt that I was different from everyone else, that there was something wrong with me, but from the moment of my brothers' arrival my feelings of being an outsider began to take on even greater proportions.

One evening I sat in the chaise watching my mother getting ready to go out, wondering whether I should tell her what was on my mind. I was confused about something that Mary Frances Griffin had said to me. Mary Frances, nicknamed Murph, was the adopted daughter of Irene Dunne and her husband Frank Griffin. She knew all about adoptions, she told me. Her mother had told her that she picked her out of all the other children at the orphanage because she was special. "When you're adopted you're special because you're wanted," Murph said with an air of superiority.

I wondered why my mother hadn't told me that I was special. I wondered if my real parents didn't want me and if that was why they gave me away to the orphanage in the first place. Then Murph asked me something strange, something that I didn't have any answer for, something that disturbed me.

"If you're adopted, why is it that you look so much like your mother?"

"I don't know," I answered. And I thought to myself, *Aren't daughters supposed to look like their mothers?*

"If your mother isn't your real mother, why do you look like each other? Only real parents and children are supposed to look like each other." She must have been reading my mind.

Now, with my mother, I decided to take a chance. "Mom, are you my real mother?"

She stopped what she was doing. Her eyes locked on mine in the mirror. "What makes you ask a question like that, Judy?"

"Murph said that only real parents and children are supposed to look like each other."

She swiveled around on her stool so that she was facing me.

"And what else did Murph say?"

Uh-oh! I knew then that I shouldn't have asked that question. She had that funny look she sometimes got when I said something that I shouldn't have. Her eyes grew narrow and her voice got cold. *She's angry,* I thought. But I didn't know why.

"Murph says that we look like each other. That's all. She asked me how come, since I was adopted."

"I couldn't love you any more than if you were my own child, Judy." The penetrating look that had scared me disappeared.

What does that mean? I wondered. *Am I her own child? Is that what she means? If I'm not her own child, does that mean she doesn't love me?* Before I could say anything, she continued.

"You know, when two people live so closely in the same household, as you and I do, as mother and daughter, it's only natural for you to pick up mannerisms, the inflections in my voice, things like that. That's probably what Murph meant when she said that we looked like each other."

"Did you want me?" There it was again; the look in her eyes was back.

"When?"

"When you adopted me."

"Where are all these questions coming from?"

"Murph's mother told her that when you're adopted, you're special because you're wanted."

"Judy, I will say it again, I couldn't love you any more than if you were my own child. And if that doesn't make you feel special, I don't know what could." She got up from her stool and went into the other room, leaving me feeling more confused than ever.

I saw that the subject of my adoption was one I couldn't discuss freely with my mother. I didn't ask many questions about it after that. But I did begin telling my friends that my mother picked me out of all the other children in the orphanage, and that made me special. If it was true for Murph, then it could be true for me.

My mother might often have been inaccessible, but my father was exactly the opposite. He seemed to be everywhere, watching everything that I did. When my mother married my father and turned the management of her finances over to him at the beginning of their marriage, she also gave him full authority over me and everything pertaining to me, including discipline.

When I was about eleven he decided I should begin my education in economics. He told me I would receive a weekly allowance of twenty-five cents, but I had to earn it. Aside from keeping my room neat, my weekly chore was to clean the brick patio. It was quite large and had many pieces of oversized upholstered patio furniture. He instructed the maid to show me how to sweep, hose, and scrub the brick floor, dust and clean all the furniture thoroughly from top to bottom, and clean all the glass-topped tables until they shone.

"She will show you only once, Judy. It will be your responsibility from then on," he said. To ensure that this job would be mine, he instructed the staff that under no circumstances were they to assist me. At the time the staff of servants was substantial: a housekeeper; the boys' nurse, Miss Smith; a relief nurse; Miss Shankey; a cook; a relief cook; an upstairs maid and a downstairs maid; a gardener; a houseman who took care of my father's clothes; and a night watchman.

Before I received my allowance, my father would hold a weekly patio inspection to see if my work was satisfactory. I dreaded those inspections. I was always fearful that he would find something wrong and that I would be told to do it again. Invariably there was some small corner that I had overlooked.

I no longer felt comfortable around him. He showed no affection toward me anymore; in fact, he frightened me, and I was anxious and apprehensive that I might do something to displease him. His lectures on my performance were an embarrassment that I endured in respectful silence. He had the tendency to talk extensively on any subject, and his tirades left me feeling desolate.

I often couldn't sleep the night before "patio inspection," worrying whether he would approve of my job or whether I would have to do it all over again. I came to believe I was incapable of performing the task well enough. I'd done it again and again, and no matter how hard I tried, it was never good enough. I could never please him.

At the same time a rebel voice in me asked why, with a full staff, it was so important that I be the one to clean the patio. But there was no one I could ask to intercede. If I went to Miss Shankey to complain about my father, she would certainly listen to me, but I knew she could change nothing. Moreover, I was afraid if she said something she might even be dismissed. If I asked any of the servants to help me, they could also get in trouble. I knew I had to handle the situation on my own.

When my mother was away, I lived for her return, feeling sometimes I couldn't tolerate the waiting for one more day. When location filming was prolonged, I often became terrified that she would never come back to get me. I became obsessed with the idea that I'd never see her again, and then what would become of me? Because that thought was too awful to hold for very long, I would fantasize about what it would be like when she finally did come home. Once she was home, I knew I wouldn't feel so totally alone. I knew she wouldn't let my father send me away, something I secretly feared.

Sometimes, just when it seemed more than I could bear, my mother would suddenly and miraculously send for me. I would go to visit her at the studio or wherever she was on location. I came to view those events quite unrealistically, as an extrasensory-perception communication between us. I reasoned that she had sensed how much I missed her and that was why she had sent for me. I didn't have to tell her my thoughts; she already knew them. My preadolescent magical thinking was confirmed when she told me, "I haven't seen you in such a long time, and I was missing you."

I told none of my worries to anyone; they were too terrifying, and I felt it would have been dangerous to voice them. I believed I had

1945. Celebrating my tenth birthday on the set of The Accused. *My mother was helping me cut my cake.*

to give my mother the impression that I was all right, that I was fine. I couldn't disclose any of my fears; otherwise, I would be a burden to her. She wouldn't want to hear that my father frightened me to the point of immobility; she wouldn't love me then.

But of course I wasn't fine and I must have unconsciously wanted to be rescued pretty desperately, or, at the very least, to call attention to my isolation and to my feelings of fear and hopelessness, because I began to invent fake injuries—a sprained ankle, a hurt wrist, an eye infection. What I really wanted was my mother's attention. I remembered that when I was in the hospital, having my ears operated on, she was there by my side all the time. *Maybe,* I reasoned, *if I'm hurt she'll be there again.* But the "injuries" weren't serious enough to attract my teachers' attention, so no one called my mother. Just as well, for I was telling lies, and that was a sin. My mother would have been very unhappy with me for lying.

It seems incredible to me now that no one at school saw my fake injuries as obvious attempts to call attention to myself. But in the forties there wasn't much information about somatic acting out; nor for that matter was there much knowledge about how anxiety affects the body.

It wasn't until a few years later, shortly after my mother brought a stranger home one Sunday, that I began to experience blinding headaches—and this time they were quite real.

My mother came home from church supporting a young boy who appeared to be about my age. He was covered with bruises, his face cut and bloody, his pants ripped, and both knees skinned raw. He looked awful.

"Quick, Judy," she said when she saw the look of shock on my face, "get some blankets from the linen closet upstairs and bring them down here to me. Then have Miss Shankey call Dr. Marxer and tell him to come over here right away, that it's an emergency." She moved by me with the strange boy leaning heavily against her and headed for the den. I couldn't seem to move.

"What happened, Mom?" I asked.

"This poor child was hit by a car and knocked off his bicycle. The idiot didn't even stop to see if he was all right. He just drove off. Hurry up now, Judy, get those blankets." Her tone was urgent.

When I came back downstairs with the blankets the boy was lying on the couch in the den, shivering. As my mother tucked blankets around him, he started to sit up. He was frightened, but my mother calmed him instantly with a steady hand on his shoulder.

As soon as Webster Marxer, our family friend and physician, arrived, he knelt down beside the boy and began to examine him, while my mother led me out of the room. When I asked her if the boy was going to be all right, she seemed preoccupied and murmured something about his complaining of having a headache and that he might have a concussion. She told me to stay outside and wait until she called me. Then she hurried back into the den.

As I sat on the couch in the big bay window, I wondered why my mother was so interested in this total stranger. Somehow it made me feel sad. I couldn't understand why she was so concerned about him. She appeared to pay more attention to him than she had to me in the past. He was just a strange boy she picked off the street, and now she was nursing him as if he were her own child.

Then I became frightened. *What if she likes him better than she does me? Maybe she'll want to keep him.* Suddenly I wanted this intruder to leave before she got too attached to him.

Later that evening my mother came into my room and told me that the boy's mother had picked him up and taken him home. "It turns out he does have a concussion, poor kid. I hope he's going to be all right," she told me. I felt a wave of happiness and relief that he was gone.

Shortly afterward the headaches came on suddenly, without any warning. They usually started at school, and this time I was noticed and sent to the infirmary. They were so severe that my mother finally took me to Dr. Marxer. Although he could find nothing organically wrong, the headaches continued to persist for some time. In the case of both the imagined injuries and the actual headaches, I still failed to realize my fantasy of having my mother by my side, taking care of me.

1947. One of the special occasions when I visited my mother on location. She was away from Los Angeles filming The Farmer's Daughter.

AUTHOR'S COLLECTION

I always knew instinctively when my mother was working on a new picture because she changed in subtle ways. It was nothing dramatic, nothing that could really be noticed outwardly, except probably by me because I was so keenly aware of her moods. She became distracted more easily and I could tell that her mind was somewhere else. It was as if, in some part of herself, she was trying the character on for size.

When she began working on *The Farmer's Daughter* she surprised me by suddenly dying her brown hair blond for the role. She had always emphasized how pretty natural-colored hair was, and I believed it was almost a crime to dye your hair. In fact, I thought women who dyed their hair were cheap, especially blondes.

Once I told her that I had plucked my eyebrows like the other girls in my class. I hadn't really, I just wanted to see what reaction I would get. She was furious and said that if she ever caught me touching my eyebrows it would make her very, very unhappy. She told me how all the young actresses in the twenties shaved their eyebrows and then penciled them in. It was the look at the time, but she told me that their eyebrows didn't grow back the same way. "You can never improve on what God gave you," she cautioned me. I never tried.

So now, to see my mother with brassy blond hair was quite a shock. Not only did she have yellow hair, but she began to speak strangely, too, in a singsong lilt, with her mouth pursed as if she were getting ready to kiss someone. She would practice with me after working all day with her dialogue coach, Ruth Roberts.

The first time I met Ruth, she was sitting with my mother on the round couch in the bay window, having coffee. I liked her instantly. She was rather plain in looks and wore no makeup, and her clothes were practical, too, with no frills, but her smile was warm and friendly and her eyes looked straight into mine.

Thereafter, she lived at our house and I can't remember a single day that she wasn't with my mother until the picture was finished. Ruth, who had been born in Sweden, was teaching my mother how to speak with a Swedish accent. When they were together I knew that they were working, even though it appeared otherwise. I had orders not to disturb them, yet somehow I never felt like an outsider with Ruth. She was gentle and warm with me, always including me in the conversation. There was a very strong bond between my mother and Ruth, but not one that excluded me.

My mother formed another strong bond on that picture, with her producer, Dore Schary, and his wife, Miriam, and so did I. I didn't realize it at the time, but the Schary family became my idealized family, the dream family that I secretly wanted and didn't have.

Dore had been a writer-producer at MGM and was now head of production for Selznick International Pictures. He was very tall and handsome, with thick dark hair and a ready, warm smile. Miriam was pretty, delicate, and petite. Their daughter Jill was my age, her sister Joy several years younger, and Jeb was the youngest of the three children. They were rowdy and affectionate with one another. There was an ease and a unity and closeness among them that I didn't have with my brothers. I wanted what they had; I envied them.

The Schary house in Brentwood was generous and comfortable, just like the family. I immediately felt right at home there, as if I were one of them. Soon I was spending sleepover nights with Jill, and she was doing the same with me. I was even included in their Sunday night family dinner parties, where everyone sat together at the same table. There were no separate "baby tables" like the ones where the children usually sat at our family parties. At the Scharys' we even had our own place cards, just like the adults.

Miriam and Dore entertained lavishly and often. Their dinner guests always included a lively group of motion picture celebrities, like Gene Kelly, Paul Henreid, Jack and Mary Benny, George and Gracie Burns, even my aunt Georgiana and her new husband, Ricardo Montalban, who was under contract at MGM. (They had been introduced by my aunt Sally Foster and eloped to Tijuana in 1945 after knowing each other only three weeks.) There was always entertainment. If one of the guests didn't give an impromptu show, like Danny Kaye's hilarious monologues, there was the latest not-yet-released MGM or Selznick International film.

What amazed me the most was the easy, natural conversational exchanges the Schary children had with their parents and their parents' friends. All three children expressed their feelings and opinions freely in public, especially Jill. She was very outspoken and articulate, and instead of being reprimanded for intruding on a conversation, she was acknowledged. She was skillful verbally and didn't hesitate to present her point of view, even if it was in opposition to that of her parents. This was unthinkable to me. Even to explore an idea that ran counter to my family's thinking just wasn't an option for me. It was simply accepted that I thought as they did, and that my opinions were secondary to theirs, if not irrelevant.

My awe and wonder at Jill's bravery grew with each encounter. She took on the proportions of "Wonder Woman," defending her right to speak. It didn't occur to me that this independence of thought and expression was an essential part of the Schary family dynamic; Dore encouraged his children to be free thinkers. It was an attitude diametrically opposed to the one in my home, where children were seen and not heard.

Dore was what the Hollywood establishment labeled a liberal. He encouraged his children to speak for themselves. The freedom of expression in this family was an unknown element to me and it was sometimes quite intimidating. Unlike the Schary children, I had no political awareness. My family's politics were conservative Republican, and Catholic. Most of their friends were like them; the discussions in my household tended to be heated religious ones.

When my parents had dinner parties I wasn't allowed to join the group as the Schary children were. I curtsied and said "Good evening" to everyone. Then after a few minutes I quietly left the room, as I'd been instructed. There was a memorably awful time when I had to come downstairs to say my bedtime prayers. It was embarrassing, kneeling down in the middle of a roomful of strangers and voicing my private prayers. Thank God that didn't last very long.

Politically, Dore, who was Jewish, was a liberal Democrat. His films reflected his passion for the underdog and were known at the time for having a "message." He built his reputation with films that made a statement, usually against various kinds of discrimination.

I loved going to the Scharys'. I loved all the noise and the laughter and entertainment. I wanted to move right in. While I didn't get to live there, I did get to go there very often. Miriam, who was a painter, said she wanted to paint my portrait. Portraits of Jill and Joy and Jeb were everywhere in the house. I don't know why she chose me, or even if she did. Perhaps my mother asked her to paint me. Maybe she needed a subject to work on and I was there, or possibly she was aware of my loneliness and was reaching out. What was important to me was that someone I really liked actually wanted to spend time with me. I looked forward to my visits to her large, light studio in the garden.

While I sat motionless, posing on my tall wooden stool, I could watch the sunbeams playing across the wood floor and over all Miriam's paintings hanging on the wall beside me. Through the glass wall I could look out into the garden, with its lush flower beds, just like the pictures I'd seen of gardens in the English Tudor homes on which the Schary house was patterned.

A strong odor of turpentine, oil paint, and cigarette smoke always greeted my entrance into the studio. It wasn't unpleasant; it was a good smell, one that came to signify intimacy. I was in heaven sitting on my stool in that airy studio, listening to the classical music Miriam always had playing softly and watching her work. I told her my thoughts and dreams and fears, though never the scary ones, the ones that woke me up at night. She was a good listener.

Just recently Jill Schary recalled once asking her mother why she had painted my ears so large. She remembers her mother answering "Because they are big, just like her father, Clark Gable's." Miriam told her daughter the truth about my parents, that I wasn't adopted but was in fact my mother's natural-born child, and Miriam cautioned Jill that she was trusting her with an important secret that she must keep to herself.

When Miriam finished my portrait she gave it to my mother, who hung it over the couch in our projection room. But she never really liked it, and when we moved from the Carolwood house it went into storage with the unwanted furniture. The portrait resurfaced two moves later at the beach house but was never hung again.

Sadly, the bonds that are formed during the filming of motion pictures often end when the picture ends, or, like my portrait, are put into storage for a while, until another picture comes along. Then that link of friendship and creative alliance is reforged, to hold just as firmly as before. The Schary family left my life when my mother finished *The Farmer's Daughter*. She had a new producer, Samuel Goldwyn, but at least Ruth Roberts remained as my mother's constant friend and coach.

Before my mother started her new picture, *The Bishop's Wife*, our family went to Lake Arrowhead for a vacation. When my parents told me I would be sharing a bedroom with Miss Smith in a three-bedroom bungalow at the North Shore Tavern, I didn't want to go. I didn't want to be in the same room with her. We didn't like each

1947. Visiting my mother on the set of The Bishop's Wife. *The entire stage was a winter scene, complete with a frozen pond, created by set designer George Jenkins. Left to right: Gabriella Maisonville, a school friend; my mother, costumed for her skating scene with Cary Grant; my cousin Gretchen Foster; and me.*
AUTHOR'S COLLECTION

other, and she was openly hostile to me, but only when my parents weren't present. I asked my mother if I could have my own room, but she told me no, that it would be too costly.

It was a lonely time. My school friends were back in Los Angeles, and although I tried very hard to play with my brothers, at three and two they were just too young for us to have much in common. My efforts to bond with them could only be in the role of a parent or a caretaker, and there was only room for one nurse, Miss Smith. She wasn't about to be replaced by me or to let me have much contact or interaction with my brothers if she could possibly help it. So I spent the days by myself, horseback riding and swimming.

One evening when I returned to the room from a hayride I found Miss Smith waiting up for me. The minute I came through the door, she began to yell at me: "How dare you write these things about me!"

At first I didn't know what she was talking about. Then I saw that she was holding a letter in her hand, a letter that I had written just that afternoon to Miss Shankey. I hadn't sealed it, and Miss Smith had found it, taken it out of the envelope, and read it. She was wild-eyed with anger, totally out of control.

While her accusation had startled me at first, I quickly remembered what I had said in the letter. I had poured out all my discomfort about the living arrangements to Miss Shankey. I told her how much I wished she were there instead, and how much I hated Miss Smith. Now Miss Smith had read the letter and knew my most intimate thoughts.

"That's not your letter. I wrote that to Miss Shankey."

She tore up the letter into shreds. "It isn't anyone's letter now."

I was so shocked that I could do nothing but look down at the floor, where my letter lay in little pieces. Before I knew it, she had grabbed my arm and was dragging me toward the open closet door. I pulled back to resist, but she was very strong and in her fury she almost yanked me off my feet.

"I'm going to teach you a lesson you'll never forget." We had reached the closet now. It was dark inside and I began to feel a lump in my throat. I was frightened.

"Please, Miss Smith, let me go." I was crying now but her grip on my arm was relentless. I didn't know what she was going to do.

"Not until you apologize for what you said." We were inside the closet by now. She reached behind her and closed the door. I felt I would suffocate in the cramped, dark place.

"I'm sorry, Miss Smith," I sobbed.

But she didn't appear to hear me. She began to shake me with all her strength, her arms pulling me back and forth with such force that I thought my shoulders would be wrenched out of their sockets. My whole body was jerked back and forth with the violence of her shaking. Suddenly the shaking stopped, and she let go of my arms. I could hear her breath coming in short gasps from her exertions. She opened the closet door and walked away.

When I finally found the strength to walk back into the bedroom, Miss Smith was nowhere in sight. The pieces of my letter had also disappeared. Exhausted, I lay down on the bed and closed my eyes. I awoke with terrible stomach cramps that came in waves, engulfing me with nausea. Violently ill, I hurried to the bathroom, where I began to vomit.

"What's the matter, dear?" My mother was standing over me as I sat on the cold tile floor.

"I don't feel well," was all that I could manage between recurring waves of nausea.

"I'm so sorry. I was afraid you might eat too much on that hayride. It's not good to horseback-ride on such a full stomach. I thought something like this might happen."

"Could I sleep in your room tonight, Mom?" *Please say yes,* I prayed silently. I knew I couldn't go back into the bedroom. I couldn't bear to be in the same room with Miss Smith. I was afraid of her and of what she would do to me.

"I don't think so, not tonight. But I tell you what, I'll stay with you until you fall asleep, and I'll leave the door open between our rooms so you can come and get me if you feel like you're going to be sick again."

Knowing that she would be by my side made me feel better and I clung to her as she led me into my room and put me to bed. I couldn't tell her what had happened in the closet. She would have asked me what I had done to make Miss Smith that angry. I would have had to tell her about my letter to Miss Shankey. I didn't want her to know that I hated Miss Smith and hated sharing a room with her. After all, Mom told me that I had to share a room. It would seem as if I was complaining about her to Miss Shankey. She'd be angry with me for doing that. I couldn't stand it if she was angry with me. I never told her about the incident.

I can still remember the rustling sound of my mother's taffeta dress as she went down the stairs on the night of March 20, 1948, on her way to the Shrine Auditorium for the Academy Awards presentation. She had been nominated for her performance in *The Farmer's Daughter.*

For a week I had been pleading with her to let me go to the awards ceremony, but she didn't believe that she was going to win. She was convinced that the award would go to her close friend, Rosalind Russell, for her performance in *Mourning Becomes Electra.*

I had made my final plea in her dressing room as she was stepping into her long, emerald-green taffeta dress with all the ruffles.

"I'd gladly let you come, Judy, if I thought there was the slightest chance I might win. But there really isn't. Mine was just a nice little picture. You can stay up and listen to the ceremonies on the radio," she told me as she pulled on her long green-taffeta gloves. I followed her out into the hallway and stood at the top of the stairs, watching her go down to meet my father, who was waiting for her in the foyer. She looked gorgeous.

Later, Miss Shankey and I listened to the broadcast of the awards, and when Olivia de Havilland read, "Loretta Young for *The Farmer's*

In her glamorous green-taffeta dress, my mother gazes at the Academy Award presented to her by Fredric March. She was named the best actress of 1947 for her role in The Farmer's Daughter.

AP/WIDE WORLD PHOTOS

Daughter," I let out a yell of delight. My mother had won an Academy Award, the highest honor an actress could receive.

A few months after that happy occasion I heard loud voices coming from my mother's sitting room.

"He's your father, Loretta. You owe him something." It was my father's voice and he sounded upset.

"I don't owe him anything. He walked out on Mama and all of us. I don't remember him at all. I've sent him money, we've all sent him money. We've all supported him, that's enough." My mother seemed very angry.

"Don't you think the least you can do is pay your last respects?"

"No. I'm not going. And that's final. I don't want to talk about this anymore."

My father stormed past me in the hall. He was very agitated, but when I went into the sitting room my mother appeared calm, as if the exchange had not taken place. I didn't tell her what I had overheard; I felt I shouldn't have been listening.

But I was intrigued. I knew nothing about my mother's father. He was never mentioned by anyone. I didn't know whether he was dead or alive. When I had asked her once, she said that he had deserted Grandma and her four children. She didn't remember him at all, she said; she was only four years old when he had left.

Grandma didn't like talking about him either; she always changed the subject. But I was curious. I wanted to know who my mother's father was and why she never mentioned him. Why was she angry when someone did mention him? And what did my father mean when he said he thought my mother should pay her last respects?

I knew enough not to ask then, so these questions went unanswered until many years later when I was doing research for this book. I came across a newspaper article that brought that argument between my mother and father to mind, for it fixed the time and the events securely in place and gave meaning and clarity to what had been so incomprehensible to me at the age of thirteen.

The headline in the *Los Angeles Examiner* of June 13, 1948, read: "Strange Story Unfolds of Dual Life Led by Father of Loretta Young." There was a picture of Aunt Polly Ann and Aunt Sally. The caption underneath read: "Attend Rites." The article described the death of a man named John V. Earle in a general-hospital ward on June 6, and went on to say that this man was actually John Earle Young, my mother's father, who had deserted his family years before.

Grandma was quoted in the article as saying,

I have not seen the children's father since he left us thirty-one years ago. If the man who died under the name of John Earle was really he, I respect his desire to die in the identity he chose and maintained in his life. He was not a mean man, but he was a weak man. He was handsome, much too handsome for his own good. He just left.

It was the most I'd ever heard my grandmother say about her husband.

Apart from recounting the "amnesia" my grandfather supposedly suffered after deserting his family, as well as the details of his "new life," the newspaper account mentioned that he had appealed to my mother for financial help through her parish priest and that she had sent money to him through her attorney. The story then went on to say that when John Young died, a woman friend of his asked his mother, Laura Young, for money to meet the funeral and burial expenses. My mother and her siblings again paid. In gratitude, Laura Young sent a note to her granddaughter, which was printed in the newspaper account:

Dear Loretta,

I am obliged to tell you but you should know, that a person who called himself John Earle died in the County Hospital of a stroke or heart attack yesterday, 6/6/48, and is to be buried in Woodlawn Cemetery, Santa Monica, at 1:30 Thursday, 6/10, from Utter McKinley, 817 Venice Boulevard.

Please notify your mother and others who should know.

Everything has been taken care of, as the monthly check I received from the Good Samaritan has not been used for provisions and I could save some of it. So again, dear, you pay.

I am just back from the Queen of Angels Hospital due to a bad fall I received trying to get up and into the wheel chair. Tricky things, when one can't stand or take a step or stop them when they start to roll away from you. That bill was also paid. I am so glad to be able to do so without having to call on you all for everything although always so gallantly and generously given. Thank you so much again. You have paid for everything.

All my love,
Grandma

Reading this, I realized that Helen Ferguson had obviously given the letter to the press on behalf of her client, the "Good Samaritan."

I cannot recall that my mother had ever spoken to me of her grandmother, although I do remember a visit I made with my father when I was about eleven or twelve. We had gone to an unfamiliar part of town "to visit a relative," he told me. I'd forgotten the incident for many years, probably because I had wanted to forget it.

The woman we visited was very old and bedridden. Her room was musty and dark, the drapes were pulled, and an unpleasant smell lingered around her. I hung back, away from the bed. I wanted to leave. I didn't know why my father had brought me there; I didn't know who she was or what she had to do with me. It must have been twenty years later that I realized that that old lady was my mother's grandmother.

My aunt Sally remembered her father's funeral very clearly. "I was pregnant with Robert and someone called and said, 'Your father's being buried today.' Your mother didn't go," Sally told me, "because of the publicity. Mama didn't go because Papa's mistress might be there, and Polly Ann didn't want to go, but I refused to go without her. I insisted, so she went along to keep me company. Jack went because he wanted to see Papa.

"It was a Christian Science burial service somewhere on Washington Boulevard. We sat on the side saying our rosaries. When the casket came in it was covered with the roses that Polly and I had sent, a bunch of zinnias, and a bunch of nasturtiums.

"There was a woman in black who was crying all the way through the service. After the service a hideous old man came up to us and asked us if we wanted to see the body. Polly Ann didn't want to, but she went because I wanted to. She barely glanced at him, but I just stood there and looked and looked and looked. He was always so vain about his clothes. And there he was in a brown suit with red stripes and a maroon tie and an old frayed shirt. I wanted to lift the casket to see his leg to see if it was really him. I wanted to kiss him. Jack was crying and crying and crying and saying he'd waited all these years to see him.

"Jack helped carry the casket to the hearse and later at the cemetery because there weren't enough pallbearers. At the cemetery the woman in black picked four roses off the top of the casket and gave us each a rose. Polly Ann didn't take hers.

"We all paid for all the funeral expenses. Later, the woman in black, who had been Papa's mistress, called Norman and me. She said that she was going to sue us for twenty-five thousand dollars. Norman scared her off and we never heard from her again."

Six months after my grandfather was buried, a loss of which I was unaware, I had a very tangible loss of my own. Sometime toward the end of the year Miss Shankey left. She was ageless to me and so it came as a surprise when she told me that she was going to retire. She was moving to Canada to live with her sister, Esther, and her nephew, John. I hadn't ever thought about what it would be like without her; it seemed as if she had always been with me.

She hadn't been young when she came to take care of me, probably already in her fifties, so she was certainly ready for retirement. Now that I was a teenager I hardly needed the care of a governess, but Miss Shankey had played more roles than that in my life. I was losing a loving parent figure. She had been my companion, my solace, and my emotional mainstay. No matter what else was going on around me, I knew I could depend on her to be there for me. Now I would no longer have her as a refuge, and her leaving was difficult to bear. I wasn't prepared for the hole it left in my life.

In June 1949 I was to graduate from the eighth grade of Marymount Grammar School. The months preceding were filled with preparations for the event. The nuns were planning a formal ceremony on the lawn, with the archbishop presiding. Our class was the first to graduate from the new building in Brentwood, built to accommodate just the junior grades, so there was much excitement.

All my friends and I could talk about was where we would buy our white dresses, what our plans for the summer were, what it would be like being in high school, if we had a boyfriend coming to the graduation, and whether Ingrid Bergman would come back to her famous brain-surgeon husband, Petter Lindstrom, and her ten-year-old daughter, Pia.

Ingrid had left them in Hollywood to go to Italy with the Italian director Roberto Rossellini to film *Stromboli*. Her letter to her husband saying she wasn't coming back had been printed in all the newspapers. The media was filled with reports that she was divorcing her husband, abandoning her child, and marrying her lover, who hadn't yet divorced his Italian wife. Hollywood was shocked and scandalized.

Joseph I. Breen, vice-president and director of the Production Code Administration of the Motion Picture Association of America, notified her in a letter that her career would be destroyed. He suggested that she issue a denial of the rumors "at the earliest possible moment." He said the rumors constituted a major scandal and he threatened that they could result in "complete disaster personally."

Ingrid didn't deny any of the rumors. She announced that this would be her last picture, and she didn't come home. I couldn't understand how this famous movie star, and mother, could just go away forever and leave her daughter behind. It bothered me deeply and I was very angry with her for causing her daughter so much emotional pain and public ridicule. Some of my friends were saying that she was no saint, laughing at their cleverness, but it wasn't a laughing matter to me. I didn't know Pia, I had never met her or her mother, but I did know someone who knew them both very well— Ruth Roberts, who was Ingrid Bergman's best friend. They had met ten years before on *Intermezzo* when Ruth was hired by David O. Selznick to be Ingrid's dialogue coach, and they had worked closely together ever since. If anyone could tell me the truth about Ingrid, Ruth could, so I decided to ask her. My mother sat quietly beside Ruth; she said nothing and I couldn't tell what she was thinking.

Ruth was doing most of the talking and her reaction surprised me. "Petter Lindstrom is a harsh and cruel man. He's been awful to Ingrid." Ruth's face was flushed, her usual calm exterior no longer serene. I had stirred something in her that I had never seen before. I was a little taken aback by her passionate and instant defense of her friend. I hadn't expected it.

"Ingrid has been honest and forthright with him about this relationship. Their marriage was over long before Rossellini came into her life. But he forces her to stay married to him. He won't give her a divorce. She tells me in her letters how unhappy she is. She cries all the time and she feels that she is an awful person for ruining everyone's life. All she did was fall in love. I've tried to talk some sense into Petter, but he won't listen to me; he won't listen to any-one."

"What about Pia?" I asked. Nobody seemed to be thinking about Pia's feelings. "Doesn't Pia have a say in this? What does she think about her mother leaving her and her father?"

"Her mother writes to her, but Ingrid never hears from her. I don't think that Petter lets Pia write back. He says he'll give Ingrid a divorce if she'll come to Los Angeles and face Pia. But that's impossible. She's in the middle of a picture. Petter knows that."

She wasn't answering my question. "I just don't understand how she could go away and never come back. I don't understand how a mother can just desert her daughter."

"Maybe Ingrid feels that she's doing what is best for Pia," my mother interjected. It was the first time she had said anything. Her attitude surprised me.

"How could it be the best thing for her daughter? Living in sin with a man who isn't her husband, and have the whole world talking about it? I don't understand that."

Ruth gently addressed my Catholic upbringing. "Not everybody feels that following your heart is a sin, Judy. Ingrid is very much in love with Mr. Rossellini and is trying to get a divorce so that she can marry him. But her husband won't cooperate. She is trying to do what is best for Pia and for her husband, but he won't let her."

"I don't see how leaving your daughter and never coming back would be the best thing for her."

My mother and Ruth looked at each other. There appeared to be some significance in their silent exchange, but I had no way of knowing what it was.

"It isn't as if she were leaving her all alone, Judy," my mother said. "Pia is with her father. She's in good hands."

"But Ruth just said that he was a cruel man," I argued.

"He's been a good father to Pia. He wasn't a particularly good husband to Ingrid," Ruth replied.

It was useless to try to explain my feelings to my mother and Ruth. Some of them I didn't fully understand myself. I felt a strong personal attachment to Pia, a girl I didn't know, and it was obvious that no one understood that. But I thought I knew how Pia was feeling. It must be unbearable to have the whole world know your famous mother didn't love you enough to stay with you and be your mother. Pia must be feeling so ashamed; I would have been, had I been her.

Ingrid Bergman had done the unthinkable, and she had done it publicly. But what frightened me the most was that if Pia's mother could do it, then mine could, too. They were both actresses. My mother often left home to go on location to film a picture. She was beginning another one now. Maybe she, too, might decide not to come back, like Ingrid. Then I'd be left with my father, like Pia. That thought frightened me even more.

I kept my fears to myself, and when a classmate of mine asked me if I'd like to go to summer camp in Rhinelander, Wisconsin, I begged to go. My mother was very skeptical and asked me, on several occasions, if I was sure this was what I wanted to do. In truth, I wasn't sure at all. The idea of spending three whole months away from home horrified me. I'd never been away for any great length of time, and when I was, I was usually at a relative's house. What had at first sounded like a fun idea had somehow gotten out of hand, and, before I could stop all the arrangements and say "I'd like to think this over," I was sewing name tags in my camp uniforms.

My mother was now very preoccupied with her new picture, *Key to the City*. She was working with Dore Schary again. He was now head of production at MGM. And her costar was Clark Gable. Before I left for camp, she asked me if I would like to come to the set and meet Clark Gable. I loved visiting my mother on the set; it was a special treat. But this time I refused. This was highly unusual behavior for me; I had never refused her anything before, and I generally did what I was told to do. Although it was quite obvious that my mother wanted me to go, I turned her down. I didn't want to meet Clark Gable. I didn't want to visit her at the studio. She asked me several more times, and each time I said no, much to her surprise and frustration.

With hindsight, I can only surmise that my behavior had some-

1949. My father, Clark Gable, and my mother, Loretta Young, in
Key to the City, *the second picture in which they appeared together.*

thing to do with how I felt about Ingrid Bergman. On some unconscious level, I was afraid that my mother was about to repeat Ingrid's behavior, that she would fall in love and leave me, as Ingrid had left Pia. My unconscious fear and anger were strong enough to risk my mother's displeasure, but ironically, in refusing to visit her, I also missed meeting my real father.

It was at camp that I heard over my transistor radio my mother had fainted on the set of her picture and had been rushed by ambulance to Queen of the Angels Hospital. I tried to call home but couldn't reach anyone. I was beginning to panic when, several hours later, I received a call from Helen Ferguson.

"Your mother wanted me to call and tell you that she's all right. She's in the hospital, and she's going to stay there overnight."

"What's wrong with her, Helen? Why did she faint?"

"Your mother's expecting another baby, Judy."

"I want to come home, Helen. I don't want to stay here any longer."

"There's nothing for you to worry about. Your mother is going to be fine. She's just tired, that's all. She'll call you as soon as she can. You stay put. That's what she'd want you to do."

As it turned out, my mother wasn't fine at all. She stayed in the hospital for two more weeks, but the doctors couldn't save the baby. She had a miscarriage. Once she had recovered, she went back to work and finished the picture.

When the summer ended and I arrived back in Los Angeles, my father was waiting for me at the airport. He had a surprise for me, he said. While I was away at camp he had sold the Carolwood house. I was being taken to a brand-new home where the family was now living. I was shocked, overwhelmed by this sudden and unexpected change, but I could only ask, "Why?"

"Your mother and I decided it was just too large to manage. She thought it was best not to tell you while you were away, so you wouldn't worry. And this way you didn't have to deal with all the confusion and mess of the move." He seemed to think that took care of everything.

From my viewpoint, everything was gone once again. All that I had known over the past four years, everything familiar, I would never see: my room with the bunkbeds; the hammock stretched between shade trees where I read my favorite books; the secret garden that Gretchen and I played in; the tennis court where I roller-skated; the swimming pool; my neighborhood friends—all had evaporated while I was gone, and I never even had a chance to say good-bye. In three short months my world had changed dramatically.

I felt apprehensive as we turned north off Sunset onto Doheny Road, winding up into the hills until we finally pulled up in front of large iron gates. They were closed, but as my father signaled someone I couldn't see, the gates slowly slid open. A man in uniform stepped out of a small stone gatehouse by the side of the long, winding driveway and waved to us as we passed.

We drove past lemon groves on our right and orange groves on our left. "This is the Doheny estate, Judy. Isn't it something? You wouldn't know it, but it's also a working ranch. There are chickens, ducks, geese, and even some pigs back there." He gestured to the right, pointing toward a grove of tall eucalyptus trees. "It's all owned by the Countess Doheny and her family. They live in Greystone Manor, over there." He waved vaguely off to the left.

All that I could see were more groves, trees, and the hills, on the other side of which lay the San Fernando Valley. We drove past two tennis courts and an Olympic-size swimming pool with a Grecian-columned bathhouse. It was spectacular. Ahead of us stood a large white house perched on top of a hill. The winding driveway curved around under a porte cochere.

My father stopped the car under the porte cochere, right in front of several flights of brick steps leading up to a wide porch and the front door. "Here we are," he said as he opened the car door. "We're home."

8 THE DOHENY RANCH

My new home was five hundred acres of privately owned land, a ranch in the heart of Beverly Hills. The developed part of the estate was a compound, fenced and guarded on the city side, but with no boundary marks along the vast hillside down to the San Fernando Valley floor. Coyotes roamed the miles of wild brush in the undeveloped virgin hills behind us.

We were tenants of the Doheny family, who lived in Greystone Manor, the mansion that oil millionaire Edward L. Doheny had built for his son at a cost of $4 million in the twenties. The main house (as our family referred to it) had fifty-five rooms, and quarters that could accommodate a live-in staff of thirty-six.

Our home—the estate guesthouse—had a mere thirty-eight rooms, with a living room that resembled a hotel lobby and an elevator to the second floor. Although the two families shared the tennis courts, the huge pool and dressing rooms, a large recreation room complete with a brick barbecue pit and rotisserie, and a lawn the size of a professional football field, I don't recall seeing much of the Dohenys. In actuality we lived on the estate by ourselves.

Living in such a grand and luxurious environment might be someone's dream come true, but it certainly wasn't mine. The surroundings were far too intimidating and isolating. I longed to live in an ordinary house, on an ordinary street, accessible to the world. It was only many years later I learned that my mother had had no say in the selling of the Carolwood house; indeed, she didn't even know it

Our "guesthouse" home on the Doheny ranch had thirty-eight rooms, including a living room the size of a hotel lobby, and an elevator.
AUTHOR'S COLLECTION

was sold until she arrived home from location and was informed by my father. She was as shocked and uprooted by the move as I was.

Shortly after our move I turned fifteen, was a freshman at Marymount High School, and had yet to go on a date. It was the year that I met Mary Eileen Hutson—Mimi—who was to become my best friend. She arrived, late for class, wearing a tight black sweater, an even tighter black skirt, and two-inch black-suede high heels. (Her uniforms were late in arriving, she later explained.) Her thick black hair hung past her shoulders, and her lipstick was dark crimson. She had a voluptuous figure and an air of sophistication and sensuality far beyond her years.

I thought she was the most exotic person I'd ever seen. Compared to me and the rest of my classmates, in our dark blue school uniforms, white blouses, and blue-and-white saddle shoes, she looked as if she had come from another planet. Not only was I not allowed to wear black (it was too mature), but the highest heels acceptable to my mother were "baby louies," short squat little numbers, saved for special occasions. As for crimson lipstick—or any lipstick, for that matter—it was forbidden. Then and there I decided that Mimi was going to be my best friend.

As I got to know more about her, Mimi's life seemed highly desirable. She lived with her family in an "ordinary house on an ordinary street" in Westwood, directly across from St. Paul the Apostle Church, where the weekly meetings of the Chi-Rho Club, a social group for young Catholic men and women, were held. Mimi was the darling of the family, and the household revolved around her. She was full of laughter, with an upbeat view of life, and she was very popular with both boys and girls. The Hutson home quickly became my recreational and social headquarters, and Mimi's family treated me as one of them.

Because her father, Clarence, was ill, and her mother, Eileen, was fearful that he might die suddenly, Mimi was never allowed to

My best friend, Mimi Hutson.
AUTHOR'S COLLECTION

spend the night away from home. "Poppy" (our nickname for Clarence) didn't appear ill, although he did walk with a cane; nonetheless, everyone obeyed Eileen's wishes and gathered at Mimi's. Apart from the fact that this was a good way for Mimi's parents to monitor her social activities, they both thrived on our teenage romances and loved having young people around. Opening their house to us was an effective way to enjoy us and keep us home at the same time.

After Chi-Rho Club meetings a group of us often crossed the street to Mimi's. A pot of something good was always simmering on the stove, and the whole family, including her aunt, grandmother, and younger brother, was gathered in the living room eagerly awaiting the latest gossip about who danced with whom and who might be interested in whom. There was always something going on at the Hutsons' house, centering around Mimi and her friends. It was a casual household. No formal meals were ever eaten; everyone just went into the kitchen and helped themselves whenever they were hungry, very unlike the rigid schedule and early curfew that my father had structured for me at home. I wasn't allowed to drive alone in a car with a boy and I couldn't date. I couldn't visit friends on week-nights, and on weekend nights I had to be home by eleven.

My father usually took me over and picked me up. I was embarrassed that I didn't have the freedom that my other school friends had. Moreover, I was totally isolated in my home on the Doheny ranch; it wasn't convenient for friends just to drop in, as it was at Mimi's house. When I did have friends over, I always had to get permission beforehand. Fortunately, once my father met the Hutsons he relaxed his strict vigilance on my whereabouts, provided I was at Mimi's.

The fact that both Mimi and her brother, Eddy, were adopted made her and her family even more attractive to me. To begin with, she and I had something major in common. At the same time, I discovered that Mimi's family, which gave so much love to their adopted children, could also give it to me. When I was with her, I was part of the family. Mimi and I had long private talks about who our real parents might be, and we shared mutual fantasies regarding our genealogy. We both knew there were secrets surrounding our births that we didn't have the answers to. We shared a sense of relief in finally being able to explore with a friend what up until that time had been internal speculation. Mimi was the only person I told that I thought my mother was hiding something about my birth, confiding in her my mother's confusing statement, "I couldn't love you any more than if you were my own child." Maybe I was her real child, and I wasn't really adopted, I told Mimi, wishing it could be true, but having no reason to think it was.

Mimi would listen quietly, not saying much, and then she told me her own feeling that she was Clarence's child by some unknown woman. Together we would examine the mystery about our early lives and talk about how we could get proof of our suspicions. The discussions always ended when it came to actually trying to obtain birth certificates. I was too frightened that I would be caught at it, whereas Mimi didn't want to know, or at least that was what she told me. What she didn't tell me then, and I later learned, was that she already knew the answers to my questions, for her parents had told her that my father was Clark Gable. She kept the secret, as she was asked to do.

My mother's career continued to flourish, and in 1950 she was again nominated for an Academy Award for her performance in *Come to the Stable,* which had a script written by her good friend Clare Booth Luce, wife of *Time* publisher Henry Luce, and herself a convert to Catholicism. I was always intrigued by Clare Booth Luce, partly because she was a playwright and very dynamic, but mainly, I think, because my mother painted her as a tragic and heroic woman. I knew that her daughter had died and that Clare was devastated by her loss. And I was flattered when my mother told me that I reminded Clare of her daughter.

I had a great deal of curiosity about the reasons why this intelligent woman had chosen to adopt my religion. I looked forward to the dinner conversations, and there were many, when she and Monsignor Fulton Sheen discussed Catholic theology. Often they differed

This picture was intended as a present to my stepfather and had been planned with only my mother and my brothers Christopher and Peter. I was included at the last minute, which is why I am wearing a costume of my mother's.

©JOHN ENGSTEAD, COURTESY FAHEY/KLEIN GALLERY

on some detail, and lively debates ensued. I was stimulated and challenged in a way I had never been before. And I realized that if these two outstanding Catholics could ask questions about their religion without risk of excommunication, then so could I.

While my mother was working on *Come to the Stable*, Tom was cowriting a script, *Cause for Alarm*, with screenwriter Mel Dinelli. Later he sold it, with himself as producer, to his old friend Dore Schary. Tom had been considering Judy Garland for the lead, believing that the combination of her acting skills and look of vulnerability was perfect for the role.

By that time my mother had finished filming *Come to the Stable*, and her agent, Jimmy Townsend, suggested that she should play the lead. When Tom balked, Townsend accused him of discriminating against Loretta Young because she was his wife. Tom wrote in his unpublished autobiography that he knew Townsend was reflecting what Loretta had said and that he was disturbed because she hadn't come to him directly.

Up to that point, my mother and Tom had an established policy not to mix their careers and their private life. In his autobiography Tom revealed that he had even consulted a priest, who advised him not to have his wife as the star because it didn't seem "healthy," but in the end they did do the film together. (What Tom wrote in his autobiography may have been distorted, and his statement that their business partnership wasn't healthy may also have been hindsight, for he wrote all that many years after he and my mother were divorced and after he had initiated a bitter court battle over their television partnership in "The Loretta Young Show.")

What was significant about *Cause for Alarm* was that it was filmed not on the usual several-month schedule, but in an unprecedented fourteen days. My mother sat in on all the production meetings, and at her suggestion the cast rehearsed for two weeks before beginning filming. The sets were small, there were no locations off the MGM lot, and the crew joined the rehearsals for the last few days to observe. Interestingly, the entire script was rehearsed and filmed in the same way that my mother's television show was to be rehearsed and filmed three years later.

Television was just beginning to make its mark, and my mother had done her homework. She once told me, "I'd already won an Academy Award; I'd reached the top in the film business. There wasn't any further for me to go. It was time for me to reach the top in television."

Cause for Alarm and her business partnership with her husband were my mother's dress rehearsal for her television career and, although neither of them knew it at the time, probably the beginning of the end of their marriage.

While my parents were preoccupied with their careers, I was pre-occupied with the opposite sex. I was blossoming into young womanhood under the stern and watchful eyes of the clergy in the basement of St. Paul the Apostle Church and with the warm support of Mimi's parents in their living room. The weekly church dances attracted boys from the local Catholic schools like Loyola and Notre Dame, and the group kept enlarging as word spread that there were pretty young girls, free refreshments, and good records to dance to. I was very shy but gradually, as time went on, I learned to feel more comfortable around the boys I met, secure in the safety of Mimi's house. My group always went everywhere together.

When Mimi turned fifteen her parents gave her a formal dance at the Beverly Hills Hotel. She and her mother arranged the guest list and chose the dates for each of the girls. Mimi was "madly in love" with John Considine, who was tall, dark, and extremely handsome, and she chose John's friend, Frank Vogelsang, to be my escort. Frank went to University High and wasn't like the boys from Loyola. He had an air of sophistication and worldliness about him that made me uneasy, but my mother gave me permission to go with him if my father drove us. I was the only girl being chaperoned in that manner.

Despite the fact that my father was producing his first motion picture, he managed to find the time to eavesdrop on my personal phone calls, especially those from Frank. I could hear the phone click

1950. Mimi's fifteenth-birthday party at the Beverly Hills Hotel. I am with Frank Vogelsang (sixth and seventh from the left); Mimi Hutson is at the far right with John Considine.

as he lifted the receiver upstairs and then the sound of his breathing, and I prayed that Frank didn't know he was on the line. It was exciting to have a boy calling me, and conversation was difficult enough without knowing that my father was listening to every word. I was always afraid that Frank would say something that I didn't want my father to hear, and so all I could safely contribute were inane comments. *He must think I'm a real idiot,* I'd worry, after putting the phone down on another unsatisfying one-way conversation. I was angry with my father, but it never occurred to me to say something to him. His eavesdropping remained a secret until one evening when he finally made his presence known.

"It's time to get off the phone, Judy." His loud voice broke into the middle of our conversation. I was so shocked that all I could do was hold my breath and wait. There was a long silence and then he added, "You're up too late. Hang up now." This was the first I'd heard about a curfew on phone conversations. Finally, after what seemed an eternity, I heard Tom hang up.

"Frank, are you still there?" I was afraid that he had hung up, too.

"Who was that?"

"That was my father. He's been listening to all of our conversations." I didn't care now; the damage was done.

"To all of them?"

"Pretty much. I'm sorry, I didn't know how to tell you. I was embarrassed."

Frank was very understanding. He told me that I wasn't responsible for my father's actions and that he understood how I felt. It was good finally to confide in someone. I hadn't even told Mimi.

Thereafter, whenever I heard a click on the other end of the line, I intervened immediately, saying that someone wanted to use the phone and that I had to get off. I didn't want to give Tom the satisfaction of listening to any more of my private conversations.

One day I made a critical error that cost me whatever minimal privileges my father had finally granted me. Mimi was visiting with Frank and John, and she and I decided that it was time we learned how to smoke. Everyone in both of our families smoked—it was the accepted thing for adults to do—but we still didn't know how to inhale. Frank and John had promised to teach us. All we had to do was find a safe place where no one could discover us, since smoking was strictly forbidden us by our parents.

On 500 acres of land there must have been innumerable places for four teenagers to find a safe spot to smoke. We obviously weren't thinking when we went to the garage, closed the garage door, climbed into my father's car, rolled up the car windows, and began our lesson on how to inhale cigarette smoke.

When Frank lit my cigarette I felt a thrill go through my hands as I cupped them over his and drew in as he told me to. The smoke filled my lungs and made me choke and cough, but I kept puffing.

Frank and I sat facing each other in the front seat, he taking a draw and inhaling, then slowly exhaling, while I mimicked his actions with all my powers of concentration. I was just beginning to get the feel of the smoke entering my lungs and chest and holding it there before slowly exhaling, when suddenly the garage door flew open with a loud bang.

The car had been backed into the garage, and when the door opened the bright sunlight hurt my eyes, which by now had become accustomed to the darkness. As I squinted through the smoke-filled haze inside the car I saw a figure standing directly in front of us. I could barely make it out; the smoke was now so thick that it had fogged up the inside of the windows.

From somewhere in the backseat, I heard Mimi gasp, "Mr. Lewis."

My God! It was my father standing only a few feet from me, directly in the path of any possible escape from our smoke-filled den of iniquity. I had thought he would be gone for the day.

We jumped out of the car, everyone talking at once.

"We weren't doing anything, Dad," I stammered.

"We were just having a cigarette, Mr. Lewis," John explained.

"I can see for myself what you were doing." His voice was cold and unforgiving and I knew this was a very bad thing for me to have done. I decided to tell the truth; it was too late now to make up any excuses.

"I'm sorry, Dad. I just wanted to learn how to smoke." I sounded and felt ridiculous.

"Sitting inside the car with the doors closed, in the dark?" There was something in his tone of voice that intimated I was guilty of a more serious offense. Now I realize that he thought that we had been necking in the car, not just smoking, but at the time that never occurred to me.

I looked to Mimi for some moral support, but she stood silently, studying the ground, saying nothing. The two boys just looked at Tom, intimidated and frightened, as was I. I was terribly embarrassed that my father was causing my friends such discomfort.

Tom turned to John and Frank. "I want you to leave now." They both nodded but made no move to go. "And I'm going to have to call your parents, Mimi, and tell them I found you smoking. I know they have rules about that, just as we do." Mimi looked at me.

"Please don't tell them, Dad. It wasn't Mimi's fault." I was sure I'd never be able to see her again.

"That'll be enough, Judy. You're campused with no more privileges. I'll discuss this with your mother."

To his disappointment, my mother was very understanding and didn't seem too upset about my smoking; in fact, she even laughed about the inappropriate hiding place Mimi and I had chosen. She told me that since she couldn't stop me, she would rather that I smoke socially in her presence at home instead of sneaking behind her back. So thereafter I smoked openly without embarrassment, but Tom still confined me to the house on the weekends as punishment for my indiscretion.

Tom managed to cast a pall over my social life. Even after Mimi's father died and she no longer had to stay at her house, she still didn't stay overnight at mine. She didn't want to. I understood, but I wasn't pleased that my friends weren't comfortable in my home. I blamed my father, whom they had nicknamed "The Bear."

If it hadn't been for Robert Dornan, I wonder if I would ever have had a formal date. I guess eventually some brave young man would have ridden up that long driveway in his car and swept me out of my castle, just as I had fantasized in my childhood dreams. But it was a brash, determined young red-haired Irishman who took on the task of knight-rescuer. It was a challenge, and Bob loved challenges. He cast himself as the patient suitor and began calling me regularly.

My father's intrusive phone interruptions didn't faze Bob; he included Tom, as if a three-way conversation was expected. It confounded my father so much that he often hung up, allowing us to continue to talk unmonitored. I was delighted that The Bear's behavior didn't disturb Bob in the least and that I finally had a male advocate.

My mother liked Bob; he made her laugh. He possessed an actor's instincts coupled with a great gift of gab and a good dose of Irish charm that enabled him to deal with whatever came up. And he passed her test; her priest friends at Loyola gave him a good report, and he was from a show business family. His mother, Mickey, and her sister, Flo (who was married to actor Jack Haley), had been Ziegfeld show girls in their youth.

Bob and my mother had in common their passion about religion, and she couldn't help laughing at his humor and charm. He didn't treat her like a movie star, and that kept her off balance; she never knew quite what to make of him. She once said to me, "Bob will either become a charming bum or a tremendous success." In fact, he became a success; he is now a congressman for the state of California, and more than once has used his Irish charm and wit to score politically.

Bob's personality and patience won my parents' acceptance and approval. He became a regular visitor to the house and was even occasionally included in small family dinner parties as my escort. When he invited me to attend a Loyola prom, I accepted and got permission to drive alone in the car with him to and from the dance. At fifteen I was finally going to have my first formal date.

The dance was on a Saturday night, and Bob came to visit on Friday, the week before. My mother, who was filming *Because of You* at Universal, had been working late hours and was spending the night at the studio, accompanied by her maid, Beatrice. My father was out for the evening, so Grandma was staying at the house as my chaperone. She had dinner with us and then discreetly left us alone. We watched television, and Bob left at eleven, my appointed curfew.

About an hour later, Grandma (who had waited up) and I were sitting in my bedroom talking when I saw the lights of my father's car come up the driveway and pull into the garage. I knew he had seen the lights from my room as he drove up, and suddenly I knew he was going to punish me for being up so late. I confided my fear to Grandma.

"But you've been talking to *me*, Judy. Why would he punish you for that?" she asked.

"I know he's going to think that Bob stayed past eleven." I was beginning to panic.

"Just tell him that Bob left when he was supposed to and that we've been talking," she reasoned.

"He won't believe me, I know he won't." I stood in the middle of my bedroom, not knowing what to do, or where to go, feeling panic rising in me as I heard the garage door close and my father's footsteps go up the outside path past my bathroom window. He would be coming in the side door any minute and somehow I knew there was going to be a confrontation.

My grandmother was watching me closely now. She got up quickly, giving me a signal to be quiet. "Don't tell him that I'm here. I'm going to be in the bathroom if you need me. I want to hear what he says." She disappeared into the dressing room, out of sight, just as my bedroom door flew open and my father came into the room.

Before I could say a word he began a tirade.

"What are you doing up at this hour? I thought I told you that Bob was to leave by eleven o'clock." He was standing a few feet from me; his voice was loud and I could smell the liquor on his breath.

"He did leave, Dad."

He didn't hear me. "When I make the rules here they are to be obeyed. You can't be trusted, can you?"

"But I just told you . . ."

He wasn't going to let me say anything in my defense; he just kept yelling at me. "It doesn't matter what you told me. I don't believe you. It's midnight and your lights are still on. Once again you disobeyed me. As your punishment you are not going to the dance with Bob Dornan on Saturday." Without waiting to hear what I might have to say, he turned and stalked out of the room.

I slowly closed the bedroom door after him, feeling numb. My grandmother came out of the dressing room and put her arms around me as I began to cry.

"I heard every word he said, Judy." She stroked me soothingly as she held me.

"You see, I told you he didn't believe me. Now I can't go to the dance with Bob. How am I going to tell him? What am I going to say to him?" I wept.

"Don't worry about anything. You're going to the dance." Her voice was calm and reassuring.

"You heard what he said, Grandma. He said I can't go."

"Never mind, Judy, I'll take care of it. I don't want you to worry about it. Everything will be all right, you'll see."

I didn't believe her. Nothing would ever be all right again, I thought as I climbed into bed. Grandma kissed me good-night, got into the twin bed next to mine, and turned out the light.

The next day my mother came into my room. "Mama told me what happened last night," she said, "and she also told me that Bob left at eleven. It's all right for you to go to the prom as you planned."

I still wasn't sure what she was telling me; maybe she didn't know I was being punished. "But Dad said that I couldn't go."

She put her arm around me. "Never mind about that, Judy. We've talked it over and it's all taken care of. You have permission to go out with Bob." I was so happy and relieved that I didn't consider whether or not my mother had had to argue for my freedom or what it might have cost her emotionally. I was just grateful that my grandmother was my witness and had taken some action.

The night of the prom Bob and I returned at midnight. My mother had extended the curfew for the occasion. It had been a perfect evening; all my friends were at the dance and I was very happy. As we drove under the porte cochere I saw a figure strolling in the dark on the other side of the driveway. Bob turned to me and asked, "Who is that, Judy?"

The night was very dark, with just a sliver of a moon, but in the darkness I could make out the figure walking toward us.

"It's my father."

"You're kidding? What's he doing out at this time of night?" Bob asked.

"I don't know," I replied.

As Bob got out of the car my father walked up to him. They shook hands. "Good evening, Mr. Lewis," Bob said courteously.

"Nice night. I was just looking at the Milky Way," Tom said. "Lovely, isn't it?"

We both gazed up at the sky. It was pitch-black with just a few stars and no sign of the Milky Way.

"Yes, lovely," Bob said, giving me a quizzical look.

"It's time you went into the house now, Judy," my father said.

Bob and I shook hands and I thanked him for the wonderful evening while my father stood there, watching us. His presence ensured that there would be no lingering at the front door and no kiss for me that night.

I remember my mother telling me some years later that she wasn't happy during this period in her marriage, but I had no sense of it then. My parents never argued that I can remember, or if they did, it must have been behind closed doors, privately, where they couldn't be heard. I assumed they were happy and thought that she was in agreement with my father's rules. She had never openly contradicted him until the incident of the prom, and although I was thrilled that I could go to the dance, I was also surprised by my mother's role as intermediary and worried that I might be responsible for causing a disagreement between my parents.

I was even more surprised when my father complained to me about Beatrice, who had been with my mother for several years. She was all but indispensable, especially when my mother was working on a film.

"I can't understand why your mother insists on Beatrice coming into our bedroom and waking her up in the morning to go to the studio," he said. "It's such an intrusion. She could just as easily set an alarm clock. Beatrice invades our privacy and I don't like it one bit."

I wasn't accustomed to being taken into my father's confidence. It was not something he had ever done before and it made me oddly uncomfortable. On the one hand I was flattered, but I was also confused by this new intimacy and I felt disloyal to my mother. I knew that he didn't like Beatrice or my mother's attachment to her, but up until that time he had never openly voiced his displeasure, and certainly never to me. I really didn't know how to answer him or what to say, so I just listened as he continued to complain about Beatrice, who, he said, "seems to mean more to your mother than I do."

It appeared that he was jealous of the time the two women spent together at the studio. At first I thought he was being silly and unreasonable. My mother had to get up very early in the morning to begin filming. Beatrice drove her to work and was her dresser on the set; she cooked her meals and tended to her many needs during the day. My mother really *couldn't* do without her.

But the more my father complained about Beatrice, the more I began to wonder myself why my mother sometimes seemed to be more attached to the people who worked for her, or even to near-total strangers, than she was to those closest to her. I wondered if Tom had ever told her how he felt about Beatrice, and if he had, why my mother hadn't tried to please him, as we were taught in church and school a good wife was supposed to do.

But *my* role then was to listen, and so of course I never asked if he had discussed his feelings with my mother. As usual, I kept my own feelings to myself. Ironically, I could understand his jealousy of Beatrice, for I had some of the very same feelings myself.

So in some ways it was easy to be drawn into my father's confidence. My mother simply wasn't available to give me her side of the story, and although in the final analysis my loyalty remained to her, underneath I really didn't know what or who to believe.

But all of this became insignificant once I discovered for myself what it was like to fall in love.

Although Bob Dornan was a lot of fun to be with, we weren't in love, just very good friends. It was his cousin, Jack Haley, Jr., who was my first real love. Jack had graduated from Loyola High School in June 1951, and was going east to attend Fordham University in the fall.

Jack's family were close friends of the Hutsons and we met at Mimi's. In typical teenage fashion, when I began dating Jack, Bob Dornan began dating my cousin, Gretchen Foster, which worked out perfectly because we could double-date. At fifteen I was happier than I'd ever been before. I had a lot of friends whom I cared about and who cared about me, I had no responsibilities, *and* I was in love for the very first time. It was the best summer of my life.

Jack lived with his mother and father on Walden Drive in Beverly Hills, a short two-block walk from the Church of the Good Shepherd. The noon mass at "Our Lady of the Cadillacs" (our irreverent nickname) was the Sunday meeting place for my gang of teenagers: Bob Dornan; Gretchen Foster; Jack Haley, Jr.; Gary Crosby (Bing Crosby's son); Leslie Gargan (actor Bill Gargan's son); and Mimi. We all walked to Jack's for brunch after church. Jack's home was as popular as Mimi's—in fact, it was much like Mimi's, very informal and always crowded, with visitors coming and going. Jack loved people; he collected them, as did his mother, Flo, a woman generous with her time and her resources, and a sucker for a hard-luck story. Flo was forever taking care of someone's sick relative, or loaning money to someone down on his or her luck, or finding a place to live for someone who didn't have any home at the moment. We loved her; she was Earth Mother to all of us.

John Hearst, Jr., whom we all called Bunky, joined our group that summer, and stayed with us for many summers thereafter. He lived

With my escort, Jack Haley, Jr., at a Loyola University dance; on the left, a friend, Don Robinson; on the right, my cousin Gretchen Foster. The boys are wearing their ROTC uniforms.

AUTHOR'S COLLECTION

Our group, gathered in front of Mimi's house. Left to right, back row: Jack Haley, Jr.; me; Eddy Hutson; Mimi Hutson; Bob Dornan; Bill Bashe. Front row: Leslie Gargan; Bunky Hearst.

AUTHOR'S COLLECTION

with his father and stepmother in New York and went to boarding school in the east, then visited his mother in California every summer, spending some of the time in the family quarters at his grandfather William Randolph Hearst's castle, San Simeon. Everybody loved Bunky; he was witty and bright. He said very little about his parents, more about his father than his mother, and even though he stood to inherit the Hearst millions he was unpretentious.

Our pleasures were fairly simple: leisurely days spent riding to Zuma Beach in Jack's Chrysler convertible with the top down, swimming in the warm Pacific Ocean and lying on the hot sand sharing our dreams for the future, or just swimming and playing tennis. Our days were usually spent as a group. At night couples went to the movies together or separately, but no evening was complete without a big juicy hamburger and a malt at Simon's drive-in on Wilshire in Beverly Hills, where we all gathered once again, going from car to car, greeting one another as if we hadn't been together just a few hours earlier.

We were our own family that summer, and whatever our personal home lives were like, whatever problems each of us had, they were forgotten while we were together. We had a common bond: We were Hollywood kids from show-biz families, but among ourselves we could *be* ourselves with no pretenses.

Most of us could, that is. Gary Crosby couldn't, although I didn't know that then. I just knew that he was very angry, and his anger frightened me. I liked Gary, for there was a sweetness, an ingenuousness that surfaced and drew me toward him. I found I wanted to know him better, to get closer to him.

One night as we sat in his car talking, I asked him why he was so ready to fight anyone who appeared to challenge him, friend or stranger. We talked about how difficult it was to be the children of famous parents, to be viewed as the "son or daughter of," with no other identity. Gary thought the only way he could protect himself from being beaten up at school as "the rich kid" was to beat up the other guy first. He had a large chip on his shoulder and he dared anyone and everyone to knock it off. What I didn't know then was that Gary was hiding an abusive and alcoholic home life from all of us. Nor did any of us know that summer that Gary was already an alcoholic himself. He had finished his senior high-school year at Bellarmine, a Catholic boarding school in northern California, and when he lost his eligibility in football he decided he was a loser and that he was never going to win at anything. None of us had any way of knowing that Gary's mother was an alcoholic or that his father was beating him mercilessly for the slightest infraction of his strict rules. By the time he was ten or eleven, Gary had become addicted to amphetamines to control a weight problem. His father insisted on weighing him once a week and he was beaten if his weight went up.

Gary had a curfew, too, although he kept the fact from us. Jack Haley Jr. was the first one to find out. Gary's father had agreed to give him an eighteenth-birthday party at home, and we were all looking forward to it. Once or twice a year Bing allowed Gary to have friends over, ten people at the most, but this was to be his first grown-up party and we were all very excited. About a week before the party Gary arrived home fifteen minutes after his curfew, so as punishment, his father called off the party. When Gary told Jack that his father had canceled the party, Jack was furious and told his parents, who were good friends of Bing and Dixie Crosby. Flo and Jack Haley gave Gary an eighteenth-birthday party at their house, and in retaliation Bing refused to speak to them for a year.

Still, when I look back forty years, I see how much simpler life was then for most of us. We were really very moral kids, raised with strong religious convictions that we shared. Our Catholic sex education was clear: denial and self-control.

No matter how much in love Jack and I were, the thought of sleeping together before marriage was not a consideration. A good Catholic girl remained a virgin until she married, and a good Catholic boy helped her. Sometimes that was easier said than done, especially when we were locked in a passionate embrace in the front seat of a car on top of Mulholland Drive on a warm summer night with the jeweled lights of the city spread out below us. But somehow we managed because we truly believed that having intercourse before marriage was a sin. The boys were raised to protect the girls, to keep them virgins.

Everyone also protected me from knowing who my real father was, both girls and boys alike. I have since discovered that each one of my friends knew that I was illegitimate and had heard somewhere the details about my mother and Clark Gable. Just recently Jack told me, "It was such common knowledge in the industry. All your friends felt that Loretta was going to let you know when you were seventeen or eighteen. Then seventeen and eighteen came and went, and then twenty-one, and then I guess after that, as you became an adult, I figured you knew. The subject never came up."

But the subject of my ears did come up.

Jack remembers: "We'd all go swimming and your hair would be back and someone came up with a remark, teasing, the way teenagers do about anyone's physical appearance. You said, 'My mom told me I used to sleep on my ears in my crib and that's how they got so big.' And we all said, 'Okay, we'll buy that.' That would have been the perfect spot for anyone who had any cruelty to say, 'Oh, yeah? Well, here's the real reason.' "

I was not only protected by my friends, but loved as well.

As Jack recalls, "I don't remember any of us ever dishing about it. And you expected it out of your girlfriends. But Gretchen, Mimi— nobody ever said anything. Never in a negative way. Well! Judy's a bastard. It never entered anybody's mind to talk about it in that kind of way."

"You looked just like Clark Gable then," Gary Crosby recalled. "I always respected your friends for not telling you, for not making a thing out of it."

Jack remembered an incident a few years after that summer, when we went to the opening night of the circus, sponsored by the Thalians, a charity group we both belonged to. Jack Oakie, a good friend of Jack's father, was one of the celebrities performing that night. Jack brought me backstage, and I waited outside the dressing room while he went inside to talk to Oakie.

As he recalls it: "I told him, 'Jack, I have someone with me, someone I want you to meet—Judy Lewis, Loretta Young's daughter.' And he said, 'Oh, yes! *Call of the Wild* . . . Clark Gable.' And he started to tell the whole story of their romance. He was going deaf and his voice was very loud. I had to put my hand over his mouth. I told him, 'Shut up, Jack. She's right outside. She doesn't know.' "

This may have been one of the reasons my mother didn't like Jack taking me to industry events. In fact, I'm not sure that she liked Jack at all then, although she came to like him. Perhaps she was worried that he would tell me who my father was.

Jack was not intimidated by my mother. Her movie-star status didn't impress him since he had grown up around stars. His natural interest and curiosity eventually enabled him to develop a relationship with my mother that no other male friend of mine would dare to attempt. He knew all the films she had made and who produced and directed them, and he was always trying to get stories out of her, encouraging her to talk about herself, against her will. He was able to tease her and make her laugh, not a role she was accustomed to playing with my friends. Ultimately he disarmed her.

Recalling my mother in those days, Jack said, "Loretta was not the kind of person you wanted to throw your arms around and give a great big hug to." She usually kept her distance until she liked or trusted someone—and she trusted few people.

When I look back, I'm sure my mother would have been happier if Jack and I hadn't been so close, but nothing she could say about him changed the fact that we were in love and thinking about getting married after he finished college.

In addition to eavesdropping, my father had begun to leave me long hand-written notes. I found them when I got up in the morning. My stomach would tighten into a hard, enduring knot when I saw the folded yellow legal pages slid under my closed bedroom door. They were never shorter than two pages and often went on for many more, listing the things that I hadn't done or the chores that I hadn't finished, the grades that I hadn't maintained, or just his general dissatisfaction with everything about me. A great deal of what he wrote didn't make much sense. As the notes became longer and more incoherent, I paid less and less attention to them. Oddly, he never referred to them, nor did I, but there were times I couldn't even read them because they made me physically sick with anxiety. Instead, I just tore them into little pieces and threw them away.

In retrospect, I see that my father was a heavy drinker and probably had been most of his life. The advertising business was structured around lunches and meetings, with numerous cocktails a part of the ritual. I know now that my parents' marriage was no longer a happy one and hadn't been for quite some time. Those long, rambling missals that I received regularly were probably a drunken man's harangue, forgotten by him the following day. I didn't forget, however; I took them seriously and they upset me.

The household help also took Tom seriously and ran interference whenever they could. If I had forgotten to make my bed it would be made for me, and I was warned when he was inquiring about my room so that I could be more vigilant. But no one was able to protect me from my father's wrath when it was unleashed.

One day when I came home from school and went upstairs to my bedroom I was shocked to find that all my clothes had been taken out of my closet and tossed over the furniture or thrown on the hallway floor. My shoes, dresses, crinoline petticoats, skirts, blouses, jackets—everything was lying in disarray everywhere. My entire wardrobe, the hangers still attached, was strewn about, as if a small hurricane had invaded my closet and hurled my belongings into the hall, blowing and tossing and dropping them in its fury.

Who could have done this and why, I wondered, as I stood in the hall, staring at the destruction. I was frightened by the implicit fury of the act, then filled with anger at the blatant intrusion into my room and the privacy of my closet. I began to gather my clothes in my arms as swiftly as I could.

"Leave everything where it is." My father was standing in the doorway to his room. I was so surprised that I dropped what I was holding without thinking.

"Who did this? Who took all my clothes out of my closet?" I demanded.

"I did. I want your mother to see this. I want her to see how many clothes you have and how much money she is spending."

I didn't know what he was talking about. All I knew was that I was deeply humiliated. My father's invasion of my personal possessions was bad enough, but I didn't want to be further disgraced by having anyone else see my things so nakedly discarded. Wordlessly I began to gather up my clothes.

"Judy! I told you to leave everything right where it is." Something in the tone of his voice made me obey. I put down the bundle in my arms as neatly as I could and turned and went into my room, shutting the door behind me.

I must have retreated into sleep because I remember I was awakened by the sound of voices through my bedroom door. "Do you see this? . . . This was Mama's. And this . . . this was Georgiana's. My dressmaker cut it down for her." My mother was very angry. I got out of bed and put my ear close to the door so that I could hear the argument taking place outside my room.

"Where did all of these clothes come from? She has far too many dresses for a girl her age." My father's voice was loud; he, too, was angry.

"Do you really want to know where her clothes come from? They're all hand-me-downs. This is one of my old dresses, this skirt was Polly Ann's, and this blouse—and that—Sally gave those to her last year."

"She doesn't need all these clothes. She's a young girl. She wears uniforms to school. You're spending too much money."

"I don't spend any money on her, Tom. I've already told you, most of these clothes are hand-me-downs from the family."

"What does she need all those shoes for?"

"We wear the same size, Tom."

I tiptoed away from the door and lay back down on the bed. I didn't like knowing I was the cause of their argument, and I felt powerless, hiding in my room behind my closed door while my mother fought my battle. Still, I was enormously grateful that she was standing up for me.

Finally, the voices quieted down and there was silence, followed by a knock on the door.

"Judy, are you there?"

"Yes! Mom, I'm here," I replied.

"Come on out and I'll help you put these things back where they belong."

Together we picked up my clothes and hung them back in my closet. As was typical of my family, neither of us discussed what had just taken place. She never asked me how I felt about my father's intrusion, and I didn't tell her that I had overheard their argument. At the time it seemed enough that she had stood up for me.

Sometime after that, my mother informed me that she had made arrangements for me to take sewing lessons from her seamstress. "I called Marymount," she said, "to see when they were going to start sewing and cooking classes for you girls. Mother David told me, 'Oh, Mrs. Lewis, our girls don't cook. We train our girls to marry well enough to hire a cook and seamstress.'" My mother was very indignant when she reported this conversation to me and insisted that I start the lessons immediately.

I was surprised by her indignation. My mother trusted the nuns implicitly. However, she had endorsed Marymount more for instilling Catholic values than for providing a well-rounded education. She had never taken much interest in my academic studies and was always more concerned about my marks in deportment and courtesy than in my grade-point average. I think she felt intimidated by anyone with a higher education, since her own education had ended at the eighth grade. Tom was the one who showed an interest in my grades and pushed me to do better, but then he was a college graduate. Not that I needed much pushing; I was a good student and liked school.

I certainly didn't want to spend my time learning to sew. It was the last thing I was interested in. I couldn't understand my mother's insistence on my learning such a menial task and I told her so one day. She countered by saying that her mother had supported her family by cooking and sewing, and I just might marry someone who couldn't afford to hire a cook or a seamstress, no matter what Mother David said.

I realized that I was going to learn to sew or she would know the reason why. She was determined and not to be deterred, for in her mind she was giving me necessary wifely skills. I had no other choice but to apply myself. Even though my mother was a career woman and had hired cooks and seamstresses since she was very young, it never occurred to her then that I might someday want a career of my own. Clearly, I was not slated to follow in her footsteps; I was going to be a wife. It's very possible, too, that she saw this as a way for me to get some new clothes without a tirade from Tom. He could hardly fault her when I was learning such a money-saving craft.

That September, just after the new school year had begun, the station wagon dropped me off under the porte cochere and I walked up to the front door, planning the rest of the afternoon in my mind. I would wash my hair before my dinner date with Jack. I wanted to look especially nice because this was our last weekend together before he left for Fordham.

The front door was wide open. I walked into the entry hall and stopped in my tracks. There, standing a few feet away in my front hallway, was Clark Gable.

I couldn't believe my eyes. He was right in front of me, and he was smiling at me. His eyes were crinkled into smile lines at the corners and he was so tall that I had to look up. He was much more handsome than I remembered him from the movies. I was stunned. *What is he doing here?* I wondered to myself. But I could say nothing. I was speechless.

"You must be Judy." *How did he know who I was? I'd never met him before.*

Finally I found my voice, but somehow it didn't sound like me. "Yes, I am. And you're Mr. Gable, aren't you?"

He laughed and said, "Yes, I am." We just stood there, looking at each other for what seemed like a long time. I felt very awkward.

"Well! I see you two have introduced yourselves." My mother came around the corner from the living room, just in time.

"Yes, Mom! We have." I was relieved that she was there. *He came to see her,* I thought. *They've worked together before; they must be friends.* That would account for his presence in my front hallway. But how did he know who I was? I didn't know what else to say to him and I was beginning to feel foolish standing there staring at him like some star-struck teenage fan. Children of movie stars don't stare at other movie stars the way I was now doing; it wasn't polite.

As the three of us walked into the living room, I headed toward the front stairs. "Where are you rushing off to, Judy?" Something in my mother's tone made me turn around. It carried a vague unspoken command. The two of them were standing close together in the middle of the large living room, both looking at me.

"I thought I'd go up and wash my hair."

"You have plenty of time to do that. Stay and visit for a while."

I was right. I hadn't imagined it. It wasn't a request, it was a command. As I walked toward them I frantically thought to myself, *What am I going to say? I don't know what to say.*

Clark Gable sat down on the couch. "Come and sit next to me, Judy."

I followed silently and did as he requested. My mother watched us, saying nothing.

"Your mother tells me that you like ballet."

All I could manage was a smile, as his eyes looked into mine. Something about him and the way he looked at me gave me an odd feeling of discomfort.

"Are you studying with anyone?"

"I used to study with Eileen O'Kane Fegté. But now I'm taking classes with Nico Charisse. He has his own dance studio." The words came out in a rush.

"Is he a good teacher?"

"Yes. I think so. He's very strict, but I like him very much."

"Tell me about your school, Judy. That's the school uniform you're wearing, isn't it?" His voice was gentle and he seemed genuinely interested. I was surprised. Usually my mother's friends paid very little attention to me. Their questions were always polite, but they weren't interested in my answers; they just asked out of courtesy. But he was different. I could tell he really cared about what I was saying. I liked him, and I began to feel more at ease.

"Yes, isn't it awful?" I hated the ugly dark blue jumper and white blouse that had identified me as a student of Marymount since the first grade. I tried every device I could think of to camouflage it, to make it look less institutional, but nothing really worked. Even Clark Gable knew it was a uniform.

He smiled and his eyes lit up. "No, I don't think it's awful at all. I think it's very becoming. You're a very pretty young lady."

I felt the blood rushing to my face and was embarrassed that his compliment had made me blush.

"Thank you," was all I could say.

"Your mother tells me you're a sophomore at Marymount."

"Yes." They must have been talking about me. Why would he be interested in my life? I looked in my mother's direction. I'd forgotten about her for the moment, but she was no longer there. The two of us were alone in the living room.

"Do you like school?"

"Yes, very much. I've made a lot of very close friends. I've been going there since the first grade."

"How old are you now, Judy?"

"I'm fifteen. I'll be sixteen in November." *Why did Mom leave me alone with him? Is she coming back?* I kept asking myself.

"And do you have a boyfriend?"

"Yes! Jack Haley. I have a date with him tonight. We're going out to dinner and a movie." I couldn't help blushing again. I liked sitting there, talking to Clark Gable. The more we talked, the more comfortable I felt. He never took his eyes off me. I didn't understand why my mother left us alone, but somehow it didn't really matter. I was enjoying our conversation, just the two of us.

"Tell me about him."

"He went to Loyola U. and now he's going to Fordham University in the east. He's three years older than I am. We have a lot of fun together. We laugh a lot. We go to the movies and parties and to the beach. There's a whole crowd of us that go everywhere together."

"You sound like you like him a lot."

"I do. Very much. He's special."

He nodded and smiled. He seemed to understand what I wasn't able to say. I was in love with Jack. I didn't talk about my feelings with anyone; I kept them to myself. Yet here I was sitting next to this man, this famous movie star, and instead of finding him difficult to talk to, as I had previously feared, I found myself quite comfortable and at ease.

Unlike most actors, he didn't talk about himself. I was used to listening to them talk about their work and their life. I was always the audience with my mother's friends or acquaintances. It was very unusual for me to be asked about myself, and particularly by a star as big as Clark Gable. It seemed strange for him to be interested in me at all. But I knew that he was, and I trusted what I felt from him.

We sat there on the living room couch and talked for what seemed like a long time. I have no idea how long it was, but what mattered was that I was alone with Clark Gable and that he wanted to know everything about my life. I forgot about my anxiety over my mother leaving us alone, I forgot my uncertainty about carrying on a conversation with him. I even forgot, after a while, that he was a famous movie star.

He was warm and considerate and caring, unfamiliar qualities coming from an adult male, especially one whom I'd just met. I liked his interest in me; I didn't understand it, but I genuinely enjoyed it. I answered his questions freely because something told me that he needed to know everything I could tell him about myself. This wasn't just polite conversation on his part. He was there with me because it was something that he wanted to do, and I responded as genuinely and honestly as I could.

It never occurred to me to ask him any questions, or even to ask how he knew who I was. But as I sat there, it did occur to me that he had actually been waiting for me to walk in the front door and that he had known when I was due home.

I didn't ask him about himself because that wasn't the role I was meant to play that afternoon, and somewhere, down deep, I instinctively knew it. This was about Clark Gable getting to know me, for his own reasons, reasons that I knew nothing about then, and can only speculate about now.

When it was time for him to leave I walked with him to the front door. We stood in the entrance hall, facing each other, as we had when we met that afternoon. He looked down at me and smiled.

"Thank you for a lovely afternoon. I enjoyed our talk."

"So did I. Very much."

He bent down and, cupping my face in his two big hands, kissed me lightly on the forehead.

"Good-bye, Judy."

"Good-bye, Mr. Gable."

He walked out the front door, down the brick steps, got into his car, and drove away.

The very first thing I said to Jack as I climbed into the front seat of his car that evening was, "You won't believe what happened to me this afternoon. I came home from school and Clark Gable was standing in the hall."

Most of my conversation that evening was about his visit. I replayed every moment over and over as fully as I could recall it, scarcely believing that our encounter had actually taken place. In my enthusiasm and excitement I didn't notice that Jack was quieter than usual. He said very little, letting me talk.

Many many years later he told me, "It broke my heart to see you so excited about meeting Clark Gable. I wanted so badly to tell you right then that you'd spent the afternoon with your father. But that wasn't up to me. I thought that visit was a prelude to your mother telling you. Surely now she was going to tell you. But she didn't."

If I *had* known, how different it might have been. I often wonder what Gable was thinking that afternoon as he sat in my mother's living room and gazed down at his fifteen-year-old daughter, looking so like him, on the brink of her adult life. When he looked at me, was I a reminder of a younger Loretta, in the days when they were together and in love? What thoughts ran through his mind as he sat next to me and listened to me talk? Why did he decide then that he wanted to meet me? Was he merely curious about my life, or did he want to tell me that he was my father? If so, why didn't he?

At times, when I feel the pain of that lost opportunity, I wonder whether there might have been a remote possibility that he thought I knew he was my father, that he was waiting for *me* to say something to him. I ask myself, if he wanted a child as much as he so often said to the press, and privately to friends, how could he see me and be with me and not tell me that I was his daughter? Did he really want a child, or was that just his actor's ego speaking? What were my father's thoughts that day? I replay the few hours that we had together over and over in my head and all I am left with is "What if?" That day—those few hours together—is all I have of my father. It isn't much to hold on to.

It was after Tom Lewis died, in May 1988, that I read a copy of his unpublished autobiography and learned that this was not Gable's first visit to the Doheny house. One afternoon in 1949 he drove his convertible up the long driveway and stopped by the pool, where Tom was watching my brother Peter swim. He was hours early for a party that my parents were giving that evening to celebrate the finish of the film *Key to the City*.

Tom wrote that he was surprised to see Gable arrive at such an early hour, and even more surprised when he told Tom that Frank

Morgan, a good friend, with whom he had been playing golf that morning at the Bel Air Country Club, had died of a heart attack. Frank had had a supporting role in *Key to the City*.

Describing that visit, Tom wrote:

> We sat on the terrace all afternoon, talking about things that one only talks about at funerals — the brevity of life, the blow of losing friends, the difficulty of accepting news that threatens to be just a little more than one can bear.

Gable confided in Tom his desire for a child.

"I always wanted a kid," Gable said. "Carole and I planned to have one, you know." Tom wrote that Gable talked about his idyllic marriage to Carole and her precognition that she wasn't going to be with him long.

Then Tom wrote of his own marriage and how he was feeling at the time:

> Talking to Gable that afternoon made me less lonely somehow, and gave me a new appreciation of my blessings — my wife, my two sons, my house.

Just recently my brother Christopher told me that his father had described that afternoon to him. Apparently, Tom had asked Gable if the rumors about my being his daughter were true. Christopher remembers his father telling him that Gable replied, "Tom, if that were true, do you think I would let anything or anyone stop me from knowing my own child?"

Christopher assured me that Tom truly didn't know whose child I was. Tom even once told Christopher that he wondered if I were Sally's daughter because of our resemblance.

If Tom did indeed ask Gable if he were my father, it certainly speaks volumes about his lack of communication with my mother. I can well believe, however, that he never asked her directly if I was her child, or even if I were Sally's for that matter. But Gable's response, as Tom recounts it, seems on the surface to be odd and perverse. Yet if that conversation with Gable did take place, as Tom told Christopher it had, it seems quite likely that Gable was protecting my mother with his answer. Obviously she hadn't told her husband the truth about my birth. At the time, her marriage appeared to be a good one; moreover, she had just had a miscarriage and was openly heartsick about it. In responding as he did, Gable did the honorable thing for both me and my mother.

What Gable had no way of knowing that afternoon, sitting on the terrace of the Doheny house, was that the man to whom he was talking was less than a good father to me. He had no way of knowing how unhappy I was. And despite his assurance to the contrary, he *did* allow everything and everyone to stop him from knowing his child.

9 THE BEACH HOUSE

In 1952 we moved again, this time to a temporary home on the white sands of Santa Monica beach. Tom had bought a town house owned by millionaire Huntington Hartford on Flores Avenue in West Hollywood and we were waiting for the extensive remodeling to be completed. The luxurious apartment complex of two-storied maisonettes with individual private gardens would provide both income property as well as a permanent home for the family. Tom had already invested in a small resort hotel, the Ojai Valley Inn, located in a lush valley two hours north of Los Angeles. Our family had been spending weekends and holidays there, and he had begun construction on a home there as well, without telling my mother. When the foundation was laid, he showed it to her and announced that it would be our family vacation home on the condition that she, and not her mother, decorated it. The fact that Grandma was traveling in Europe and would be away for some time fit in nicely with Tom's plans, and my mother accepted his challenge.

The beach house that we leased was Harry Warner's home on Ocean Front in Santa Monica. One of the sharpest memories I have of that house is the sight of my mother sitting at a table in her bedroom in front of the picture window overlooking the pool and the ocean, beading sweaters. She had always enjoyed working with her hands. She loved to sew and was extremely creative, but I was never so keenly aware of her almost obsessive sewing and beading as during that period. The fact that she was home more than I ever re-

The beach house was Harry Warner's home in Santa Monica.
ANDRE R. WILLIEME

membered should have been a clue that her career was dormant, but I didn't give that a thought, I was just so glad to have her available.

She was decorating cashmere sweaters for everyone in her family, and most of her friends as well. Her designs were finer and more intricate than any to be found in the stores, where beaded sweaters were very much in vogue, and, had she wanted to, she could have made a great deal of money designing and selling them. But she wasn't sewing for money, she was sewing because she wasn't happy—not in her career and not in her marriage.

Few film offers were coming in. My mother believed that after winning an Academy Award her career could only go downward because she had already reached the summit. She had always put a great deal of faith in timing, and now the time was right to move on. She wanted to get into television, much to the dismay of her agents at William Morris and her industry friends, who called her a defector and said she would ruin her career. But she was aware that Lucille Ball already had her own series, "I Love Lucy," produced by her husband, Desi Arnaz. She wanted a series of her own and she wanted her husband to help her get it. So Tom began conducting some viewer research and talked to successful friends in television like Desi Arnaz, Ozzie Nelson of "Ozzie and Harriet," and Jim Backus, costar with Joan Davis in "I Married Joan."

I was now in my junior year at Marymount and in love again— this time with Russell Hughes. Although Jack Haley and I wrote to each other constantly while he was away at Fordham, I was lonely. The short holidays we spent together weren't enough to keep our fairly new relationship alive during the long stretches of the school year.

Russ, who was seven years older than I, was attending the University of Southern California when we were introduced. I was naturally thrilled that this extremely handsome, older college man, with thick, dark, curly hair, would find me attractive, and before I knew it we were seeing each other exclusively.

My mother liked Russ well enough. While he didn't come from as wealthy a background as some of the sons of her friends, he was

1952. A family portrait taken in the living room of the beach house. Left to right: my brother Peter, my mother, me, and my brother Christopher.

personable, working to put himself through college, and, most important, Irish Catholic. She didn't approve of our going steady, however. She thought I was much too young to be serious and she told both of us so. She encouraged and even arranged evenings with other eligible boys, none of whom interested me in the least. I endured these dates because I was told to, not because I wanted them. All I wanted was Russ.

In an attempt to divert me, my aunt Georgiana got into the act. A friend of Ricardo's, a young actor and newcomer to Hollywood named Burt Reynolds, wanted to take me out. But I had no interest in anyone other than Russ, so I told Georgie that I wasn't interested in dating any actors. She seemed quite disappointed; I think she felt she had come up with a good match.

While at first my father was fairly cordial to Russ, he nonetheless treated him with a touch of condescension, which angered me. I wanted the two to like each other, but no matter how hard Russ tried, he was met with great reserve on my father's part. From time to time Russ worked as a parking attendant at the Beverly Hills Hotel. When my father would see him there he always acknowledged Russ's greeting with a silent nod, as if he didn't know who he was. I know it hurt Russ.

Getting my driver's license was a turning point, for it brought me more freedom. Santa Monica was miles from my friends and Russ, but now that I had the family station wagon to go to and from school, I was no longer "territorially undesirable." In my tumultuous race from the confines of oppression toward my newfound independence I drove with my foot down hard on the accelerator. I was a menace. I made more than one frantic call to Russ while an irate driver waited for me to give the particulars that might get my license revoked. The accident was usually my fault. Russ would come to my rescue, soothing the offended driver and offering to pay for any damages. Then he'd arrange for the station wagon to be fixed before my father could see it. It was usually nothing drastic, but there would have been hell to pay if the damage had been discovered. The summer between my junior and senior years, when I worked as a

Russ Hughes and me relaxing on the beach.
AUTHOR'S COLLECTION

salesgirl at Desmond's department store in Westwood, my entire salary was spent on repairs to the car.

One afternoon I borrowed Russ's car while the station wagon was being repaired. As I drove into the driveway my father pulled in behind me. He got out and came around the driver's side and, leaning down, his face close to mine, he asked, "Whose car are you driving?"

"It's Russ's," I replied.

"Why are you driving Russ's car?"

"He loaned it to me just to see how I liked driving it," I lied. *Please, God,* I prayed, *don't let him ask me where the station wagon is.* I didn't have a ready answer.

"And how *does* it drive?" he asked.

"Great, just great. It's a wonderful car."

"That's fine, but it's the last time I want you driving Russ's car. It's much too intimate a thing to do." He turned and went into the house, leaving me in a state of shock. What could possibly be intimate about driving another person's car? I wondered. However, I was so relieved that he didn't ask about the station wagon that I didn't pursue it, although his odd comment stuck in my mind.

As the construction and decoration of the Ojai house escalated, my mother spent more and more time there with Tom, Christopher and Peter, and the boys' new nurse, Mary Coney, whom I liked immensely. She was gentle and kind to the boys and to me, and she adored my mother. After the boys no longer needed her, she stayed on and took care of my mother as her housekeeper.

At first I reluctantly spent the weekends with them, but after a while my mother said that I could stay at the beach house if I wanted to. It *was* easier not to have me around. When I wasn't there I couldn't be a source of friction between my father and mother. Tom was constantly objecting to my social life and my boyfriends, and my mother felt obliged to come to my defense because his hostility couldn't be dismissed; it was too obvious. In all honesty I didn't feel comfortable at Ojai. Everything centered around the new house my mother was decorating, a house built for her family with Tom, a family that I was becoming less and less a part of.

There were times when my mother took the entire household staff with her to Ojai. Since I was reluctant to stay alone in the empty beach house, I prevailed on Russ, and once again he was there for me. He gave me his bedroom in the two-bedroom duplex apartment that he shared with his widowed mother, Lucy Hughes, while he slept on the downstairs couch.

His home became my home and I saw more of his mother than my own. She was quite unlike my mother: a plain, gray-haired middle-aged woman with simple tastes, not at all sophisticated or glamorous. She had been widowed for many years and had worked hard most of her life raising three children, the youngest of whom was Russ. She was always very kind to me and I often wonder what she must have thought about the daughter of the wealthy movie star who was her frequent houseguest on weekends.

I was more or less resigned to the nonrelationship that I had with my father, but Russ was not. It upset him and he wanted to rectify it. When he offered to act as my emissary and set up a meeting with my father, I didn't have the heart to discourage him. I thought Russ might be able to tell Tom, man to man, how much I wanted and needed a father instead of an unyielding disciplinarian. I wanted love and affection from my father and I hoped and prayed that perhaps Russ would be able to accomplish what I seemed unable to achieve for myself: make my father care for me.

They had their meeting late one afternoon. When Russ came to pick me up later, he was uncharacteristically quiet. Finally, after much coaxing on my part, he told me that he couldn't understand my father. Russ had expected Tom at the least to listen to what he had to say. Instead, he was belligerent and uncooperative. Some angry words were exchanged. Russ wouldn't tell me exactly what was said. He was angry with himself for attempting something that he now knew to be impossible, but he was angrier with my father for his behavior toward me and toward him. "What's wrong with the man?" he kept asking me.

I had no answer, for I secretly believed there was something wrong with *me*, and that our relationship, or lack of it, was my fault.

I asked Russ if my father had said anything about me at all. He looked at me for a long moment before he reached over and touched my face gently with his hand. "He said, 'I'll give Judy credit for one thing—she has guts, and she'll need them if she's going to marry you.'"

At the time I was too young to understand what a slap in the face that statement was to this young man who loved me. I regarded it as a compliment, about the only one my father had ever given me. Russ understood, however, and he was silent when I replied, "Well, at least that's something. He thinks I've got guts."

Their meeting passed without any comment regarding it from my father; it was as if it had never occurred. Only several years later did my mother tell me how angry Tom had been when he came home that afternoon. "Do you know what that young man had the nerve to say to me?" she said he had barked. "He told me that I didn't deserve to have such a loving daughter and wife and that I didn't realize how lucky I was." She told me that she was surprised and more than a little pleased by what Russ had said. Whether it precipitated an argument with Tom, I don't know. If it did, my mother kept it to herself.

After that, an uneasy truce existed between the two men. They were polite to each other, but like strangers, wary and watchful, careful not to offend; too much had already been said. Russ was always respectful of Tom, but Tom was often not as courteous and he used his parental power to get even.

Once, when I was on vacation with the family in Ojai, Russ came to visit me by bus since his car was being repaired. I was upset and very disappointed when he told me that he had to go back to Los Angeles the following day to take his mother to dinner on her birthday. That meant we had only a very short time together and he wouldn't be able to get back in time for a party that I wanted him to attend with me.

My mother intervened and offered to let him borrow the station wagon so that he could visit his mother and then drive back in time for the party, but my father overheard the plans and insisted that he didn't want Russ driving the family car. When my mother asked him why, he gave no reason but simply said, "He got himself here, he can get himself back," leaving my mother and me very angry but helpless to do anything about it. Not wanting to cause any further upset in an already embarrassing situation, Russ solved the dilemma by hitchhiking, arriving back just in time for the party.

When I look back now at Tom's behavior, I realize that there were circumstances I wasn't aware of then, as well as some subconscious emotional elements. Tom was jealous of Russ and overprotective and possessive of me. My parents' marriage was undergoing some radical stresses and strains. Perhaps, for whatever reasons, Tom felt unable to retaliate at my mother and so he used me instead. In a way I became the scapegoat for both of them. They could argue about me, instead of dealing with the very real problems of their deteriorating marriage.

"Mom, I'm late with my period. Do you think something might be wrong?" When I recall that announcement made at the dinner table, I am astounded by my innocence.

My mother looked at me. "I don't know, but we'll discuss it after dinner."

"Are you pregnant?" she asked later, when we were sitting side by side on my bed.

I was shocked and embarrassed by her question. "No, of course not, Mom. I wouldn't do that to you." It never occurred to me until that moment that she would jump to that conclusion. Well schooled, I believed that having intercourse before marriage was a mortal sin. Russ and I necked pretty heavily, but that was as far as our sexual exploration had gone. I chose celibacy willingly because I felt it was the right thing to do.

She just looked at me for a moment. "Forget what it would do to me, Judy. Think of what it would do to you." That thought had never crossed my mind; I had thought only of the shame my pregnancy would have caused her.

My announcement must have been a terrible shock to my mother, her identification with me so complete that she must have believed immediately that I was repeating her mistake. In reality, I was so indoctrinated with the Catholic teaching of chastity before marriage that Russ's and my heavy-petting sessions left me afraid that I might die and go to hell before I could rush to confession the next day and vow never to commit that mortal sin again. My sexuality was in constant conflict with my religion.

In the early months of 1953 the house in Ojai was finished, and so was my mother's last film commitment, *It Happens Every Thursday.* Now she was free to be where she longed to be, in television. While I was finishing my senior year at Marymount, she and Tom began developing her series. She was forty and he was fifty-one. Both were beginning new careers. "Letter to Loretta" was an anthology series;

a different story was presented each week, with my mother playing a different character. The pilot presentation left nothing to chance, and the series was sold to Procter & Gamble on that first presentation. There were thirty-nine stories scheduled for the first season.

There was barely time to set up a corporation, Lewislor Enterprises, Inc. The start date came so quickly after the sale that production had to begin almost immediately to create a backlog of shows in case of emergencies. The stock in Lewislor Enterprises was divided equally between my mother and Tom, with each one contributing one percent to Robert F. Shewalter, the accountant who was handling the business affairs.

As my high-school graduation drew near, my mother was totally absorbed in plans for the series. And if she wasn't in meetings or at the studio, she was in Ojai with the rest of the family. So I began staying with my cousin Gretchen Foster. I didn't mind the arrangement; it was pleasant not to be alone. Gretchen was in her junior year at Marymount, and we were both absorbed in school activities. I was elected a candidate for prom queen, and Gretchen was my campaign manager.

The night of the junior/senior prom Russ drove me to the Church of the Good Shepherd before we went to the Marymount auditorium, where the party was being held. "I have a surprise for you," he said as he led me up the aisle. We knelt together in front of the altar. He took my hand in his and, looking into my eyes, said, "I love you, Judy. Will you marry me?"

I whispered, "Yes, I'll marry you." We sealed our love and devotion to each other with a kiss in front of God in the quiet beauty of the church. I wasn't the prom queen that night, merely a princess, but I was so happy that I was going to marry the man I loved that nothing else mattered.

My happiness was short-lived. When Russ and I told my mother about our plans she was not pleased at all and insisted that we delay our marriage for at least a year. All my protestations against that long a delay went unheard. She was immovable. It cannot have escaped her notice that I was the same age she was when she had eloped

1953. Irene Dunne and my mother costumed for my Marymount High School graduation party at the Beverly Hills Hotel.
ALEXANDER P. KAHLE

with Grant Withers. (At the time, I couldn't understand what might underlie her reaction because not only did I not know about my own father, but I had no knowledge of my mother's first marriage. It was only when I was older that she confided in me.)

"You're only seventeen years old. One more year won't make that much difference. If you two really care for each other you can still get married at the end of the year. I won't stand in your way and I'll give you a big wedding," she promised. No amount of pleading on my part could change her mind, and Russ, wanting to keep peace, reasoned with me, saying since it meant so much to her, perhaps we should consider waiting.

Neither of us was prepared for what happened next: My mother suggested that I go to school in Switzerland.

"Think of the opportunity you can have to live in a foreign country, to travel, and to meet all kinds of different people. Then, after the year is finished, you can come home and marry Russ if that's what you still want to do. You'll never have another opportunity like this." She was very persuasive, using every possible inducement she could think of.

But I had already been making my own plans, telling no one. I wanted very much to go to college. Most of my classmates were already enrolled: Mimi in Immaculate Heart, others at U.S.C. and U.C.L.A. My grades were acceptable and I had already gone through the preliminary enrollment procedures at U.S.C. I planned to major in philosophy and minor in psychology.

I hadn't discussed any of this with my parents because I wanted to wait until I was accepted and then tell them my plans. It never occurred to me that my mother would try to separate me from Russ for a year, and I stubbornly refused to be sent to Switzerland, no matter how glamorous she made it sound. She dropped the idea of Switzerland, but she was not going to be thwarted for long. She had made up her mind and she was determined to have her way.

Without my knowledge I was enrolled for a year at Duchesne Residence School, a girls' finishing school in New York City run by the Religious of the Sacred Heart. My plans to attend U.S.C. were ignored along with my dreams and desire for a college education.

In April my parents, with Irene Dunne and Frank Griffin and a group of Marymount parents, hosted a large pregraduation party at the Beverly Hills Hotel. My mother had taken me to the studio costume department, where I chose a sexy thigh-length pink-and-black-sequined can-can costume that showed off my legs. The wig department fitted me with a jet-black wig complete with bangs, and I wore a tall pink plume in my hair. We spent the rest of the day choosing a costume that Russ might feel comfortable wearing, nothing silly or overdone. We came home with three choices. I was surprised and hurt when Russ refused to wear any of them, saying he didn't feel comfortable in a costume and that he had decided to wear his army reserve uniform. Nothing my mother or I could say would dissuade him. My mother took this opportunity to point out that if

1953. My Marymount High School formal graduation picture.

Russ didn't care enough about me to wear a costume to my party when he knew how much it meant to me, what was he going to be like when we were married? She made a convincing argument out of a very minor circumstance. She was angry with him for refusing her choices. And, vulnerable to suggestion, I was disappointed, too.

At long last, graduation day arrived, a beautiful sunny California day. As my classmates and I slowly walked down the long stretch of lawn and up the steps of the auditorium to take our seats, I could hardly believe I was leaving this school, the most consistent and reassuring part of my life for more than ten years. I cried as I listened to Mimi's commencement address and again when I received my diploma, and yet again when my mother and father kissed me and said, "Congratulations, graduate."

They were tears of joy, not like the tears I had shed a few days earlier when my mother had told me that I didn't have permission to stay out all night with the rest of the class. The entire class and their dates were celebrating that evening at a party at the Ambassador Hotel's Coconut Grove. Following the dinner and dancing, other after-hour parties were planned that were to last until the next morning. I was the only graduate who didn't have permission to stay out all night.

Graduation night, a little before midnight, a waiter brought me a folded sheet of paper. He leaned over as he handed it to me. "I was told to deliver this to you in person. You don't have to answer it."

I opened the message and read:

> You can stay out as long as you like. Have a wonderful time.
> Love,
> Mom

Once again my mother had interceded with my father to give me a perfect ending to a perfect day.

My mother and father accompanied me to my school in New York; they were meeting with NBC executives, and my mother was going to be doing publicity appearances, promoting the launch of "Letter to Loretta." I remember little about the trip except that I cried most of the way. When I wasn't crying I was reading the novel I'd chosen for the plane ride—of all books, *Gone with the Wind*. My parents, however, were in a festive mood. They had celebrated their thirteenth wedding anniversary a month earlier on the set, and the word of mouth for the show was positive.

During the trip my mother introduced me to someone who was traveling in first class with us.

"I'd like to introduce you to my sister Judy," she said.

At first I thought I had misunderstood her. "Did you just call me your sister?" I asked.

Her face flushed and she looked surprised. "Is that what I said?"

"Yes, Mom, you called me your sister," I replied. Turning to the man standing in front of us, I extended my hand.

"I'm her *daughter* Judy, not her sister."

He smiled as he took my hand. "Well," he said, gazing at my mother, "you certainly look young enough to be her sister."

"Thank you," she replied, giving him a dazzling smile.

This slip of the tongue on my mother's part repeated itself so often over the years that we would both laugh routinely and dismiss it as a "private family joke." Now that I understand more fully my mother's strong unconscious need to keep herself young, I'm not at all surprised that she introduced me as her sister. Having a grown daughter heightens any mother's awareness of her own aging process, but my mother was also a forty-year-old movie star beginning a new career in which she would be playing women far younger than her actual age. A grown daughter of seventeen entering college was a liability, not an asset, to her career. If she felt threatened, I in turn felt shocked by her introduction. I keenly sensed her competitiveness as I had in many more subtle ways before; I needed a mother, not a rival.

Duchesne Residence School, originally a private home, was a magnificent building on East Ninety-first Street. The front entrance was set back from the street within a private enclosed cobblestone driveway. Mother Claire Krim, the school's headmistress, greeted my mother and me in the large circular marble entrance hall. She appeared to be about sixty, although it was dificult to tell since her habit hid everything but her round and somewhat wrinkled face. She came from a wealthy Boston family and her carriage and deportment reflected her aristocratic background.

The school year was not to begin for a few more days, so this initial visit gave my mother an opportunity to see the school, and me a chance to choose my room. Mother Krim led us first into the parlor, a large comfortable room with dark, paneled walls. A crystal chandelier hung from the high, ornately decorated ceiling, and bookcases filled with books, all obviously well read, lined the room. There were couches upholstered in dark-colored velvet; an Oriental rug covered the inlaid-wood floor. This rather cluttered East Coast elegance was not at all what I was accustomed to, and I longed for the bright California sunlight and Grandma's spare Oriental style of decoration. Mother Krim pointed out certain pieces that were rare antiques and gave a brief history of the donor. At the time I wondered why she remembered such inconsequential details about a person's background, especially the financial status.

As Mother Krim led us down a third-floor hallway, pointing out the students' rooms, I wondered how I was ever going to choose a room when I didn't want to be there in the first place. At the end of the long hall we entered the largest bedroom I had seen there. It fronted on Ninety-first Street and, because it was at the corner of the building, it had more windows than the others and was much brighter. There were five single beds with night tables and matching bureaus, and a long closet hidden by curtains at one end of the room. This was a dormitory.

"Well, Judy, you've seen all the rooms. This is the last of them. Have you decided where you want to live for the next year?" Mother Krim asked. My heart sank. I had always had my own room and never had to share my living space with anyone for any length of time, least of all with total strangers. Now I had to make some kind of a decision. Time had run out.

"This is fine," I answered. At least it was big and bright, I reasoned.

We followed Mother Krim into a large domed-ceilinged room, surrounded by leaded-glass windows and tall marble pillars; frescoes decorated the walls. "This is the ballroom where we hold our monthly tea dances. You will meet a lot of nice young men, Judy. There are quite a few Catholic universities near here and the men enjoy coming to the Sunday dances."

My mother glanced swiftly at me as I turned away to hide the tears that were now beginning to well up. I could only nod in response. I didn't want either of them to see how very lonely and lost I was feeling.

I wasn't the only student to cry herself to sleep that first week. One of my roommates' sobs continued far into the night, long after I had exhausted myself, muffling my tears in the pillow. She was from somewhere in the Midwest, and was a shy, silent girl who kept to herself. I felt sorry for her and knew that whatever grief she was experiencing would probably overwhelm her if she continued in her depressed state.

Then suddenly, at the week's end, she was gone. Her clothes no longer hung in the closet, her bed was stripped bare, even her pillow was missing. It was as if the sad and frightened girl in the corner of our room had never existed, simply an echo of our own homesickness. Her sudden disappearance did not remain a mystery for very long, however. That evening before dinner everyone was called to a meeting in the large assembly room, where Mother Krim informed us that my roommate had been secretly married without her parents' knowledge to a boy they did not approve of. "He is a plumber," Mother Krim said. "And his family is not of the same caliber as hers. There was no alternative but to have her return home."

Midway through Mother Krim's remarks, the urge to rise from my chair and walk out of the room in protest was so strong that I can remember it to this day. Most likely the many years of family and Catholic-school training about manners and etiquette overrode my inner rage at this woman's crass dismissal of a young girl's pain. I hated the demeaning way she said *plumber,* as if it were cause for shame; I hated the total lack of respect for the girl's feelings and for her relationship with her husband. Judgments were being made on the basis of his social status and what he did for a living, not on the kind of man he was. I was swept by fury; its power kept me rooted, shocked into immobility by its intensity.

In Mother Krim's words I heard the echo of the voices of my own family—my grandmother saying, "Why, Russ doesn't have the same breeding as you, dear, he's common." That from a woman who barely knew him.

My father: "You have guts to marry Russ."

And my mother: "When you're married, do you really want to spend Saturday night having dinner with his *mother,*" saying the word *mother* just as Mother Krim had said *plumber.*

I didn't do battle with my family, but I could do battle with Mother Claire Krim, and that night in the assembly she became my mortal enemy, and Duchesne Residence School my battleground. We were at war.

Duchesne was not a conventional school. It really was a residence. Our days began early, with a nun ringing a bell up and down the corridors. There were classes like music appreciation and modern history, outings to the Metropolitan Opera and the theater, and courses in marriage and child development, taught by a Sacred Heart alumna with a raft of children who extolled the virtues of a Catholic marriage. Sometimes she even brought her husband, as if to affirm what she was saying. There was even a course in the correct protocol for being presented at Court.

Most of the actual education was supplied by professional schools off the premises. Some students attended the Juilliard School of Music, the New York Academy of Dramatic Arts, or Ballet Arts. How I would have loved to attend the New York Academy of Dramatic Arts had I known of its existence in advance. However, my mother had arranged for me to take cooking classes at the New York YWCA, and typing at a business school on Forty-second Street. She told me that if I was going to be a wife I'd better get the cooking classes that Marymount had failed to provide. She also felt that I should have some useful business skills, or at least that was what she led me to believe. Perhaps she had some future plan in mind for me. One thing I am sure of, though—none of this was my choice, and secretarial work was the last thing I wanted to do. The curriculum also required us to spend a certain number of volunteer hours at some charitable institution in Manhattan. I chose the New York Foundling Home, where I enjoyed taking care of the infants who had been left on doorsteps all over the city. The orphan in me reached out to them.

The majority of the twenty-six girls enrolled at Duchesne when I was there came from Latin American countries. Duchesne was a safe and protected home away from home, a far cry from the volatile political situations in which many of their parents lived. Some were the daughters of diplomats, a few the daughters of presidents, but all of them were extremely wealthy, as evidenced by their designer clothes and lavish jewels. They had substantial bank accounts and unrestricted charge accounts at New York's finest stores. There seemed no limit to the money these young girls had.

I, on the other hand, had a minimal bank account that barely supplied walking-around money. After I had taken buses to and from my classes, there was little money left for anything else. Fortunately, Russ, who had graduated and was working as a salesman for Reynolds Aluminum, sent me whatever spending money he could spare, and that is what I had. I don't know why my parents put me on such a tight budget, what their thinking was, or if they even considered the costs of living in New York. All I know is that if it hadn't been for Russ's generosity I would have had insufficient pocket money. Recently a mutual friend recalled how angry Russ had been at the time, telling her, "Judy barely has enough money to put a dime in the pay phone and call me collect." That pay phone at the end of the hall was a lifeline for me and for my close friend, Frances

Lederer. Franny was as unhappy as I was. She called her family in Chicago practically every night, begging and pleading to go home.

My collect calls to Russ were limited because he was on a tight budget himself, but those calls were the only thing I looked forward to and what got me through the week. Every night before I went to sleep, I wrote to him: long letters telling him what I was thinking and feeling. In the beginning I also called home, but my mother was usually at the studio and couldn't be disturbed. The show was now absorbing all her time and attention. When I did get her and begged to go home, she said that was out of the question and she didn't want to hear any more about it.

On Sunday, September 20, 1953, "Letter to Loretta" premiered at 10 P.M. on NBC-TV. At Duchesne lights were usually out by that time, but Mother Krim gave me and the rest of the girls permission to stay up and watch my mother come twirling through the door in an elegant gown designed by Marusia; it was an entrance that would be her trademark for nine years. After the show was over, everyone congratulated me, telling me how much they had enjoyed it. I was very proud of my mother that night; she looked absolutely radiant and her performance was wonderful. Now she was a star on television, too, and I was thrilled and excited for her. I called to congratulate her and she seemed genuinely happy to hear from me and pleased that I had liked the show.

My celebrity status was short-lived, however. My personal war with school had brought an accumulation of demerits, eliminating any free time on the weekends. Mother Krim seemed to be winning. She had all the power and enforced the rules, and for every infraction more hours were added to my name in the demerit book. I couldn't help myself, I wouldn't conform.

It seemed utterly foolish to me for a bunch of young girls to wear dresses or suits, stockings and high heels to dinner. Who were we getting dressed up for? There weren't any men (I believed then that a woman's main motivation in dress was to please a man). I wore the dress and jewelry, everything just so, but on my feet I wore my white-fur bedroom slippers; more demerits ensued.

I hated the business school. It was located in an unpleasant neigh-

"Letter to Loretta," later "The Loretta Young Show," premiered on September 20, 1953. My mother's entrances in glamorous gowns would be her trademark for nine years.

borhood, Forty-second Street and Eighth Avenue, in an office up four flights of stairs. But it was the tea dances that really did me in. They were held in the ballroom on Sunday afternoons at two o'clock sharp; attendance was mandatory if you were in residence that weekend. I was usually in residence every weekend, working off my demerits.

Mother Krim presided over the party with an unparalleled vigilance and dedication, not unlike a zealous madam managing her "girls." A whistle was attached to a cord hung around her neck, and its piercing sound constantly interrupted the music on the record player: It meant someone was dancing too close, or someone was spending too much time with one partner. "Time to change now," she'd call, and everyone was obliged to change partners. As she watched, I could see her mentally pairing couples. Again, I declared silent war. She wasn't going to pair me with anyone; I was already paired. And so I refused to attend the tea dances, making up some excuse, pleading illness. More demerits went next to my name.

Franny Lederer was also relentless in her attempts at liberation from Duchesne. Her single-mindedness finally wore her parents down and she won her freedom, leaving before the Christmas holidays. I was sorry to see her go. She was my closest friend except for Anne Crossin, who was a day student.

At Christmastime I packed all my clothes and other belongings into cartons and shipped them home. I had made up my mind. I wasn't coming back to Duchesne after the holidays.

In California there were parties to attend, friends to see, presents to buy, and time to be spent with Russ, but there was no time to discuss with my mother the cartons that lay stacked one on top of the other, filling my bedroom. My mother didn't ask, and I avoided bringing up the subject. I was too busy having fun. I lived every waking moment with Russ, so glad to be home that I forgot the past months as if they had never happened. Then one afternoon my mother stopped me on my way out of the house.

"I want to talk to you, Judy," she said.

"I don't have time now, Mom. I'm late meeting Russ. We're joining some friends for dinner." I tried to move on, but she blocked my way.

"You'll have to make time. This won't wait." She led me into the living room and shut the door. I knew immediately that she was going to discuss school, and I hadn't thought of what I was going to say. I wasn't prepared in the slightest for this.

"You've decided you're not going back to school, haven't you?"

How did she know that? I wondered. I hadn't told her. Why did she always know everything, and why did she always surprise me before I was prepared? She always caught me off guard.

"I *have* decided that I'm not going back, but how did you know?"

She smiled and shook her head. "It's pretty obvious, isn't it? All your clothes arrived home. What else am I supposed to think?" Of course, how stupid of me not to realize she knew, and even more stupid to procrastinate in telling her. Before I could say anything, she spoke.

"Do you admire me, Judy?" Again she caught me off guard.

"Of course I do. You're my mother."

"No, I mean not just because I'm your mother, but do you admire me as a person, who I am?"

"Yes. You know that I do. Why do you ask?"

"Part of the reason you admire me is because I always finish a job that I start, no matter how unpleasant and how distasteful it may seem to me at the time. When I was very young I got up at the crack of dawn, took the trolley car, and transferred many times before I got to the studio. Sometimes when I stood at the top of the hill looking down at that studio I wanted to throw up I was so frightened. I didn't want to go there. But I walked through those gates and put in a full day's work, doing my job.

"Now, you can stay home. I can't make you go back to school if you don't want to. You turned eighteen in November. I can't force you. It's really up to you, the choice is yours now. You're old enough to make up your own mind." Before I could answer her, she turned and left the room.

There was no discussion, no argument, no chance to voice my feelings, to tell her why I didn't want to return to Duchesne, to explain to her that Mother Krim's materialistic values were totally opposite from the ones that I was just beginning to formulate for myself. Nothing that I wanted to say was said. She was gone before I could utter a word. I felt ambushed, yet it appeared to me that everything was left in my hands. I could decide my own fate. I thought she had given me the power to make my own decision.

The truth, as I see it now, was that I had no power. She possessed it all, and she had already decided for me. She knew me well; in order to win her admiration and respect, the things I most wanted from her, I had to return and finish what I had started. In order to win her love I had to be like her, to mirror her, as I had always dutifully tried to do in the past.

And so I returned to Duchesne to finish out the year. I didn't want to feel ashamed of myself for not completing a job I had begun. I believed that I was building a strong character and that I was making the right choice. Not following my heart was probably the biggest mistake of my young life, the first of many made primarily to please my mother.

Years later she revealed that before I arrived home at Christmas she had received a letter from Mother Krim. "You can't believe how shocked and surprised I was when I read that my perfect daughter, who always had marvelous grades and had never been any trouble to me or to anyone, was behaving so rebelliously," she told me. Mother Krim had written her that unless I changed my attitude and abided by the school rules she wouldn't accept me back. My mother couldn't risk Mother Krim's having to expel me; she had to think of a way to convince me that returning and finishing the year was my idea, a choice made for my own good, and she succeeded.

In the early months of 1954 after my return to Duchesne I had to have my tonsils and adenoids removed. It was decided that I would have the operation in New York rather than in Los Angeles. Mother Krim assured me that the surgeon she recommended was one of the best in the city, and Anne Crossin's mother promised she would take me to the hospital and stay with me.

When I awoke from the anesthetic, Agnes Crossin was right by my bed, just as she had said she would be. A widow, Agnes lived in a comfortable apartment on Park Avenue with her unmarried sister and her only child, Anne, my close friend. Agnes was small in stature, but vast in kindness, and Anne generously shared her mother's affection with me.

One afternoon, as Agnes and I were chatting, there was a knock on my door, and in walked Irene Dunne, impeccably dressed, as always, in a designer suit, with a fur hat on her head and a fur coat tossed over her shoulders. In her gloved hands she carried a potted plant.

"Mrs. Griffin, what a surprise!" I didn't even know she was in New York. "I'd like you to meet Agnes Crossin." She crossed the room and Agnes rose and shook her hand.

"Your mother called and told me you were in the hospital. She sends her love." She came over to my bed and put the plant on my nightstand.

Her visit was very brief. She inquired about my operation, asked me how school was progressing, and promised to call my mother with a report. Then she was gone, almost as swiftly as she had appeared, having made the thoughtful gesture, the duty call.

"She's a very attractive woman, isn't she?" Agnes's voice brought me out of my reverie. And suddenly, for the first time, I realized how distant my mother's close friend really was, compared with Agnes Crossin. That woman sitting next to me had known me only a few short months, and yet she was by my bedside when I awoke, she held my hand when I was in pain, and cared for me as if I were her own child, giving me real warmth and love.

"Yes! She is," I replied, wanting to add more. She was everything a movie star should be, glamorous and elegant, a loyal friend, a good Christian performing good deeds. But I felt no warmth from her presence. I never had. I called her Mrs. Griffin, even though she'd asked me to call her Aunt Irene. Somehow that didn't suit her. I'd known her and gone to school with her daughter, Murph, since I was six. Our families took vacations together and still she remained inaccessible. It always amazed me when I watched her old movies. I couldn't reconcile the uproariously funny comedienne on the screen with the Mrs. Griffin that I knew. But it had become clear to me that the charmer on the screen was the actress, and the distant woman who had just left my room was the real person.

Once I had recuperated, I settled back into Duchesne's routine. My battles with Mother Krim didn't have the explosive intensity they had before; the fire of nonnegotiable rebellion had been pretty well extinguished. We continued to have our disagreements, but none that couldn't be rectified. I hadn't yet declared peace, but I was resigned to "finish the job."

Despite our dicey relationship, Mother Krim was not above requesting favors. Through my mother's intercession, Rosalind Russell gave the entire student body tickets to *Wonderful Town*. Roz and her producer husband, Freddy Brisson, were good friends of my mother. Although the Brissons were at a great many of my parents' dinner parties, I hadn't formed much of an opinion of them, except that he was a rather stuffy Englishman and she was loud.

Rosalind Russell and her husband, Frederick Brisson. I fell in love with her and the theater when I saw her performance in Wonderful Town.
UPI/BETTMANN

But the night I saw Rosalind Russell on the Broadway stage I fell in love with the theater and with her. I finally understood what everyone meant when they talked about Roz's comedic talents. She was sensational, a star, and watching her in that dark Broadway theater, I was far more impressed than I had ever been by anyone in Hollywood.

At her request all of us trooped backstage to her dressing room after the performance and I presented her with a bouquet of flowers that by then had wilted from being clutched all night in my hot hand. She kissed me and thanked all of us for coming back to see her. She made me feel important that evening and I loved her for it.

Russ and I still wrote to each other daily and talked weekly on the phone. He had supported my decision to return to school and agreed with me that it was right that I finish out the year. "After all, honey, six months isn't that long a time. We'll have the rest of our lives together," he said. It was a comfort knowing that he was waiting for me at home. He didn't mind if I had dates; in fact, he encouraged me to have a good time. We loved and trusted each other and nothing could change that.

By the time the final six months had passed I was no longer at war. Mother Krim and I had declared peace and parted friends.

Russ met me at the airport with open arms when I returned home. He enfolded me in his embrace, kissed me, and said, "I love you. Will you marry me?" And I told him yes. That was what we both had waited for so long, what we wanted and had talked about for a year. The arms around me were the same familiar ones that I knew and loved, but I had a vague feeling of unease as I climbed into the front seat of his car and we headed home to the beach house.

My mother and father had already begun filming the second season of the show, which had been renamed "The Loretta Young Show." In the beginning of the first season the ratings had been low and some changes had to be made. As the ratings began to climb slowly, Tom decided he didn't want to grant Procter & Gamble its option to continue sponsoring the show. He had another sponsor waiting in the wings and figured that he could get more money. But my mother and her agency joined forces, and Tom was voted down. Procter & Gamble renewed, and my mother was nominated for an Emmy.

The friction of working together was already telling on my parents' marriage. My mother was spending most of her waking hours at the studio. I saw very little of her. After a long day's filming she stayed late, viewing the dailies with the editor, and arrived home in time for a light snack and bed. Now that I had finished my year at Duchesne, Russ and I approached her about formally announcing our engagement and setting a wedding date, as she had promised we could.

"I can't think about that right now," she told me. "Can't this wait?"

I felt it couldn't, but I didn't want to upset her. She seemed exhausted. So I dropped the subject and waited for a better time to discuss it. That time never seemed to come. Our wedding plans were put on hold.

But Russ could wait no longer. He bought my diamond engagement ring and slipped it on my finger one evening at the Mocambo nightclub. I proudly showed it to my mother the next day and asked her, now that I had my ring, when I could formally announce my engagement.

"I don't have time to give you a party," she told me. "I'm much too busy with the show, but maybe Polly Ann would."

My aunt Polly Ann agreed. She and her husband, Carter, acted as the official family host and hostess, giving an informal swimming party at their home in Coldwater Canyon in Beverly Hills. Both our families and friends attended, but still my mother didn't instruct Helen Ferguson to issue a formal press release. The large wedding that she had promised seemed further and further away.

It was clear to both Russ and me that my family was not happy about our engagement. My father had already openly voiced his opinion that he didn't think Russ made enough money to support me in the manner to which I had become accustomed, ignoring the fact that Russ was working long hours and beginning to move up the corporate ladder. Nothing Russ did seemed acceptable.

My mother continued to delay any formal arrangements for a wedding, saying that her strenuous shooting schedule was all that she could handle and that she was exhausted. Indeed, she was beginning to look it. She was smoking nonstop, lighting one cigarette while another still burned in the ashtray. She was losing weight at an alarming rate. She had already stopped doing all her favorite charity activities: the Holy Family Adoption Service, which she and Tom had helped to found; and St. Anne's Maternity Hospital for Unmarried Mothers, which she had promoted vigorously since 1944, when she became president of the board of trustees.

I decided to enlist Grandma's help, thinking maybe she would intercede with my mother. It had worked in the past, and I was getting desperate. But Grandma was having her own problems. The construction and decoration of the Flores town house and surrounding luxury apartments were absorbing all her time and energy. She had long ago far exceeded the budget Tom allocated, and still the expenses continued to escalate. Nothing was even remotely near completion. She was under constant pressure from both the accountants and Tom to finish the job. My mother was anxious to move into her new home; the commute from the beach to the studio during the week and to Ojai on the weekends was taking a physical toll on her, so she, too, was pressuring Grandma to finish.

Grandma had no time to run interference for me. In fact, she advised me to put my wedding plans aside for the time being, until my mother had finished filming and she had completed the house. "After all, dear, there's no big rush, is there? This will give you and Russ more time to be together, to get to know each other a little better. You've been apart for a year now. A lot can happen in a year. You might decide that you don't want to get married after all. I think long engagements are a good idea, don't you?"

No, I didn't at all, but I didn't tell her that. Nor did I tell her how heartsick I was that she didn't want me to marry Russ, that nobody in my family did, how let down I felt by everyone.

I began experiencing excruciating abdominal pains, and when they had become so severe that I couldn't bear it any longer I finally told my mother and she advised me to see Dr. Marxer. He prescribed medication for an acute case of colitis and then, ever intuitive, he asked me, "How are things going at home, Judy? Is everything all right?"

"Everything's fine, Dr. Marxer, just fine," I replied. Strange as it seems now, looking back to those days, I actually did think everything was fine. I was so accustomed to keeping my problems to myself and feeling that I was the singular cause of them that I didn't see any correlation between my intestinal discomfort and my basic relationship with my father, my conflict with my mother about the wedding, or the troubles I was having with my family's reaction to Russ. After all, I reasoned, my family life was what it had always been. As a matter of fact, my relationship with my father appeared to be changing for the better. With my mother spending more and more time at the studio, my father was more available and our conversations together were actually more cordial than they had been in the past.

In retrospect it is quite obvious that Dr. Marxer knew my colitis was a somatic symptom of extreme emotional distress. He was my mother's physician before she married Tom, and now he was a confidant to both of them. He often took Tom flying with him in his private plane. He knew everything was not all right at home, and like everyone else, he also probably knew about my origins and no doubt was aware that my mother hadn't told Tom. As my doctor he wanted to be a sympathetic and impartial listener, hoping to alleviate some of my emotional burden. God knows I could have used such a wise listener, but I wasn't aware of it at the time, nor did I really trust anyone, other than Russ, enough to confide everything. (I later learned that my mother had enlisted Dr. Marxer's cooperation as a mediator with Tom. When he wouldn't take sides, she felt betrayed and dismissed him as her physician.)

On August 11, 1954, Walter Winchell announced in his column that the Lewis marriage was over. Helen Ferguson swiftly denied it, and a few days later Winchell reported that Tom and Loretta had celebrated their fourteenth wedding anniversary.

I remember that Tom did seem lonely and distracted, but I attributed it to the fact that my mother was never home. I thought that perhaps the rumors about their marriage were true, and I was secretly angry with my mother for putting her work ahead of her family's needs. I needed her to plan my wedding, and Tom needed her at home with him. He began to seek me out when he came home, eager to share his day with me, unusual behavior for him, but I enjoyed the attention, nevertheless. At times he tactlessly told me his personal feelings about my mother and that became awkward and more than I was willing to hear. But, eager to please, I often commiserated with him, for I was feeling as abandoned as he was. When I told him about Dr. Marxer's diagnosis, Tom's response was: "You know what your problem is, Judy? It's Russ—he's your problem."

The lack of cooperation on the part of my family and the delayed plans for our marriage were finally affecting my relationship with Russ. His patience was wearing thin. He wanted to marry me and he didn't want to wait any longer. I, on the other hand, wanted everything to be right. I wanted my family to approve; I wanted them to love Russ as much as I did. Nothing was working out the way I wanted it to. I kept hoping things would change, and when they didn't, I began to wonder if maybe my family was right. Maybe my problem really was Russ and not them. Maybe he wasn't the right man for me after all.

The year in New York and now the aching disappointment of this endless stretch of time with no wedding date to look forward to was a hellish limbo for me. I was floating in an emotional vacuum, alone and unsure, and the longer I waited, the more unsure I became. Finally, any action seemed more bearable than none. Instead of marrying Russ against my family's wishes, as I should have, I gave him back his ring.

"I broke my engagement and gave Russ back his ring." I stood in front of my mother's dressing table, tears streaming down my face. I could still see his pain-filled eyes as he had turned away from me a short time before. I had just said good-bye to my love, my future, my protector, and my best friend. All my dreams, my life with Russ, our plans for children—all of it was gone. The world was empty and I was alone. I felt I would never be happy again.

My mother looked up from the mirror, her face shiny with the thick clear grease she applied to remove her film makeup. She carefully took a large swipe with a tissue, cleaning off a portion of her forehead.

"I think you did the right thing, Judy."

She seemed so detached. Couldn't she see how much I was hurting, how I wanted some comfort? Couldn't she just put her arms around me and hold me until that ache went away? Instead, she sat looking at me, and finally reached over and handed me a tissue.

"You'll feel better with time."

10 *THE FLORES HOUSE*

My mother's prediction proved correct. I did heal with the passage of time and life went on, only not quite as before. Most of my friends were now in their sophomore year in college and I found that I had less in common with them than I had had before. While I had been focusing on my marriage plans, their lives were filled with new people, new experiences, and intellectual stimulation. I envied them and considered enrolling in a university, but I found I would have to begin as a freshman since my year at Duchesne afforded me no college credits. My pride wouldn't let me. Silly as it seems now, I didn't want to be the oldest in my class (appearance was so important back then). Somehow, my previous ambition to major in philosophy and minor in psychology seemed impractical.

In 1955 the attitudes were a bit different from what they are today. There were fewer options for women, career opportunities were more limited, and, in my world, at least, college was regarded as a place to have fun, meet a man, and get married. Marriage was what women did, their primary and universally accepted lifetime career. Now that I was no longer engaged to be married, I didn't know how to define myself. I'd been raised and educated to get married and be a wife.

My mother came to the rescue by offering me a secretarial job at the studio: "I haven't seen very much of you since you've been home and I think you'd be an asset to the show. I need your young ideas," she told me. This was the third season and Lewislor now owned "The Loretta Young Show." But my mother and father had fought bitterly over contract negotiations and Tom was no longer producing the show.

I liked the idea of being needed. Moreover, this was an opportunity to learn the television business, so I accepted her offer. I went to work in the accounting department and a few months later was thrilled when my mother's old friend Ruth Roberts, now story editor for the show, asked me to be her assistant.

I was spending my nights and weekends working at the Players Ring Theater, a small, highly regarded neighborhood theater. In exchange for my free labor in the box office, I was invited to join a weekly acting class given by Ralph Senensky, the staff director. Although I was strictly a beginner—some of the other actors in the group were far more advanced and already working in television—I knew that this was the work I wanted to do.

We had finally moved into the Flores house. Grandma had done a superb job of redesigning and redecorating. Our house had white-marble floors in the entry and black marble in the atrium; the ceilings were high and the rooms flooded in sunlight. Word spread rapidly and the maisonettes were occupied by members of the movie community, Joan Crawford and Rod Steiger among the first tenants. But my mother had little opportunity to enjoy her beautiful new home. She all but lived at the studio in an apartment furnished by Grandma, with a maid in attendance; her workdays ran from early morning until late at night. She attended all the story meetings, production meetings, and casting sessions. She even viewed the dailies after the shooting day ended, instructing her editors about which takes to use and which to eliminate. She was not only an actress but an executive and part owner as well. There wasn't one small element of "The Loretta Young Show" that she didn't oversee.

On March 7, 1955, when she accepted her Emmy, she set a new precedent—she was the first star to have won both an Oscar and an Emmy. But the long and difficult work schedule, together with the emotional stress of her deteriorating marriage, was taking its toll of my mother's already fragile body. By the time she had finished her second season, in February 1955, she weighed less than 100 pounds,

The Flores house, the apartment complex of private maisonettes that my grandmother, Gladys Belzer, designed.

well below what was normal for her five-foot-six-and-a-half-inch frame. Her doctor prescribed three months of total rest before she began to film the next season's shows in June.

I was in my studio office when the telephone call came from my aunt Georgiana Montalban on April 10, 1955. She was calling from Ojai and she sounded very upset.

"It's your mother, Judy. She was taken by ambulance to St. John's Hospital in Oxnard."

"What's wrong with her?" I asked.

"We don't know yet. She began to have abdominal pains while we were driving up here yesterday. Tom called the doctor and he came and examined her and told her to rest. But when the pains continued and your mother wasn't getting any better, I told Tom to call him again. Tom had the nerve to tell me that there was nothing wrong with her, that she was imagining it. She wasn't. She was in serious pain and nobody was doing anything about it. I insisted that an ambulance be called and she was just admitted to St. John's."

"I'll come right up, Georgie."

"No, Judy, that isn't necessary. There's nothing you can do. She's being taken care of, she's in good hands, but she's in a lot of pain. I'll keep you posted."

"I'm glad that you were there, Georgie. Promise that you'll let me know how she's doing, and when I can see her?"

"Yes, Judy, I promise I'll keep you posted."

News of my mother's illness spread quickly and the next few days were filled with rumors. Helen Ferguson worked hard to keep the press away from the hospital. We were all alerted not to take any calls, not that there was any information I could have given anyone since I had none myself. Ruth and I continued our work with the staff writers, getting the next season's scripts ready, but things were very unsettled at the studio. No one knew for sure if there would be a "Loretta Young Show."

The cause of my mother's intense abdominal pain and illness was an ovarian cyst that had burst, causing severe peritonitis. When she was admitted to the hospital, her condition was very serious and she was judged too frail to undergo surgery. It was decided to keep her hospitalized until she was strong enough to undergo a hysterectomy. While my mother lay in her hospital bed for several months enduring incredible pain, the press reported all sorts of rumors, the most persistent being that she had cancer. Meanwhile, the family held firm to its collective "no comment" stance.

Those months in the Flores house, waiting to hear about my mother's condition, mostly fearing the worst, were torture. I had come to realize that Tom resented my working at the studio and he vented his anger and resentment by withholding information from me. Tom and Helen Ferguson were in daily communication, however. My mother's illness had a curious effect on Tom. I once heard him exclaim to Helen Ferguson, "Finally I have my little Gretchen back," his voice full of elation. I realized then that my mother's illness had reduced her to a powerless little girl, and that in some way it made Tom happy. In that moment I hated him more than I'd ever hated anyone and I silently vowed to protect my mother from him.

But there was no way that I could possibly have protected her from what he proceeded to do. I heard about it many months later from Ruth Roberts, long after the fact. He instructed the William Morris Agency to cancel the NBC contract, explaining that my mother was too ill to think of acting since she was facing a prolonged hospitalization, followed by surgery. Shortly thereafter, Helen Ferguson called Tom and asked him to meet her and Abe Lastfogel, president of the William Morris Agency. They informed Tom that when my mother had heard what he had done she had called her own meeting in her hospital room. She announced that the contract was to remain in effect and that she was now officially in charge of Lewislor and the show, and that orders were to come only from her or her representative, accountant Bob Shewalter; together with their combined shares, they could outvote Tom.

Abe Lastfogel then promised Procter & Gamble that the agency would provide some of Hollywood's top stars to fill in for my mother until she was well enough to return. "The Loretta Young Show" would continue as always, with one stipulation: The doorway would remain closed until Loretta was well enough to walk through it again. In June 1955, "The Loretta Young Show" began filming its third season without its star.

"We're the PCT Club. No one but us can belong. Just the three of us—Peter, Christopher, and Tom. We three stick together, don't we?" My father's voice drifted up the front hallway and into my bedroom; it was loud and he sounded as if he'd been drinking again. "Where shall we go on our next club trip?" he went on.

"San Francisco, on the train!" eleven-year-old Christopher shouted excitedly.

"San Diego! San Diego!" ten-year-old Peter shouted even louder.

Tom was laughing. "Maybe we'll go both places. Maybe we'll even go to New York and never come back."

I got up from my desk and walked out into the hallway.

"When can we go, Dad? When?" Both boys were talking at once.

"Pretty soon now, I should think. No one seems to care what happens to us anyway. Everyone around here is too interested in their jobs at the studio."

"Mom cares about us," Christopher said.

"So does Judy," Peter chimed in.

"Oh, Judy! She's only interested in her friends and her job. Besides, this is a family trip, for the PCT club. She isn't family," Tom replied.

"Yes, she is. She's our sister." Both boys were talking at once.

"No, she's not, not really. She's adopted. She's not related to you. She has nothing to do with you. She's not part of our family."

Before I knew what I was doing I had run down the stairs, through the front hallway and into the living room, where I found my father sitting on the couch between my two brothers.

"I don't believe what I just heard you saying about me to my brothers. How dare you!" I was shaking with rage. I thought my knees were going to buckle, but I stood my ground.

For a moment Tom looked shocked. I had surprised him with my sudden appearance and my rush of anger, but he recovered quickly and stood up.

"You were listening to our private conversation. How characteristic of you, sneaking around so no one can hear you."

"I stood at the top of the stairs and heard you tell my own brothers that I am not part of this family. And I have also heard you talk to Helen Ferguson about my mother when she wasn't here to defend herself, she was too sick. So don't you dare talk to *me* about sneaking around."

He turned quickly to Peter and Christopher, who were sitting in stunned silence on the couch, and pointed his finger at me.

"See, you see! Look at her. That's what I was talking about—that's what I don't want you to become. I don't want either of you to ever be like her." He was shouting.

The family gathered around the piano in the living room of the Flores house. Left to right: me, my mother, and my brothers Peter and Christopher wearing their St. John's Military Academy uniforms.

"They would be lucky if they were like me. They are lucky to have me as a sister. No matter what you tell them, I am still their sister. I have done everything I possibly can to be a good daughter to you. But you've been a rotten lousy father to me. You've gone out of your way to be cruel and mean. You never tried to love me. I don't want anything more to do with you ever again." I was both shouting and crying uncontrollably, just exactly what I hadn't wanted to do, but at least I had finally said what I wanted to say, what I felt.

Tom moved toward me quickly, his hand raised, and as his arm swung down, I grabbed it and held on tightly. My power and strength surprised me, and as we stood locked together, Tom looked startled.

"That is the last time you will ever touch me. Don't you ever raise your hand to me again. You are no longer my father. I want nothing more to do with you, you mean nothing to me," I said, as I flung his arm away from me and walked out of the living room.

That evening marked a major shift for me. Although I was very upset by our encounter, at the same time I felt detached and resolved. I meant it when I told Tom I wanted nothing more to do with him, that he could no longer influence me. This man whose love I had spent so many years trying to win was no longer important in my life. He was not my father, nor would he ever be. I was finally free of any obligations to him. He could no longer affect me in the ways that he had in the past. We lived together in the same house, passing each other silently in the halls, but I no longer cared about him. I shut off all feelings toward him. It was finally true that he meant nothing to me; he was merely a presence that I endured without any feeling of connection at all.

The next time I visited my mother at the hospital, I told her about my confrontation with Tom and my feelings of absolute detachment. She not only understood but seemed sympathetic. No doubt she was feeling much the same detachment herself.

covering bones. Her arms were covered with black-and-blue marks from the intravenous feedings that she had been receiving for the last three months. She looked as if she had been beaten up and starved, like the prisoners in Dachau in World War II.

I couldn't hide my thoughts from her. "Not a pretty sight, huh?" she said.

"I've seen you looking a bit more glamorous."

She managed a smile. She was very weak, and Marie and I all but carried her between us while she made a supreme effort to walk. She weighed so little that I could lift her with ease.

When she finally got back into bed, Marie began to insert the needle for the intravenous feeding into the vein in one hand. My mother winced and looked away. "Do you have to put that thing in again? I hate needles. They hurt all the time. They hurt when you put them in and they hurt while they're in there."

"I'll try to be as gentle as I can. Just imagine that you're getting caviar instead of liquid," Marie said patiently, and they both laughed.

"Did I tell you that the only thing I could eat in the beginning was caviar? It's the only thing that appealed to me and made my digestion work."

"Yes, Mom. You told me."

Once Marie had finished taping the needle to my mother's hand, Mom looked at her and said, "Leave us alone now, would you please, Marie." Her tone had changed slightly; it was a command.

As soon as Marie had gone, my mother turned her gaze on me. "What's this I hear about you signing with an agent?"

"That's right, I've signed a one-year contract with Myer Mishkin."

"And when were you planning to tell me this news?"

"When you were out of the hospital and feeling better."

"Did you think I'd take it better then? I don't appreciate hearing about things after they're already in the paper. Why in the name of God do you want to be an actress?" Her voice was beginning to rise. It wasn't as weak as it had been before.

"It's what I'm interested in now. You know that. You sit in the living room and see me walk out of the house every Wednesday night to go to class. Every Wednesday you ask me where I'm going, and every Wednesday I answer you, 'To acting class, Mom.' You know I've been working nights at the theater."

"Yes, I know all those things." She dismissed my reasoning. "Why acting?"

"Because I think I have talent. I like the work. It's what I want to do."

"Do you want to end up like me? Do you want to end up lying in a hospital bed half-dead, weighing next to nothing, with no life, no show, nothing. Is that what you want, Judy?"

What did all that have to do with me? I wondered. But all I could manage to say was, "No."

"It's a terrible life. A terrible life. You don't want it. You think it's easy because you've only lived with the gravy. You don't know about the rest of it. It may look easy, but I can assure you it isn't."

"Mom, please let's not argue about this. I don't want you to get upset."

"Upset? I'm already upset. You upset me by not telling me what you'd done. I want you to call Myer Mishkin right now and tell him you've thought it over and you've decided that you don't want to sign with him."

"I can't do that, Mom. The contract is signed and he wants to handle me."

She gestured toward the phone on the bedside table and held out the receiver to me. She was sitting straight up in bed, her back stiff. She was no longer the sickly, frail woman I had seen just a short time before; she was the powerful movie star.

"You can get his number from information."

I held my ground. I was determined not to give in. "No, Mom. I'm not going to call him."

"If you won't, I will, and you don't want that, I can assure you." Her voice was getting quite loud; she was very angry.

I tried reasoning with her in a calm, quiet voice. "Mom, please, he has already spoken to two studios about me. They may be interested in putting me under contract."

She began to yell. "I will see to it that Myer Mishkin will never work in Hollywood. I will ruin him. I will destroy him. He doesn't know who he's dealing with here. I will destroy him, I promise you."

Her voice was so loud that Marie and a nun came bustling in.

"What's going on here?"

"Just a family discussion," my mother answered, her voice calmer.

"Mrs. Lewis, you know you're not supposed to get upset." Marie's voice was soothing.

"Well! What are you going to do?" my mother asked me. They all looked at me.

"All right, Mom, you win. Nothing is worth your getting upset and having a relapse. Okay, fine. I'll take care of it, don't worry."

Her whole body seemed to relax and she sagged against the pillows and let Marie straighten the bedclothes around her.

"When?"

"Today."

When I got back to the studio, Ruth didn't have to ask how the meeting went. She could tell by my face. Myer Mishkin phoned later that afternoon. I told Ruth to tell him that I had gone for the day. I just couldn't talk to him, not then, anyway. But he was persistent, and finally, a few days later, I told him that I'd given it a lot of thought and didn't feel I was ready to start a career yet. I thanked him for his interest in me and said I hoped I hadn't inconvenienced him.

"You've seen your mother, haven't you, Judy?" he asked me. I lied and said no, that she had nothing to do with it; this was my decision. I didn't tell him that I believed that she did have the power to ruin him, and that she would use it if she had to. I was afraid of that power. I was afraid of her.

After my mother left the hospital she faced a long convalescent period, just as predicted. Although the operation was a fairly simple one, her condition prior to it had been almost life-threatening. She now had to build up her strength and regain her lost weight before she could undertake the grueling television schedule.

Although Bert Granet, who had a solid reputation as a writer and producer, was hired in Tom's place, my mother still guided her show from the sidelines. No one was going to control "The Loretta Young Show" but Loretta Young. Although she was unable to attend any meetings, no decision of any importance was made without her approval. She and Ruth Roberts, now associate producer, spoke daily. What "Loretta wanted" governed everyone's thinking, and when she finally returned, in October 1955, and walked through her door, which had been shut for five months, everybody on the set applauded, calling out, "Welcome home." There wasn't a dry eye anywhere; everyone was crying with happiness, including my mother and me.

When the show finished filming in February 1956, I began making plans for a trip to Europe. Norman Foster was traveling to Denmark on business and wanted to take his daughter Gretchen with him. My mother asked me if I'd like to accompany them, and naturally I said yes. We planned to fly to Copenhagen. After spending a few days sight-seeing, Gretchen and I would then leave Norman in Denmark and fly to Rome.

My mother was very enthusiastic about the trip and wrote ahead to Clare Booth Luce, who was then the American ambassador to Rome, to let her know that we were coming. Georgie and Ricardo Montalban were expected to visit Rome at the same time we would be there, so we had plenty of contacts, should we need them. My mother wasn't worried about two young women traveling alone in Europe, but my aunt Sally was far less sanguine about our independence and safety, and when she found out that an old friend of hers, Lansing Brown, was conducting a tour throughout Europe, she booked us on it. Finally, all that was left for Gretchen and me to do was get our passports.

"There's nothing to it, Jude. Daddy and I went downtown and we stood in line, we handed them our birth certificates and pictures, and got our passports. It only took about half an hour."

Gretchen's words kept going through my mind as I sat on the bench at the Hall of Records in downtown Los Angeles. Forty-five minutes had passed since Helen Ferguson disappeared with some official behind the glass door opposite me. Why was this taking so long? I wondered. Gretchen told me that it was a simple process, but it didn't seem so simple. Why hadn't Helen and I stood in line like the rest of the people getting their passports? Why had Helen made an appointment, and why had she left me sitting waiting for her to return?

Something wasn't right, but I didn't know what it was and I was

Helen Ferguson stands beside Sister Mary Winifred, administrator of St. Anne's Maternity Hospital for Unmarried Mothers, as she receives a check from my mother, representing the proceeds from an auction my mother planned to establish the St. Anne Adoption Service.

AP/WIDE WORLD PHOTOS

getting anxious. We were leaving in six days. Everything was arranged: the airline tickets, hotel reservations, everything. What if I couldn't get a passport? What if something went wrong and I couldn't go?

Maybe there was something wrong with my baptismal certificate. "Here," my mother had said as she handed it to me. "You'll need this. Give it to Helen." Why didn't I have a birth certificate like everyone else? Why did Helen Ferguson, of all people, come with me? For that matter, why did Helen or anyone have to come with me? Why, I wondered, did I have to be different?

My mother said she had sent Helen because, as she pointed out, "I'd be recognized and there would be a crowd. It's much better if Helen goes with you." But why couldn't I just have gone with Gretchen and Uncle Norman? It would have been easier. I hated these uncomfortable feelings. There were too many questions that I didn't have answers for, and yet try as I might, I couldn't push them out of my mind as I had so many times before. Where was my birth certificate? Even though I was adopted, there must be a record of my birth somewhere, and if there was, where was it, who had it, and were my parents' names on it? Why was a baptismal certificate the only legal document my mother seemed to have for me, when everyone else in the world had a birth certificate? What was wrong with me, and why was this taking so long?

An hour had passed before Helen finally emerged. She was alone and she was smiling. She came over to me and sat down. "Well! It's all done. You have a passport, Judy." Her eyes were sparkling; she looked happier than I'd ever remembered seeing her before.

"What took you so long, Helen?" I asked.

"Just a few details that had to be ironed out." She waved her hand in dismissal. "This is a very important document, Judy, probably one of the most important you'll ever receive in your whole life. You now own an official United States passport in the name of Judith T. Lewis, and nobody can ever take that away from you." She handed me a black-leather passport case with my name stamped in gold at the bottom, a present from her. I thought it odd that the letter *T.* had been added to my name. It most likely stood for my confirmation name of Therese, which I never used.

I didn't know what to say. Helen had never given me a present before. In fact, she'd never been this animated or friendly toward me before. There was something in the way she spoke, in the expression in her eyes; I couldn't identify it, but I knew that she was proud of what she had accomplished.

"Well, aren't you going to look at your passport?" she asked somewhat impatiently.

I opened the leather case and drew out the green passport. My name, Judith T. Lewis, was printed on the inside above the large red seal.

"Here, Judy, sign it and make it valid," Helen said as she handed me a pen. "You have to put your signature above your picture. Sign it in the same name that appears on the passport," Helen instructed, and as I signed she reached over and gave me a kiss on the cheek. "Congratulations, Judy, you are now legally an American citizen with a United States passport. You can travel anywhere in the world with that."

It wasn't so much the kiss that marked that day in my memory, although that, too, was highly unusual behavior for Helen—it was the unspoken message I received that there was a great deal of significance in my having a legal document in my name. I knew from her behavior that she felt she had brought something off. In fact, she *had* achieved the impossible. She had obtained a passport for Judith Lewis, for whom there was no official record anywhere. She didn't exist. My birth certificate read "Judith Young," and my baptismal certificate read "Mary Judith Clark." Helen must have taken some state official into her confidence and probably even risked exposing her client's past. More than likely she paid someone to keep silent. No wonder she seemed so elated, and no wonder I remember that day so clearly. It was then that the questions that I had kept repressed suddenly became intensified. I felt more than knew, from Helen's attitude, that there was something hidden and secret and that it involved me.

As strange as it may seem, to this day I still don't know when I actually realized that my mother was my mother. Before I finally confronted my mother, I don't ever remember a moment when I said to her: You're my birth mother, I'm not adopted, I'm your daughter, aren't I? And her affirmation of that fact. If that did happen, and I doubt that it did, in all likelihood there was so much anxiety surrounding it that I have blocked it out of my mind. I probably knew, on some primitive level, that most likely she would not tell me the truth and the only way to keep her was to remain her adopted daughter. If unconsciously I had suspected the truth, it was Helen's attitude at the passport office that finally confirmed my suspicions.

When the fourth season of "The Loretta Young Show" began, Tom Lewis was still living at home, while my mother was now living full-time at the studio. When she came home on the weekends, Tom left with the boys for Ojai; they rarely saw each other now, and when they did they barely spoke.

My mother had already spoken privately to Chet LaRoche, imploring him to find Tom a job in New York, so she wasn't surprised when, in September, her husband packed all his belongings and drove back east, where he went to work for his old friend and mentor, creating a television department for C. J. LaRoche, Advertising.

My mother replaced Bert Granet with John London as producer and signed two new actors for the upcoming season: Hugh Beaumont and John Newland. John was, without a doubt, my mother's favorite leading man, and, as John told me, she was of major importance in helping him shape his career both as an actor and a director.

I responded immediately to John Newland when I met him. He was warm and friendly, never condescending, and he never dealt with me in a demeaning manner as my mother often did. He was more a father figure than anything else, although I was flattered that he paid attention to me, listening to my worries about my life and the conflicts that I was having with my mother. Not the least of these was my longing to work as an actress on the show, something that she consistently discouraged.

In retrospect, I don't think my mother was pleased with the friendship that developed between John and me, perhaps because she didn't understand it, perhaps because she viewed me as competing with her for John's affection. John recalls that she once asked him, "What in the world do you and Judy talk about? You're so much older than she is and you see her on the set. What can you possibly have to talk about?"

"We talk about her problems, about her life," he answered.

One afternoon at lunch I poured my heart out while John listened patiently. My mother had just insisted that I stop seeing an actor I had been dating. She didn't approve of him: Bad enough that he was an actor, but worse, she stated adamantly, was that he was never going to be a star and just wasn't good enough for me. I was angry and hurt about that, but in addition I was frustrated because every time Dick Morris (another director) or Ruth Roberts or John London had suggested me for an acting role on the show, my mother had flatly refused.

I implored John to intercede for me. "I know she'll listen to you," I told him. I also told him that all I really wanted to do was act. I knew I had talent, and my confidence was growing daily both in my classes with Agnes Moorehead and at the theater. A year had passed since my mother and I had had that dreadful scene in her hospital room, and I hoped that if John spoke to her, maybe he could persuade her to change her mind.

As John remembers it: "I went to your mother and said at some prudent moment, 'Why don't we use Judy as an actress on the show? I know that's what she wants to do.' As I recall, her answer to me was, in a circuitous and polite fashion, Just mind your own business. She didn't say it like that. She was very clever. But she ended up by saying, 'Judy's working for me on this show, and to be an actress in Hollywood is the very last thing that I want for her because you know the odds. It's a dreadful profession.' I knew I couldn't win. I acceded to her and simply withdrew."

Hearing John admit that he knew he couldn't win and so he gave in made me feel enormously relieved. So many times over the years, looking back on my life and the choices that I've made, I have asked myself why I let myself be stopped from doing what I wanted to do. It helped to know that in the face of my mother's power, even John Newland, whom she respected and admired as a peer, shared my helplessness.

When I asked John about this he replied, "Your mother's persona is truly unique. I have worked with many many big stars and I never remember anyone who had so conveyed the sense of 'I am the king of this room'—in a restaurant, in her house, on the stage, in the commissary, anywhere. What I remember of you is that you were always being enormously prudent and tactful because she was sometimes very harsh with you."

One day, when the entire company was rehearsing, the large sliding doors on Stage 6 had been left wide open to let the sun into the dark, musty interior. John was standing with his back to the door. I stood beside my mother, with a notebook in my hand, taking down any dialogue changes or director's notes for the scene.

As John remembers it: "All of a sudden the stage got absolutely quiet and no one was doing anything except looking over my shoulder at the door. I turned around and there stood Clark Gable in the doorway. He looked at Loretta and said, 'Hi, Slim,' and then he moved on.

"It was one of the most electrifying moments I've ever experienced. My remembrance was an unmistakable visual: how you looked like him and looked like her, too. My immediate thought was that whatever charade has been played, there's never been a moment that was so absolutely a testament to the parental involvement of this man with you.

"Loretta simply looked at him and went to her dressing room. It was one of those moments when we all pretended to be doing something because it was so obvious."

I wonder how many other occasions in my life I might have

turned around or looked up to see my father standing there. I can only ask myself once again, Was he keeping in touch with me in subtle ways? Was his presence that day just a coincidence, or did he know I would be there?

"Maggy Louis has a wonderful man that she wants you to meet, Judy." My mother was matchmaking again, this time assisted by Maggy Louis, dress designer Jean Louis's wife and my mother's close friend.

"Don't tell me, Mom, let me guess. He's a nice Catholic man."

She laughed. "As a matter of fact, he is. Maggy met him at early-morning mass. He's never been married and he's from New York. I've invited him to dinner Saturday night. I want you two to meet. Maggy says he's a lot of fun and she knows you two will hit it off."

Her reference to never being married was a reminder to me of the ineligibility of the man I had met over the Christmas holidays and was now dating. It was Maggy Louis who knew he was divorced, and it was she who had informed my mother.

"I already have a date for Saturday night, Mom." It was with my divorced friend.

"Change it. This man's leaving for New York the end of next week. I can't entertain during the week. I'm working. It has to be this Saturday night."

"What does this nice Catholic man do for a living?"

"You'll be pleased to know that he's a television director. At the moment he's unemployed and he's out here looking for work."

"Well, at least we'll have something in common."

She smiled. "You may even like him, Judy. Who knows?"

Which was how I met my husband-to-be, on January 16, 1957. My first impression of Joe Tinney was that he was a typical easterner. He wore his hair in a crewcut, and his clothes were stylish and tastefully conservative. He teased me about the black-and-brown heels that I wore with my plain black dress. I teased back, explaining that on the West Coast we preferred more casual attire and my shoes were perfectly acceptable, thank you. He laughed, a winning laugh. He was attractive, with bright blue eyes, a wicked Irish sense of humor, and the gift of conversation. He and my mother entertained each other while I sat by, the observer. It was quite obvious that she liked him and that the feeling was mutual.

A week later Joe invited me to dinner, "to reciprocate," he said. I found myself relaxing in his comfortable presence. Joe was easy to talk to and I confided my plans to move to New York in a few months when "The Loretta Young Show" season ended. I had finally realized that the only way I was going to have an acting career was to leave Hollywood and my mother far behind. Joe was the first person with whom I shared those feelings.

He listened attentively, and he agreed when I explained that New York seemed the perfect answer since my family wouldn't accept my leaving home and having my own apartment in California; it just wasn't done. The more I talked to Joe, the more supportive he seemed and the more interested I became. It was wonderful how easily the conversation flowed, perhaps because we had so much in common; we were at similar transitional stages in our lives.

Joe was very sympathetic. He told me that he knew first-hand what it was like working with family because, after graduating from the University of Pennsylvania and serving as an ensign in the navy, he had gone to work at a television station in Philadelphia where his father was vice-president and treasurer. Thereafter, he had gone off on his own and moved to New York, where he got a job as a staff director for the William Esty Advertising Agency, directing the weekly live variety shows sponsored by the agency.

But the television industry was changing rapidly; agencies like William Esty were no longer producing their own shows, preferring to let large companies like ZIV-TV and Revue Studios in Hollywood handle production, enabling the agencies to cut their overhead, including their staffs. Joe's talent as a director was no longer needed and he was laid off.

Since Joe had already met with executives at both Hollywood TV studios and no job was available, he was leaving the next day for

New York. He wrote his address and telephone number on the back of a matchbook and handed it to me, telling me to look him up when I got to New York. Then, in April, Joe came back to California with a three-month job at Dancer-Fitzgerald-Sample supervising "The Spike Jones Show."

By then I had already told my mother my plans to move. She began pressing me to stay in California. "Why do you want to go to New York now that Joe is here?" she asked.

Actually, I made my decision to go to New York one evening when Joe said to me, "When you do go to New York, I hope I miss you so much that I'll have to call you and ask you to come back." That wasn't what I had wanted to hear. I wanted him to tell me not to go, the standard line from a romantic Hollywood script. Instead, he was telling me I should go so he could find out how he felt about me.

"I simply don't understand why you want to go to New York. You have a perfectly fine job here at the studio. There are plenty of people who would give their eyeteeth for it." We were in my mother's dressing room and she was putting up her hair.

"I know, Mom, and I'm grateful for it, but it's time that I move away from home. I want to see what it's like living on my own."

"What are you going to do for money? You don't have a job. And where are you going to live?"

"I've saved six hundred dollars, and Mrs. Crossin, Anne's mother, has offered to let me stay with them until I find something. It's a beautiful apartment on Park Avenue. I won't be alone and I'll be safe. And Joe has a lot of friends. He's already told them I'm coming and that I'm looking for work. I'll be fine, Mom, really I will."

She watched me in the mirror. "I think it's perfectly foolish of you to go running off to New York when Joe is here in California. It doesn't make any sense."

"Maybe that's one of the reasons I am going to New York—so he can call me and ask me to come back."

"That seems a long way to go just to make someone miss you. Can't you accomplish the same thing staying here?"

"That isn't the main reason that I'm going, Mom. There are other reasons, too. I've stayed here as long as I have because I thought that you needed me."

She put her comb down with a sharp slap and swung her stool around, facing me, her eyes flashing.

"I don't need anybody." Her mood had shifted so swiftly that I was surprised by the sharpness and intensity of her response. But I also felt suddenly released from any further obligation to remain in my mother's house.

"In that case there doesn't seem to be any real reason for me to stay, does there?"

The following day I left for New York City.

New York hadn't changed, but I had. Three years before I hadn't wanted to be there. Now I loved everything about it. The hectic pace was stimulating, whereas before it had been intimidating. It seemed to me, walking along the busy streets, that everyone had a place to go and something important to do when they arrived. Everybody appeared successful and I was determined that I would be, too. I knew I was finally in the right place.

I set out to conquer New York. I had new pictures taken and, with the guidance of a close friend of Joe's, I wrote a professional résumé. I registered with modeling and acting agents and followed every possible and impossible lead that presented itself. I read the casting newspapers daily, following up on everything that I felt I was right for. I began my job search with a vengeance and I was having a wonderful time doing it.

My diligence paid off and in a month's time I landed a small part on "Kraft Television Theatre." The excitement of a live nighttime drama far surpassed the leisurely pace of a filmed show. I could finally say I was a New York actress.

My mother, Joe, Ruth Roberts, John London, and Mimi Hutson all sent congratulatory telegrams. Mimi followed up with a long letter telling me that she was in love and was announcing her engagement in a month.

She also wrote:

> I am so glad for you, too, Judd, that you have found the answer to so many things. I felt that this trip to New York would be so important for you, in so many ways, and I am so happy that my feelings turned out correctly. I was sure you had all the needed attributes, plus more, but it was just becoming aware of this within yourself that you needed. For some unknown reason you did lack confidence, and undoubtedly this lack sprang from the length of time you worked for your family, plus no encouragement offered on their part.

The first week in May, 1957 my mother flew to Rome for a private audience with Pope Pius XII, then returned via New York, where she stayed with Tom in his apartment at 2 Tudor City Place. She had just won her second Emmy and she was making headlines again, but not the kind that she cared for. The papers reported that the purpose of her audience with the pope was to discuss a special dispensation

My mother holds her second Emmy. Robert Young stands beside her. She had set a precedent—she was the first star to win both an Oscar and an Emmy.

UPI/BETTMANN

to divorce Tom; that was a rumor she wanted to dispel. In a concerted effort to keep up a positive public front, she invited me to have cocktails with them. "Just make an appearance, for my sake, Judy." Although I had no desire to see Tom again, I went to please her.

It was an uncomfortable evening. My mother was very tense and Tom was noticeably cold and distant. I felt sorry for my mother. She was trying so hard to be the gracious hostess, but she wasn't fooling anyone.

She and Tom went to the theater with Chet and his wife, Clara, to see Clara's sister Rosalind Russell in her hit Broadway show *Auntie Mame,* and they also made the social rounds of New York together. As a result, by the time my mother arrived back in California in June, columnist Radie Harris was printing retractions in the *Hollywood Reporter.* She wrote from New York that Tom Lewis was coming back to the West Coast, adding, "In the meantime Loretta will remain here for a month's holiday with him and their daughter, Judy." In point of fact, I saw them only that one evening. Under the circumstances I could only have been an irritant.

In June, when Christopher and Peter finished their school year at St. John's Military Academy in Los Angeles, they joined their father for the summer in New York. Tom took a leave of absence and the three of them vacationed in the Caribbean with my mother's blessing.

I was on a free-lance assignment for the WCBS network in Washington, D.C., when Joe's letter, telling me that he was flying to Rockport, Massachusetts, for his new job on "Harbor Master," a series for ZIV-TV, was forwarded to me. I flew up as many weekends as I could and we spent an idyllic summer together in Rockport, a picturesque little fishing village on the rocky shoreline of Massachusetts.

The free-lance Washington assignment ended and I was working sporadically in New York in small television roles, building my credits and keeping my expenses low by sharing a friend's apartment.

Joe had rented a funky one-room attic apartment above the Blue Lantern store, on Bearskin Neck, a spit of land jutting out into the sea. In keeping with our Catholic morality, when I stayed in his apartment he slept downstairs in a small guest room in back of the store.

The first week in September Joe and the company went back to Los Angeles and I moved into a small one-bedroom, ground-floor apartment in Greenwich Village, which I shared with a roommate. My funds were running dangerously low and so I welcomed the job offer as a program coordinator on the weekly WCBS television news program "Eye on New York." I was back in production again.

My mother wrote that Christopher and Peter weren't coming home as planned. She sounded upset and asked me to pray for patience for her. In late August Tom had taken the boys to visit the Trappist monastery at Gethsemane, Kentucky, for a few days. He told them that the purpose of the visit was to pray and decide whether they should stay with him or not. He then wrote my mother that the Lord had advised them that they should stay together and so he had enrolled the boys in St. David's Preparatory School in New York.

My mother didn't take this news lightly. She immediately hired a lawyer and enlisted her good friend Cardinal James Francis McIntyre to act as her emissary with Tom. Tom and my mother exchanged many letters until finally Cardinal McIntyre flew to New York and met with Tom at Cardinal Spellman's residence. He told Tom to return the boys to their mother, where they belonged, or, at the very least, to put them in a parochial school since both he and their mother strongly objected to St. David's, a non-Catholic school. Cardinal McIntyre had previously voiced his strong disapproval of Tom's living in New York, and he ordered him to return to California to avoid any further scandal or disgrace.

Cardinal Spellman, on the other hand, sided with Tom. So each of my parents had their own Church prelate as an ally, and what had been a private family matter was now an issue for the Church, with the boys in the middle.

My mother paid an unannounced visit to New York and called me from her hotel suite, saying she was only in town over the weekend and that she'd like to see me. When I arrived she was extremely upset. It was a windy and rainy night and she'd just left Tom's apartment, walking back alone to her hotel. This was a last-ditch effort on her part to take the boys back with her to California. She had failed. Peter and Christopher both told her that they wanted to remain in New York with their father. Through her tears she said, "I've done everything in my power. It's in God's hands now." She left the following day to return to her television show.

A few days later she wrote a warm and loving note, saying how glad she was to see me, that she thanked God for giving me to her, and that I was a "most satisfying girl." She sent her love and said she was praying that whatever God planned for me, I'd not only do it well but enjoy doing it.

I had been on my WCBS job a month when I got a call from my agent telling me that Hal Prince and Bobby Griffith were producing a Broadway comedy called *Soft Touch* and that I should audition for it. The part was a "Marilyn Monroe" role, and even though I would be against type, my agent urged me to try out for it.

When I arrived at the Adelphi Theatre I waded through a line of Marilyn Monroe look-alikes, most of them wearing low-cut, body-clinging dresses. I felt ridiculous in my demure pale blue shirtwaist dress with its Peter Pan collar and long sleeves, but I dismissed the strong impulse to walk away. It was fortunate that I did, because George Abbott, the director, selected me for the part.

It wasn't until I had taken the long subway ride to my apartment in the Village that my euphoria evaporated, and I suddenly realized that I had to quit my production job, which I did with mixed feelings.

If my job with WCBS ended abruptly, so, unfortunately, did my dream of acting on the Broadway stage. Two weeks into rehearsals it was clear that the script needed drastic revisions, and it was announced that we weren't going on the prebooked tour. The show closed before it ever opened. This possibility had never occurred to me, although the stars, Elsa Lanchester, Loring Smith, and Russell Nype, had seen it coming.

I was now without any job to speak of; I had been replaced at WCBS, and there seemed nothing left for me to do but return to California. As luck or Providence would have it, at the very last minute, a few days before I had planned to leave, I was hired to work on "The Verdict Is Yours," a television courtroom drama using real attorneys, with actors playing the witnesses. The format was all improvisational, and what was even more exciting was that I was the star. It was a prestige show and my salary for the week was $650, more than I'd ever earned before. My living expenses were covered until Christmas.

As the days grew closer to the end of the year and my scheduled arrival in California for the holidays, Joe called me more frequently than ever before. He spoke of how much he missed me and how much he looked forward to seeing me, telling me of the times he spent with my mother at Ojai or at the Flores house with the rest of the family.

I felt vaguely uneasy and didn't really know how to respond. I wasn't quite sure how I felt about him. I knew I cared about him a great deal, probably even loved him, but when he had left for California in September I had felt relieved, and that bothered me enough so that I wrote to my mother about my feelings. She wrote back that she understood what I was saying and that she wouldn't push or pursue it either, and yes, there were other fish in the sea. She counseled that in her experience when someone wanted something too much, that was just the time Our Lord withheld it for our own good. Maybe that was it, I reasoned; maybe I wanted to get married too much, and maybe this just wasn't the right time, or person.

Joe proposed on New Year's Eve, right in front of the Flores house. Mimi and her new husband, Chrys Chrys, just back from their honeymoon, had spent the evening with us, and we were all leaving

The newly engaged couple, me and Joseph Tinney.
AUTHOR'S COLLECTION

together for a midnight dinner at Scandia. As Joe opened the car door for me to get in, I heard him say, "Will you marry me?" He closed the door before I could answer.

"Did I hear what I thought I heard?" I asked as he slid in next to me on the seat.

"Yes," he replied, "you did."

Before I had a chance to answer, Mimi and Chrys joined us and we celebrated the new year by getting drunk on champagne. I accepted Joe's proposal that night.

A few days later television producer Albert McCleery's office at NBC called. I was to begin rehearsals in California on "Matinee Theater" the following week. No sooner had I said yes than my New York agent called with wonderful news. I had a running part on "Kitty Foyle," a new soap opera. In all the holiday excitement I had totally forgotten about my audition for it shortly before I'd left New York.

"But I just accepted 'Matinee Theater.' What am I going to tell Mr. McCleery?"

"You let me handle it. That's what agents are for."

"But I've already made a commitment. And besides, I've just gotten engaged."

"Congratulations on both counts, then. Don't worry, I'll take care of everything. Enjoy yourself and I'll get back to you with all the particulars. I just wanted to give you the good news."

I wasn't so sure that Joe would consider a job in New York good news. I was suddenly feeling quite frightened by his proposal and surprisingly unsure about getting married. He was very understanding, however, reassuring me that he believed in our love and that he was willing to hold off our engagement and wait while I got the acting experience that I wanted so badly. He even suggested that I date other men should I want to, assuring me that he loved me and wanted me to be positive about my feelings for him. I agreed to a ten-week commitment on the soap and left for New York.

The next ten weeks were filled with the excitement and challenge of my new role on "Kitty Foyle" and with letters and phone calls between Joe and myself. We were planning a party for our friends and Joe's family on the East Coast. Georgiana and Ricardo Montalban and their family had been living in New York while Ricardo costarred with Lena Horne in *Jamaica* on Broadway. Since my mother was still filming her series, the Montalbans agreed to host the party if I found the place and made the arrangements. We finally settled on a Sunday in the middle of March, at the Little Club, a small, elegant Manhattan restaurant.

As the months went by, my mother was busy in California making wedding plans without me, which made me feel upset, unsure, and left out. Joe wrote soothing letters assuring me that he was watching every detail. As if he sensed my unease he told me:

> If you get buck fever and feel you don't know me or if you doubt your emotions, go ahead and doubt. I'll wait. I know you love me and we are right for each other, but if you want time, take it.

Reassured, I wrote back, "You are my strength now."

In March Joe arrived in New York a week before the party, and a few days later I came down with Asiatic flu. I spent the next four or five days in a feverish fog, aware of little, eating nothing, waking periodically, then falling back once more into a stupor. I had no way of knowing that two days before the party, Tom Lewis's attorney filed a complaint in Los Angeles charging my mother, Robert F. Shewalter, and Lewislor Films Incorporated with "dishonesty, mismanagement, and unfairness."

Up until this time my mother had denied any marital problems both publicly and privately. She had managed to keep all details of the family's personal life confined to the family and the Church. In the interest of propriety, Joe had even written Tom to ask for my hand in marriage, and Joe's family and friends had expected to meet the bride-to-be's father. All the pretenses had to be dropped now that every newspaper in the nation carried the story that the famous movie and television star Loretta Young was being sued by her husband.

Tom called Georgiana to explain that under the circumstances he regretted he couldn't attend the party, and Georgiana assured him, in no uncertain terms, that he wouldn't be missed. I was too sick to attend, so Joe brought a picture of me to show those Philadelphia friends of his family that I hadn't met, and the party went on as scheduled, without me. Joe had instructed my roommate to hide all the newspapers from me, but she forgot that Sunday, and when Joe arrived, happy and jubilant from the party, I had already read the story about the lawsuit and was in tears.

We left the next day for California, where, on March 29, my mother entertained family and friends with a black-tie dinner dance to announce our engagement formally; the engraved invitations read

March 29, 1958. My engagement party. A family portrait taken in the living room of the Flores house. Left to right: Joe's parents, Joseph and Marie Tinney; my mother; me in my Galanos gown with Joe.

"Mr. and Mrs. Thomas Howard Lewis," as if nothing was wrong. Joe's parents flew in from Philadelphia and were my mother's houseguests for the event. It was a beautiful party. The garden looked like a fairyland, totally tented, with a dance floor covering the swimming pool. Sprays of yellow daffodils and tulips covered the tables and adorned the tent, and the evening was lit by tall, flickering candles in silver candelabra.

I wore my mother's engagement present to me, an elegant James Galanos dress. "You look beautiful," Joe said as he took my left hand in his and slipped three diamond bands on my finger, one white, one canary, and one coffee, each in a gold channel setting. He kissed me, saying, "I love you." I put my arms around him and held him close.

"I love you, too, Joe." I was very happy.

By April Lewislor had countersued Tom, and he notified my mother that he would not attend my wedding. I was greatly relieved; I hadn't wanted him to give me away in the first place. I asked my godfather, Carter Hermann, to do the honors. I did want my brothers to share my wedding day with me, though, and so I wrote to Tom, telling him that I had written to Peter and Christopher, asking them to attend. I told him how happy it would make me and said that Joe would like them to be ushers, ending my letter by saying, "It would make our day complete." I suggested that the three of them get together, talk it over, and let me know. I never heard from any of them. (After Tom died in 1988, Christopher found my three letters among his papers. He returned them to me, saying, "I don't remember Peter and I ever receiving these letters. Dad must have kept them from us.")

The wedding date was set for June 21 at the Church of the Good Shepherd in Beverly Hills. Cardinal McIntyre planned to marry us but later changed his mind. He told my mother that his adviser had said to do so would make him appear partial to her, and he had to retain a neutral position since he was a spiritual adviser to Tom as well as to her.

As the preparations, showers, and parties began in earnest I grew more and more distressed, so much so that my mother's doctor prescribed a tranquilizer. When I recall this period of my life, it seems I was existing on an emotional roller coaster. My mother was orchestrating my wedding and I had little to say. It was true I was experiencing the normal anxiety and tension that surround all large weddings, but something more important than that was bothering me. I felt I didn't know who I was. There were questions that hadn't been answered about my family history, and the closer I got to my marriage, the less I could repress my anxiety about them. A great deal of attention was being paid to the exterior appearance of my wedding day and none to my interior questions about myself and who I really was.

Jean Louis designed my gown, an Empire sheath of white engraved satin with a classic high neckline and long, fitted sleeves. A four-yard trapeze train flowed from my shoulders. It was just what I'd always dreamed about. When Jean showed me two designs for the veil, I chose one, but my mother opted for the other, a simpler one, which was the one I wore: a tiny coronet of white satin edged with velvet rosebuds holding a cathedral-length tulle-net veil.

What upset me was that old familiar feeling of being left out, having no say in anything: this time no say in my own wedding. Joe reminded me that weddings were often more for the parents than for the couple, and together we held our ground on the important issues, like what church I wanted to be married in, who I wanted to marry us, and who my bridesmaids would be. But as my wedding day grew nearer and nearer I began losing weight and sleep. My dreams were nightmares, confused jumbles with agitated moments at the altar, not knowing my own name.

One Sunday morning, about a month before the wedding, Joe and I were sitting in the living room when my mother walked by and casually tossed a folded, yellowed document onto the coffee table in front of us. "Here. You'll need this to get your license," she said. It was my baptismal certificate.

What I didn't know then and later learned from Joe was that Aunt Polly Ann and Uncle Carter were pleading with her to tell me who my father was. They both felt very strongly that I had the right to know before I got married, but she adamantly refused, fearing that if she told me I would cancel the wedding. This was the first time she had shown Joe my baptismal certificate. Even though her manner was casual, she had no way of knowing at the time how he would react, or how much he already knew about who my father was. It must have been a very uncomfortable moment for her, to say nothing of how Joe must have felt. (Later, referring to my baptismal name, Mary Judith Clark, he told me, "I thought, What a dumb name to use if you're trying to hide something.")

The following day we took the certificate to the courthouse in Santa Monica and got our marriage license. I was forced to write "Tom Lewis" in the space for father—a lie, and this time on a legal document. I was terribly upset. I knew Tom hadn't adopted me, so I wasn't legally Judy Lewis, but I didn't know who I was. I was afraid and worried that my lie could make our marriage license invalid. All I could think about was making sure that my marriage would be honest and binding.

Later that night I told Joe, "I can't marry you. I don't know anything about myself. I don't know who I am or what genes I'm carrying, or my medical history. I don't know what I'm bringing into this marriage. You know everything about yourself, and I don't know anything about me."

We'd talked about this before and I had told Joe my suspicions about my mother being my real mother, and I had also told him I didn't know who my father was. She had told me about her relationship with Spencer Tracy, and I wondered if perhaps he might be my father, but I knew nothing for a fact. None of it had seemed that important until now.

Joe listened quietly until I was finished and then he said, "You're wrong. I know everything about you."

"What do you mean? What do you know? I don't understand."

"It's common knowledge, Judy."

"What's common knowledge? What are you talking about?"

"Your father is Clark Gable."

"How do you know that? Who told you that?"

I was suddenly very angry, furious with Joe for knowing all along and not telling me and, at the same instant, furious with him for telling me. How did *he* know? Some part of me didn't really believe what I was hearing, and yet it all made terrible sense—the operation on my ears, Gable's visit to the Doheny house. At that moment I hated Joe for knowing the truth that I had sought. He had held the key to my missing father all along, and he just casually tossed it out as common knowledge. All my rage and frustration, built up over the years, were now unleashed against my fiancé, instead of on all the people around me who had known and didn't tell me, and of course, the only person who could give me the truth—my mother.

"Who told you?" I demanded again. I didn't want him to know how upset I was. I was fearful he wouldn't tell me anything more, like all the others in my life.

Joe looked surprised. "Phil Krim told me."

"Who's Phil Krim?" My voice was calmer.

"He works at the Ted Bates Agency. It was before I met you. He knew that Maggy Louis had set up the dinner party, and he said to me, 'I hear you're going to have dinner at Loretta Young's.' I said, 'Yes! I'm going to meet her daughter.' He said, 'Well, that's Clark Gable's kid.' And then I met you and you had those dark circles, just like him."

"You had this information all the time I've known you and you've waited until now to tell me?" I was still in shock.

"It didn't seem important until now."

"It didn't seem important! It's the most important thing in my life, to know who my father is. How do you think it feels to have everyone around you know something as important as that and you don't? I didn't know anything about Clark Gable."

Joe just looked at me and shook his head. "There's no mistaking that you are your father's child, Judy. It's clear Clark Gable is your father." He said it with such sincerity and conviction that I could no longer question it.

So I had been a topic of casual conversation between two men I didn't even know. They had known about me, though, necessary and important things I hadn't known until this very moment. Twenty-three years of my life had passed and everyone in the world knew about me. I felt like the butt of a bad joke, someone to be whispered about behind closed doors. I began to cry and no amount of Joe's comforting me stopped the flood of tears.

I awoke the following morning with new resolve and called Father John Fitzgerald, the priest who had baptized me at St. Paul the Apostle Church. I wanted to see for myself what my name was on the church's baptismal register. I reasoned that even if my baptismal certificate was a lie, my actual name and parents' names would legally have to be on the official register. *He'll tell me the truth,* I thought. *He's a priest, he can't deny me.* But I was wrong. I never heard from him; he never returned my numerous calls.

After three days passed and I still hadn't heard from him, I knew that he was avoiding me. He had probably called my mother and she had instructed him not to return my calls. I then turned to another member of the clergy. Monsignor John J. Devlin was the pastor at St. Victor's, our parish church. He was a friend of Cardinal Mc-Intyre's and had agreed to marry us. I liked and trusted him. When I met privately with him I told him that Joe had just informed me that my father was Clark Gable. I also told him that Father Fitzgerald refused to return my calls. Since Monsignor Devlin had known the family for some time and was close to my mother, I told him that I was going to ask her to tell me the truth. He advised me not to. He reasoned that if she hadn't already told me, with the wedding only weeks away, he was certain that she wouldn't tell me now.

I showed Monsignor Devlin my baptismal certificate. "You see, it says 'Mary Judith Clark.' It's all a lie. I have no legitimate document stating who I am. I can't get married until this is cleared up."

"May I keep this for a while?" he asked.

"You may keep it as long as you like. I hope I never have to see it again," I replied.

"I may be able to arrange that for you. In the meantime, try not to worry. I'll find a way to fix this."

I thanked him and left, feeling desolate.

A few days later he called me.

"Judy, I've talked to a lawyer I know and he assures me that if you are publicly known in the community for seven years as Judith Lewis, that is automatically regarded as your legal name."

"Even though Tom didn't adopt me?"

"That's correct. So you don't have to worry about your marriage being a legal one. It will be."

"Are you sure, Monsignor?"

"Yes! Judy, I am, but it sounds as if you're not. So, to ease your mind, in the wedding ceremony I'll say only your first names. Will that help?"

"Yes! Monsignor, I'll feel better that way."

"Then that's what I'll do. Now, go and enjoy your parties and stop worrying. You'll be married in the eyes of God and it will be binding, I promise you."

Six days before the wedding I received another call from Monsignor Devlin. He wanted to see me. When I arrived at the rectory he handed me two baptismal certificates. One was for "Mary Judith Clark" and had the same information as the original that I had given him, except that it was dated *May 27, 1958*, and was signed by Reverend John F. Fitzgerald with the seal of St. Paul the Apostle Church.

The other was for "Mary Judith Lewis," listing no parents, no sponsors, and stating that I was baptized in St. Paul the Apostle

Church by Reverend John F. Fitzgerald. It was signed by Reverend John J. Devlin and dated *June 15, 1958*, with the seal of Saint Victor's Church.

"You are free to use whichever one of these documents you please as your baptismal certificate," he said.

I thanked him and left. The two documents in my hand told the tale. Father Fitzgerald had issued a new certificate on May 27, obviously at Monsignor Devlin's request, but he would change no names. On June 15 Monsignor Devlin wrote a new certificate for me, signing his name and putting the seal of his church on it. That was the document I chose to use thereafter.

Joe's family arrived a week before the wedding, as did Anne Crossin, who was a bridesmaid and my houseguest. We had a joyful reunion, and when I told her my news that Clark Gable was my father, she surprised me by saying, "I already knew that."

When I asked her why she hadn't told me, she looked shocked that I would ask such a question.

"I thought that you already knew. And if you didn't, it certainly wouldn't be my place to tell you."

She was right. It wasn't her place, but I made up my mind that I would go to someone who would tell me.

"Grandma, I'm going to ask you a question and I want you to give me a simple 'yes' or 'no' answer."

I had gotten her undivided attention for once. "Why, yes, dear, what is it?"

"I want to know if Clark Gable is my father."

"What on earth gives you that idea?" She drew in her breath and began to giggle, as she often did when she was embarrassed. It unnerved me; it certainly wasn't the reaction that I was expecting.

"Please, Grandma, all you have to do is give me a 'yes' or 'no' answer. Is Clark Gable my father?"

"I can't imagine where you'd hear a thing like that," she replied, tugging at the undergarments between her ample breasts, a familiar gesture when she was nervous.

"Grandma, please, can't you just answer my question?" *Why won't she tell me what she knows?* I wondered. Then I answered my own question: *She's avoiding the truth; I know she is.*

She looked straight at me. "I'm really not able to, dear."

"You mean you won't, Grandma. All right, you give me no choice but to take your avoidance as a 'yes.' "

She said nothing, just looked at me as I turned around and walked out of the room.

When I arrived home, Anne was waiting for me. "What did she say?" she asked eagerly.

"She avoided my question totally. She wouldn't answer me." I took Anne by the hand. "Come with me. I want to take another look at the invitation list. I want to satisfy my curiosity."

Tom's room, which was in the back of the house across the hall from my mother's, now served as an office. There were unopened wedding presents in piles on the sofa-bed. The wedding invitation list laid on the desk. Anne stood beside me as I scanned the alphabetical listing of names until I found what I was looking for: Mr. and Mrs. Clark Gable. "Regret" was written in my mother's handwriting.

It's very hard to remember exactly what my feelings were; there were so many of them in those days just before my wedding, all coming so fast and furious that it was impossible to identify them. My mother remembers me in tears most of the time.

To this day I keep asking myself why I didn't go directly to my mother and confront her, and my answer is that I knew without a doubt that she wouldn't tell me. But the very fact that she had invited Clark Gable to my wedding when she had included none of her other leading men in movies was significant. In some strange way, seeing his name on the invitation list seemed to confirm what

Joe had told me, and yet, odd though it may be, until my mother actually told me herself, years later, I really never knew for sure. Until I heard the truth from her, there was always a margin of doubt.

The morning of my wedding, as I was getting dressed I suddenly felt very nauseated and promptly got sick. A great deal of confusion ensued; my bedroom was filled with people, my mother, Anne, Gretchen, and Mimi all telling me to be calm, that I had wedding-day jitters and that there was nothing to worry about. The next thing I knew, my mother's physician, Dr. John Sharpe, was standing next to me, having arrived seemingly from nowhere. He took a hypodermic from his black bag and gave me a shot.

I have no way of knowing what medication he gave me, but I do know that I walked through my wedding day in a fog. I remember little about it; all my feelings had been put on hold. I look at the movies with regret, realizing I missed my own wedding. I didn't experience the wonderful party that my friends raved about. I was there in body but not in spirit; I was anesthetized.

Many years later Anne Crossin confirmed my recollections. She told me, "I don't know who sent for the doctor or how he got there. He just seemed to appear. But I saw the shot take immediate effect on you and that you were zonked. You appeared to be fine, you did everything you had to do, you just didn't have any emotions. I decided that I would stay as close to you that day as I possibly could."

Knowing what I know now, I think my body was reflecting what I was truly feeling. There were too many questions unanswered about my life. I had too many unresolved doubts. I had tried to deaden my feelings. If I ignored the doubts about the man I was marrying, then they wouldn't exist; and if I didn't ask my mother who my father was, then I didn't have to feel the loss of him. The morning of my wedding day my feelings erupted and were anesthetized into numbness.

I remember standing in the living room before I left for the church and looking out the bay windows into the garden. It was even more

June 21, 1958. Me on my wedding day leaving the Flores house on the way to the Church of the Good Shepherd in Beverly Hills. Jean Louis, who thirty-five years later would become my mother's third husband, is holding my veil; his wife, Maggy Louis, follows behind.

© JOHN ENGSTEAD, COURTESY FAHEY/KLEIN GALLERY

beautiful than it had been for my engagement party. The entire garden was tented in white. Once again, a dance floor covered the swimming pool, and the long banquet table for the wedding party was groaning with arrangements of white flowers. Large white bouquets were draped over the iron balconies of the house, and fresh green sprays intertwined with flowers were wrapped around the poles of the tent.

"It's so beautiful, Uncle Carter." I reached over and took his hand, and he squeezed my hand in his.

"Yes, Judy! And so are you," he said, as he leaned over and kissed me on the cheek.

"Thank you for being with me today. It is the best wedding present you could ever have given me."

"I wouldn't have missed this day for anything."

The living room was beginning to empty, the bridesmaids were putting on their gloves, all chattering at once. Anne leaned toward me. "I'll see you at the altar."

I nodded at her, smiling as I stood in the middle of the room watching them all disappear out the front door. My veil hadn't arrived yet; it was 11:30 and the wedding was scheduled to begin at noon, but I wasn't upset or nervous. I felt no anxiety; nothing.

My mother emerged from her bedroom wearing a pale blue chiffon dress with a matching blue feather hat. She looked lovely. She circled me, oohing and aahing over my gown, and I did the same to her. She kissed me on the cheek, then walked to the mirror in the hall and pinned her corsage to her waist. She blew several kisses in the mirror to everyone, then was escorted out the front door to her waiting limousine.

A few minutes later the veil, delivered to the church by mistake, arrived; Jean Louis placed the coronet on my head while the fitter fastened it securely with bobby pins and adjusted the netting. It was a testament to my state of mind that I never asked to see a mirror.

"Dear friends in Christ: As you know, you are about to enter into a union which is most sacred and most serious, a union which was established by Christ himself."

Joe and I stood at the altar with Gretchen at my left side and Joe's father at his right. Monsignor Devlin, in his ornate gold robes, stood facing us. Behind him the tall white marble altar was decorated with

*M*r. *and Mrs. Joseph Lewis Tinney on the steps of the Church of the Good Shepherd after the ceremony.*

LOS ANGELES *EXAMINER*/AUTHOR'S COLLECTION

gold-embroidered cloth and banked with two large bouquets of Madonna lilies and white orchids. White flowers adorned the pews, and garlands of Madonna lilies were wound around the church pillars.

After the marriage instruction, Monsignor Devlin looked at Joe. "Joseph, will you take Judith, here present, for your lawful wife according to the rite of our Holy Mother the Church?"

Joe held my right hand tightly in his. He looked at me and said, his voice shaking, "I will."

"Judith, will you take Joseph, here present, for your lawful husband according to the rite of our Holy Mother the Church?" I answered, "I will." I was surprised to hear my voice shaking, too.

Monsignor leaned toward us and said, "Join your right hands, and repeat after me."

Joe passed my hand into his right hand and turned to face me and said his vows. His voice no longer shook; it was loud and sure.

Then I followed. My voice now matched Joe's in clarity.

We knelt down as Monsignor Devlin gave us his blessing. He'd kept his promise; no last names were used. I meant it with all my heart when I whispered, "Thank you, Father."

I was married. My nightmare of not knowing my name was a thing of the past and I could look forward to a long and happy life as Mrs. Joseph Lewis Tinney.

THE HOLLYWOOD HILLS HOUSE

We returned from our honeymoon in Hawaii to a pretty apartment on Spalding Drive in Beverly Hills that had been decorated by my grandmother. Shortly thereafter my mother invited us to dinner. When she asked Joe to tell her about our trip, he surprised us both by replying, "Well, Loretta! We dance great, but we fuck lousy."

I was terribly embarrassed; up until then it had been only my own private thought, but now by having said it, my husband had made it real. I didn't want to face that kind of reality. But I was also shocked that he would expose our intimate inadequacies so indelicately to my mother; it wasn't like him. We all laughed nervously and passed it off as a joke; the horribly uncomfortable moment passed, but it wasn't forgotten.

To the outside world we were the picture of a happily married couple, with everything in the world going right for us. In truth, we worked very hard to create that impression. It was important to both of us that our storybook wedding have the classic "they lived happily ever after" goal. But it was work. It didn't come easily, and I slowly began to realize there were problems, that I wasn't as happy as I had expected to be. These exceedingly unwelcome thoughts intruded on my idealized version of what marriage should be, so I systematically pushed them to the back of my mind and went on with my life, keeping reality at bay because I couldn't tolerate its harsh light.

I longed to get pregnant. I wanted a large family, at least four

The happy honeymoon couple on the boat to Hawaii.
AUTHOR'S COLLECTION

children, as did Joe, but the pregnancy that we both hoped and prayed for wasn't happening. In the early months of my marriage my mother often asked if I was pregnant. Her questions were difficult to field. They always left me feeling vaguely restless, as if I had left some important chore unfinished, and until I had accomplished what I was obliged to do I would remain incomplete. When I was forced to reply "Not yet," I was also forced to face my disappointment and all the accompanying feelings that I was trying so hard not to experience. Finally, eight months after we were married, my worries ended. I knew the moment that my child was conceived, and there were no two happier people alive than Joe and me when the doctor confirmed what I had already felt in my heart.

I loved being pregnant, and there were times during my pregnancy when I wondered how my mother felt while she was carrying me. Now that I had my first child growing inside me, I wanted to ask her, but I couldn't. I didn't want to risk having her insist that I was adopted, or, worse, admit I was hers and that she hadn't wanted me and how terrible it had been for her. As I write this, many years later, it seems sad that she and I missed the opportunity to share this common experience, one that mothers and daughters and good friends have been sharing for generations. My mother and I couldn't be mothers together during one of the most important periods of my life. There is so much that we never shared because of the lie that was begun when I was born.

My due date came and went. Finally, when I thought that I was destined to walk the earth perpetually rotund and that I would never view my feet again, my child decided it was time to arrive. On November 16, 1959, after almost fourteen hours of labor my daughter Maria was born. I will always remember seeing her perfect little body for the first time; it was the most beautiful thing I had ever laid eyes on. I was the happiest woman in the world. I finally had the baby that I had prayed so hard for.

Holding my newborn daughter close while she nursed, I wondered if my mother had nursed me and what my first few days of life had been like. I thought of the note she had written to me when she had learned I was pregnant. She wrote that no matter what I did in my life, I would never accomplish more than giving birth. How right she was.

The years 1958 and 1959 were spectacularly successful ones for my mother. Not only did she win her third Emmy, but the show was nominated as Best Continuing Series. NBC bought 176 installments of "The Loretta Young Show" from Lewislor for syndication, paying my mother, who was now president, approximately $4 million. She had to pay Tom half the profits of a large portion of the sale. She also paid privately as well. It became quite clear that what had begun many years before as a romantic marriage had by this time totally disintegrated into a bitter and violent ongoing legal war over money, a war waged from opposite coasts. Where once there had been love,

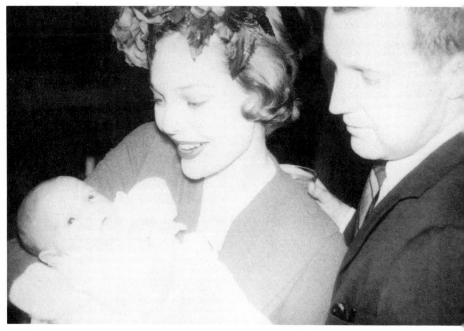

December 13, 1959. Maria's baptism. Above: Joe and me with our infant daughter. Below—four generations (left to right): my grandmother, my mother, three-week-old Maria Tinney, and me.

1960. Maria's first visit to her grandmother's set of "The Loretta Young Show." Left to right: my husband, Joe Tinney; Maria Tinney; my mother; and me.

there now seemed to be only hatred and a dogged determination to bleed the very last penny from each other. The more successful my mother became, the angrier and more resentful Tom became, blaming her for forcing him out of Lewislor, blaming her for his having to begin his career again in New York, while hers continued spiraling upward with each new season. He was determined to make her pay, literally and figuratively, and so he took some prisoners—their sons.

Christopher and Peter were casualties of the war between their parents, and they were both injured by its emotional violence.

By the time Maria was born, Peter had returned to California and was now living at the Flores house with our mother. I knew very little about his years in New York with his father, nor about any of his problems, other than the fact that he had difficulties adjusting to St. David's in New York and refused to attend. Nor did I know how he was faring living with our mother. But I did know that Peter was troubled and he told me that he was getting professional help. Not wanting to pry, Joe and I let him know that we were there if he ever needed anyone to talk to.

I was glad that Peter was nearby. I had always felt close to him. I think I knew early on that we weren't our father's favorites, and I was probably drawn to my younger brother for that reason.

While I was not without my own wounds, they were different from those of my brothers. Tom Lewis was not my father, and once I was an adult I no longer had any investment in the relationship; he meant nothing to me. I was glad when he left my life, for he could then no longer affect me. But my brothers didn't have that luxury. He would always be their father, and because of that they would always be affected by him.

However, I gave little thought to Tom, or to my mother's marriage, which I considered over whether she chose to think so or not. At this point, I was too preoccupied with my own marriage and the battles that I was having with my husband.

I had moved so often as a child, always without warning and without any acknowledgment from either of my parents of my feelings of loss, that my deepest wish when I married was to settle down finally in one place and stay there. To my sorrow, Joe and I had been married less than two years when he announced that he wanted to move from the apartment and buy a house. This didn't seem to be the right time since Joe had voluntarily, with my encouragement, left his production job at Revue Studios because he wanted to go back to directing. Although we had some savings, I was still worried about our financial future. And I feared having a husband who was without a job, remembering my mother's experience with Tom.

Joe kept insisting and looking at houses. I finally decided I needed some marriage counseling. I desperately wanted my marriage to work and I was willing to do whatever was needed. At the suggestion of my aunt Sally, I went to see a Catholic priest at Loyola University who was giving Cana Conferences (Instructions on Marriage) for married Catholic couples, and he agreed to see me once a week.

I was naïve then and knew nothing about the process of marriage counseling, so it didn't seem unusual to me that the priest didn't insist on seeing both Joe and me. I considered the difficulties in our marriage *my* problem; so did Joe, and he and I both agreed that I was the one who needed help, not him. Now, after years of psychological training, I know that there was no possible way that this counseling could have been beneficial without both of us participating. Our marriage didn't need a Band-Aid; it needed major psychological surgery, although neither of us was aware of it. The truth of the matter was that we were basically incompatible.

I plunged into my weekly sessions with fervor, dedication, and attention to detail. I felt I could now take charge of my life and change things. There was hope. At each session I was given specific assignments to perform and was instructed to report in detail on them the following week.

After a while, when the novelty wore off, and I was instructed to demand little of my husband and expect less, everything began to have a vague uncomfortable resonance, one that became more and more difficult to disregard. My weekly sessions were reminiscent of the weekly patio inspections with my father when I was eleven. In the beginning I looked forward to my sessions with the priest, but I began to dread being told that my work was unsatisfactory and that I must go back and do it again. I knew nothing then about transference, but it is now obvious to me that I had exchanged one inept patriarch for another.

Finally, after about six months of private sessions, I terminated the therapy. My inability to change my relationship with my husband on anything other than a surface level left me feeling that I had failed. Given this unpleasant experience, it's a wonder that I ever found my way back into therapy. When I finally did, and when many years later I decided to become a therapist myself, I vowed I would never repeat what was done to me. The treatment that I received may have been well intentioned, but it was psychologically harmful, nevertheless.

The Hollywood Hills house — two views: the front entrance; a side view.

In October 1960, Joe, who was now working part-time as a realtor, found a house for us on Hollywood Boulevard in the hills and he convinced me to move. It had been built sometime in the early twenties. Half of the second floor had been converted into a separate apartment, as had the entire third floor. Both had tenants with leases, generating income that would pay the mortgage. It suited our needs perfectly.

On November 6, my twenty-fifth birthday, I sat in the warmth of the early-morning sun, feeding Maria on the sun porch that we had just finished enclosing with a new roof and a large floor-to-ceiling window overlooking the city below. I realized that I had just completed my seventh move in twenty-five years. I promised myself that I was never going to move again; this was the last time. This house was now *my* home and it would offer what my parents' homes had not—stability and permanence. I wanted that for myself and my child, and I was determined to have it.

The loud ring of the telephone interrupted my thoughts and caught me right in the middle of spooning cereal into Maria's eager little mouth.

Joe's voice greeted me. "Have you got the radio on?"

"No. Why?"

"You might want to turn it on. I just heard on the news that Clark Gable was taken to the hospital early this morning with a heart attack."

I felt the breath leave my lungs as if I had just been hit in the pit of my stomach.

"Is he all right?"

"They didn't say; just that he had suffered a heart attack and was taken to Presbyterian Hospital by ambulance. Maybe turn on the television, too. They're bound to have a news flash somewhere."

"Where is Presbyterian Hospital?"

"I don't know. Why? You're not thinking of going there, I hope."

I had a strong urge to get in the car and drive there—wherever "there" was. But it passed as quickly as it had come. "No! of course not," I lied.

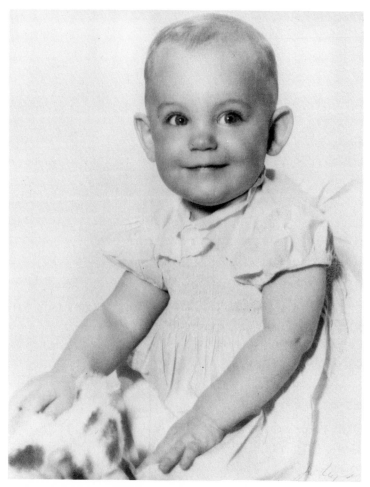

Maria Tinney's first formal baby picture.

I hung up and turned on both the television and the radio, waiting for a bulletin. I couldn't help the thoughts that were hurtling around in my head as I continued to feed my little daughter her breakfast.

My father may die. My father may die and I never knew him and he never knew me. As I watched my child's happy face and listened to her chattering sounds, I realized that, just as I never knew my grandfather, now my daughter wouldn't know hers either.

I have to do something. I have to tell him I know that he's my father. He has to see his granddaughter. I have to see him before it's too late. I could find out where the hospital is and drive there right now.

And when you get there? Then what? my practical inner voice challenged. What will you tell them when they ask who you are? You know there'll be all kinds of people protecting him. Will you tell them that you're his daughter and that you want to see him?

Why not? It's the truth, isn't it?

Is it? *Are* you his daughter? You don't know for sure, do you? You know only what Joe has told you, isn't that right? Joe said that it was common knowledge, but that doesn't make it true, does it?

No! I guess it doesn't.

And even if it were true, what proof do you have to show that you're his daughter? They'll ask for some kind of proof. His name isn't on your birth certificate or any legal document in your possession. In fact, you don't have any proof at all, do you?

There's only one person who can tell you the truth, and that's your mother. She's the only one. And until you hear it from her mouth, you really don't know.

The news report broke into my thoughts: "Clark Gable was taken by ambulance, early this morning, to Presbyterian Hospital. His physician, Dr. Fred Cerini, confirmed that the actor suffered a coronary thrombosis. A specialist has been brought in as consultant. Mrs. Gable remains by her husband's bedside."

It was true. Hearing the words confirmed it for me. He did have a heart attack, but he must still be alive. They didn't report that he died. So there was still time.

Later that morning I knelt in church and prayed for my father's recovery, and for my mother to tell me the truth before it was too late. I held my daughter close to me and imagined what it would be like to introduce her to her grandfather. Please, God, don't let it be too late; I want Maria to meet her grandfather.

Every time the phone rang that day my heart skipped a beat. Each time I anticipated my mother's voice and each time I was disappointed. I kept the radio tuned to the news station for any further developments on my father's condition, but none was given.

We had been invited to my mother's for dinner. "Do you think she'll tell me tonight?" I asked Joe as we were getting dressed.

He looked at me in an odd way. "Why would she tell you now, when she didn't tell you before you were married?"

I felt tears of frustration beginning to come to the surface. I didn't want to cry, and I didn't want to get into an argument with him on my birthday. Lately, we were arguing often, and always about my mother.

"Well, this is a little different. After all, my father's had a heart attack. He may not recover. If there's any time that a mother would tell her daughter who her father is, it would be now."

"Don't count on that, Judy," he replied.

It wasn't what I wanted to hear. I wanted to keep my hope alive that that evening would be different; that my mother would give me my father and I would finally have all my questions answered.

The other guests were already there when Joe and I arrived, making it impossible, as usual, to have any kind of intimate conversation with my mother. As the evening wore on and the conversation remained general, my anticipation began to rise to an almost unbearable level. I could scarcely contain myself.

After dinner I followed my mother into her bedroom. I couldn't stand it any longer. Maybe she didn't know; maybe she hadn't heard the news yet. Maybe I could catch her by surprise, with her guard down. This was the perfect opportunity, with just the two of us, alone.

Today was my birthday. She must have been thinking about the day I was born, and the man who was the father of her child. What better time to confront her than today? What better birthday present could she give me than my own father?

I've asked myself so many times why I didn't just ask my mother point-blank that night if Clark Gable was my father. Time was running out; it was then or never. But at the time I felt to do so would have threatened the happy family facade and forced my mother to confess to her "mortal sin." I would have risked her wrath. We were a family of avoidance, and I had always cooperated by not confronting my mother. Now, once again, I avoided alienating her. I think I felt that if I had asked, I would not only lose the father I never had, but my mother as well. I had never experienced unconditional love, and I certainly couldn't risk losing what love I did have.

"Have you been listening to the radio today?" I asked as we stood side by side in front of the mirror, combing our hair, our reflections staring back at us.

"No. I've been studying my script," she replied.

"Then you don't know, do you?"

"Know what, Judy?" She continued to comb her hair.

"Clark Gable had a heart attack. He's in the hospital in intensive care." I stared at her mirror reflection, searching her face for some reaction, something that would tell me the truth.

"When did this happen?" Her voice was calm; there seemed to be no reaction at all.

"Early this morning, according to the news reports."

"That's really too bad. I'm sorry to hear it." She turned away from the mirror and said, "Shall we go and open your presents now?"

Defeated, I followed her back to the living room.

The card accompanying her present thanked me for the joy and the gentleness that I had given her and told me that she was proud of me, I had been a wonderful child, and was now a wonderful woman. I *had* been a wonderful, docile child; she was right. But why, I wondered, was it always easier for her to write loving sentiments rather than to say them to me directly?

In the days that followed I kept tuned to the radio reports of Clark Gable's recovery. He rallied swiftly. Within a few days he was sitting up and improving, although the doctors reported that he was still not out of danger. I kept praying that he wouldn't die.

My mother's apparent disassociation from any feeling about him confused me. Maybe he isn't my father after all, I decided. And then another thought occurred to me, one I didn't want to acknowledge because it was too painful. Maybe he is my father and he doesn't want anything to do with me. Maybe that's why my mother won't tell me. She's trying to protect me. Maybe he never wanted me to be born and is so ashamed that I exist that he wants nothing to do with me or my mother. After all, he could have sent me a message if he wanted to see me. He's a powerful movie star. If he cared anything about me at all, he had the means to contact me without letting anyone know, even my mother. But that's never happened. He lives right here in Los Angeles. Maria's birth was announced in the papers. He must know that he's a grandfather. Still, I've never heard a word from him.

Wait just a minute, I argued with myself. Aren't you being unfair? Have you forgotten the time when you were fifteen and he spent the afternoon with you? Is that the way a father would act if he didn't want to acknowledge you?

Why didn't he say something to me then? Think of all the years we could have had together. He could have told me he was my father that afternoon, but he didn't. Why? Did he think I knew? Was he waiting for me to say something to him? Why? Why? Why?

The next ten days were spent on an emotional roller coaster. I asked myself questions that I couldn't answer, that no one could answer—except my mother, who remained silent; and my father, who was unreachable, under sedation, in the hospital.

On November 16 we celebrated Maria's first birthday. I baked her a cake and she blew out her one candle while we watched and applauded. The cake had vanilla icing and a sagging middle; all those cooking lessons hadn't taught me how to bake. I made a silent wish that her grandfather would be there with us to celebrate her second birthday.

I didn't get my wish. That night, at twenty minutes to eleven, my father died. Time had run out on all my dreams; harsh reality intruded on the beautiful fantasy world where I had lived "happily ever after" with my father.

It's significant to me that my father died on Maria's birthday. November 16 will forever carry a mixture of sadness and joy for me. It reminds me that while I lost my father, I also gained my daughter.

As I write these words I am surprised at the depth of the sorrow I still feel, and I now understand why this has been the most difficult chapter for me to write. There is probably nothing more wrenching to endure than the realization that what could have been will never be. I delayed feeling the pain of the absence of my father for most of my life. Experiencing that feeling now, as I write, will, I hope, be my release from the past and my doorway into the future.

I can only wonder what my mother's world must be like. All her life she has repressed the loss of her own father with the fierce denial of the abandoned four-year-old child within her, in order not to feel the overwhelming anger and grief at his abrupt departure.

A few days after my father died, Grandma said she had something very important she wanted to discuss with Joe and me. I was convinced that she was finally going to tell me that my father was Clark Gable. My excitement and expectation were shared equally by Joe. It was too late by then to know my father, but at least, after twenty-five years, I would have the truth.

She began: "Now, children, I know you've been wondering what all this secrecy has been about."

Joe and I looked at each other. *Please, hurry up.* I thought, *I can't stand another minute of this.*

"Georgiana told me yesterday that Ana told her cousin, who works for Georgie, that she's going to leave unless she can have her own room."

I didn't know what she was talking about. "What do you mean, Grandma?" I asked. *What,* I wondered, *does this have to do with my father?*

"Ana doesn't like sleeping in the same room with the baby. She doesn't have any privacy."

The secret wasn't about my father at all. It was that our housekeeper wanted her own room. It was all I could do to keep the tears of disappointment from spilling down my cheeks. If Clark Gable was my father, how could my mother and my grandmother have let him die without telling me the truth?

As the days and months went by and Joe wasn't hired as a television director, our marriage became more and more strained. It had never been his intention to abandon television. Real estate was to be just a sideline until he could get his directing credits built up, but somehow that wasn't happening. He was now working full-time, without salary, only commission, as a broker at a real estate firm. He felt upset about his career, and it was affecting our relationship.

In the beginning I had been supportive of his decision to work as a free-lance director. I knew he was unhappy and unfulfilled at Revue Studios, and we both thought that he could easily find work. But the business was very competitive, and the person who could hustle the best and the fastest got the job. Neither of us had developed those skills, and, like myself, Joe depended on his agent.

It made me uncomfortable when he was at home for long stretches. It reminded me of the years when Tom Lewis was always at home. I remembered how my mother had complained about it. I resented Joe's intrusion into my daily routine at home, and I was worried about our financial situation. I know I didn't make it any easier on him. I probably added to his confusion by urging him to go out and get a regular, paying job so that we could return to what I wanted and what I hadn't had in my own family—the ideal fairy-tale marriage with the wife and child at home and the husband at work.

In retrospect, I suspect that part of the frustration and anger that Joe was experiencing over his career centered on the fact that my mother didn't hire him as a director, which had probably been an unspoken expectation of his. It would have been natural to have such hopes, with a mother-in-law in charge of the most successful show on television. But even before we were married, Joe was adamant about not wanting to work for her. Indeed, he even told her

Early 1960s. One of the rare occasions that I accompanied my mother to an awards function. My husband, Joe Tinney, and I pose with my mother at the TV Guide *Awards.*

that it wouldn't be a good idea for her son-in-law to be her director. We all agreed with him; it would have been an impossible situation for all concerned, and it would probably have compromised our marriage even more.

Nevertheless, I believe that secretly, in his heart of hearts, Joe had his own dreams, and they didn't exactly match what he said publicly. He must have been terribly disappointed when my mother hired other directors with comparable credits; that was a bitter pill to swallow. I believe it hurt him deeply.

My mother could be very generous. She gave many unknowns, both actors and directors, their first break. She also didn't hesitate to hire established members of her family; her brother-in-law Norman Foster directed many of the shows, and Ricardo Montalban starred in many. It was very possible that she would have considered hiring Joe, but since he had been so vehemently against it, she simply took him at his word.

Today, I think in all honesty that Joe married "Loretta Young's daughter" with all the perks that that seemed to promise. It must have been a shock when he realized that his dream of being the director son-in-law was just that—a dream—and that he would have no assistance of any kind from my mother. On top of that, I was making demands on him that he found impossible to meet. *His* expectations and hopes and dreams about his marriage weren't being realized either, whether he was consciously aware of them or not, and my constant pressure on him wasn't making things any easier.

In the summer of 1961 I was hired by the producer Frank Telford to play Connie Masters in "The Outlaws," a one-hour prime-time western series on NBC. Joe shared my excitement when I told him the good news, but unfortunately my mother didn't. Ironically, the 1961–62 television season, the year that I was starring in my first series, was the first time in eight years that she didn't appear on television. The negotiations for a ninth season among my mother, her new sponsors, and NBC had broken down and "The Loretta Young Show" was canceled.

When I brought my news to her, she had already said good-bye to her cast and crew, closed down the Lewislor offices, and returned home to the Flores house with no show of her own and little to look forward to. My own elation was such that I never considered what she might have been feeling when I told her that I was starring in a series on the same network that had canceled her show. I was very excited and all I could think of was how proud of me she'd be and of how much we now had in common.

She listened quietly while I told her everything. I wanted her to be as thrilled as I was, so I just kept talking, my enthusiasm building, until I finally ran out of steam.

"Well! What do you think? Isn't that exciting news?"

"Yes! Very exciting." I could see that she didn't mean it. "So you've made up your mind. You're sure this is what you want to do?"

"Mom, of course I'm sure. It's a lead in a series. I'd be crazy not to want to do it."

"Well, then, I have only one piece of advice to give you, and it's this—you're too nice."

Her tone was one of reluctant acceptance, not the elation that I was anticipating, and I was deeply disappointed. Still, I wanted to make the most of her advice, although I couldn't fully comprehend it. What I suppose I was looking for was a shared camaraderie with my mother over my achievement, but at that moment I was willing to settle for any advice from her if it meant her affirmation of me.

"I don't really know what that means, Mom."

"Judy, if you're going to be in this business, you're going to have to learn to be tough, to pick your battles, and learn when to stand your ground so that people can't walk all over you. You don't know that yet. You're much too nice."

She had a point, but then she'd raised me to be nice. How could I change a lifetime in an instant? She had placed a doubt in my mind; I didn't have what it took to last. I didn't want to hear what she was saying.

With hindsight, thirty years later, I think that my mother had good intentions. Her observations came from her own long and sometimes difficult and painful personal experiences, and she knew that I lacked what she had gained in the school of hard knocks. The problem was that I valued her judgment, so I believed her when she suggested that because I was too nice, my success would be short-lived.

"The Connie Masters Story," which introduced my character, was the fourth "Outlaw" show to be filmed. When the time came for Frank Telford to look at a rough cut, he asked me if I would like to see it with him and suggested that I invite my mother. That was the first time he had ever asked me to a screening. I had been too timid to ask if I could see my dailies, even though I knew I could learn from them—what *not* to do, if nothing else.

Naturally I was delighted and accepted his invitation. When I invited my mother, she said she wasn't sure whether she could make it and that she would let me know. A few days before the screening I called her again and she told me that she'd try to make it, but if she wasn't there to proceed without her. I couldn't persuade her to make a firm commitment.

My mother never arrived at the screening, nor did she phone. After waiting for half an hour, Frank told the projectionist to begin. I was both disappointed and embarrassed that my mother didn't come. I would have welcomed her emotional and professional support. I felt it was yet one more example of her inability to acknowledge me.

But there was another element. My mother was still very powerful, and power is what drives Hollywood. I am familiar enough with the Hollywood system to know that in other people's eyes, the children of stars carry their parents' power with them. Frank Telford was politically savvy. He invited my mother to my screening for his own reasons, and her absence that day may well have rendered me powerless in his eyes. Even if it didn't, I *felt* powerless. It was too easy then to forget that initially Frank Telford hadn't known who my mother was when he cast me. I quickly believed that I wasn't valued for myself, but only because I was my mother's daughter. When she didn't show up, I felt humiliated.

The network was publicizing "The Connie Masters Story," and the fact that I was my mother's daughter. *Life* magazine had also featured me in an article about new television starlets. I, too, wanted to advertise, so I asked Helen Ferguson to help me with an ad to be placed in the Hollywood trade papers. Above my picture she wrote the words, "This is Connie Masters," and below it, "We invite you to meet her, to see and hear 'The Connie Masters Story,' to visit her with us every Thursday evening from now on. Don Collier, Bruce Yarnell, Slim Pickens." In very small print at the bottom of the page was written: "Connie Masters played by Judy Lewis," with my agent's name and address.

My name was so small that the entire ad had to be read to see it, and most people didn't. I had a lot of calls the following day from

friends and business associates who had missed the show, saying, "Why didn't you tell me your starring show was on?" When I told them that I had advertised, they recalled seeing the ad and thinking that it was for an actress named Connie Masters.

If Helen had intended to bury my name, she was successful. She was not my mother's publicist for nothing; her client was forty-eight years old and without a series, while her twenty-five-year-old daughter was beginning hers.

Now that I have a married daughter with two children and am older than my mother was then, I can look back to that period in our lives and speculate on some of the feelings that my mother might have been having about me and my budding career. There's no doubt in my mind that my mother had some competitive feelings. She made that obvious when I was seventeen and she introduced me as her sister; at that time she was beginning her television career and she might have felt the unconscious need to deny the fact that she was old enough to have a daughter my age.

By this time she was eight years older, a grandmother, and no longer a television star with a series. Her marriage was over, and filled with bitter recriminations. I seemed to have everything my mother didn't—a happy marriage, a daughter whom I could openly acknowledge, and the beginnings of a career as a star in my own series on her old network. From my mother's perspective, then, it must have appeared that I indeed "had it all"—marriage, motherhood, and career right in my pocket, just as she once had.

Perhaps if she had come to my screening, she would have had to face her feelings watching me on the screen. Whether or not she understood or was even aware of these feelings, she chose to stay away. By staying away, she hurt me deeply. To my mind, she once more affirmed that she didn't love me, that I wasn't good enough, and that I didn't belong in her world. I had no perspective then, as I do now, about my mother's possible feelings of loss and aging. I was simply hurt and angry that she wasn't there to support and encourage me in my career.

Although it may have seemed to my mother that I had it all, it was far from the truth. I alone knew the struggle I was having in trying to keep my fairy tale alive; reality kept getting in the way. I enjoyed my work in the series, but I missed spending time with Maria and Joe, and I often felt guilty when we were invited to a social function and I couldn't attend because I was shooting, or because I was too exhausted.

At times I even feared that I might be losing my family, and I wondered if I could be repeating my mother's life. I didn't want to be my family's breadwinner. It was too high a price to pay. Whenever Joe pointed out some similarity between me and my mother, I became instantly defensive, denying the reality, the likelihood that I could be making her same mistakes. I wondered, too, what Maria was feeling and if she was missing me as much as I had missed my mother. On the days that I worked, I felt torn when I had to leave her, and when I was home I redoubled my efforts to spend more time with her, remembering my own childhood feelings when my mother was gone for long stretches of time.

Although Joe had been generally understanding, he drew the line when he discovered that I was scheduled to work the very week that we had made arrangements for a year-end skiing vacation at Lake Tahoe. He suggested that I ask Frank Telford to rearrange the shooting schedule to accommodate our plans. Frank flatly refused, which didn't surprise me. I hadn't expected him to say yes, but I, too, had already made a choice. I had decided that if I was forced to choose between my husband and my job, I would choose my husband. This vacation was important to us and to our marriage, and I was determined to have it, no matter what the cost.

My part in that script was insignificant—a few scenes that wouldn't be missed—so I asked Frank to write me out of the show that week. He was very surprised and asked me if I was sure that was what I wanted. When I assured him that it was, he reminded me that if I didn't perform, I wouldn't be paid any salary. In my single-minded determination to get what I wanted, I hadn't bothered to check my guaranteed number of shows and which one I had been written out of. When I arrived back from my holiday and discovered that it had been my last show, and that my job was over, I was very sad.

My vacation had cost me more than my salary, and unfortunately it hadn't been the remedy that both Joe and I had hoped for. The intimacy that I had imagined us enjoying together never materialized. Joe was silent and indifferent, and no matter how much I pleaded with him to talk, he remained detached and uncommunicative. Unable to reach him in any way, I was left with a sense of frustration and anger. We returned home more estranged than ever.

I should have seen that Joe was depressed. I knew that he was very unhappy, but then so was I, and I was blinded to his feelings. Until recently, Joe had always been the primary wage earner. Neither of us had ever regarded my work as an actress as anything more than an avocation. My jobs had usually been sporadic, and my earnings provided for luxuries, not essentials.

The television series changed all that. Through circumstances neither of us could control we changed places, and I became the primary wage earner. Neither of us talked about it. We pretended to ourselves and to others that nothing was different, but it was. The fact that my career appeared to be growing while Joe's remained at a standstill had a profound effect on our relationship.

So my sadness at the loss of my job was mixed with a sense of relief that I no longer bore the financial responsibility. I hoped that our life could resume a more normal pattern. But, once more, in my desire to have the fairy tale come true, I overlooked the reality of how we were going to continue affording our way of life.

Joe became the realist for both of us. "The Outlaws" was officially canceled in March 1962, just at a time when we were forced to evict one of our tenants. Joe told me that he was leaving for New York to look for work. He explained that he just couldn't accept that all his years in television might end in his driving people up and down the Hollywood Hills looking at houses. I agreed with him and was relieved to see him go. But I had mixed emotions; I was glad that he had finally made some decision about his career, but I didn't want to consider the consequences of his trip east and what it might mean for me.

So I filled my days with my daughter, my friends, and my home. Because of the exposure from the series, I was now receiving a lot of attention in the business, much more than I had ever been used to, and some job offers were already coming in to my agent. Life seemed good and I was happy.

Then, very early one morning, the phone rang, jarring me awake. It was Joe, calling from New York. He had accepted a job as head of commercial production for the Colgate Palmolive Company and was looking for a place for us to live. I was shaken at the thought of leaving my work, my home, my family, and my friends. It frightened me that I had been happy without Joe. I wondered if that was how my mother had felt when she lived in California and Tom lived in New York. I had grown to love my home and I desperately wanted to stay there, but I also knew that in order to do that, I would have to forfeit my marriage.

Although we had been married only four years, I could see that our marriage was at a crossroads. Joe kept reminding me that I was his wife and I should be where my husband's work took him. I wasn't willing to lose my husband, and I certainly did not want to risk Maria's losing her father. My marriage, my dream for happiness, was still far too important to me—the most important thing in my life.

So with a sorrowful heart I had all our furniture and belongings packed and put them in storage, shipped the car east, handed our lovely home over to a real estate broker, and said good-bye to my family and friends.

As Maria and I drove down Kings Road I gave a farewell look to my majestic house on the hillside with the late-afternoon sun glistening on the living room windows and made a fervent promise to myself to be back in two years' time.

The two years came and went. I would never again set foot inside my house in the Hollywood Hills.

12 *THE MACKENZIE GLEN HOUSE*

Maria and I arrived in New York at the tail end of a long and bitterly cold winter. Our days together were spent confined in a minuscule one-bedroom apartment that Joe had sublet at 1 Gracie Square on the Upper East Side of Manhattan.

When our sublet ended, we moved into a spacious three-bedroom apartment in The Eldorado Towers on Central Park West, and once our furniture arrived from California and everything was in place my life became occupied with the everyday demands of New York. My thoughts of California slowly began to fade, except perhaps on those endless cold winter mornings in the park when the wind penetrated skin and bone; it was then that I longed for my garden in the Hollywood Hills where Maria could run naked in the hot sun.

My mother had now acquired a new sponsor, Lever Brothers, had a new production company, LYL Productions, and a new concept. In September 1962, "The New Loretta Young Show" made its debut on CBS. But the concept didn't work; the ratings were low and the show was canceled in 1963 after only one season, forcing my mother into retirement at the age of fifty.

In June 1963, my mother and Peter came to New York for my brother Christopher's graduation from Collegiate School. She and Tom had been living on opposite coasts for six years now. Although they had still not settled their legal differences, and were separated but not yet divorced, she called and asked if, as a favor to her, I would invite Tom to dinner. I didn't want to entertain him, but I couldn't bring myself to say no to her. When Tom arrived for dinner with us, he was clearly loaded. I took him into Maria's room to introduce him to my daughter for the first time.

"Maria, do you know how Daddy is your father? Well, this man's name is Tom Lewis, and he's my father."

Maria looked at Tom and then looked back at me, and without a moment's hesitation she said, "I don't like that man, Mommy."

Unhurt, Tom burst into laughter, relishing her three-year-old spontaneity. I was momentarily taken aback, yet I marveled at my child's canny instinct; she had said the very words that I had wanted to say to my mother: "I don't like that man; I don't want him in my home." It struck me as curious that Tom laughingly repeated this story many times over the years to friends and acquaintances. Perhaps he had such an inflated opinion of himself that he didn't see there might really be something unlikable about him.

What had begun as a mildly uncomfortable evening ended abruptly. Tom had continued to drink throughout an interminable evening, and after dinner his drunken monologue turned maudlin. Determined to convince me that he had been a good father, he grew adamant in his own defense, and I felt rage begin to rise inside me. Unable to tolerate his pretense any longer, I said, "It's time that you leave." That was the last time my stepfather was ever in my home.

I was very relieved and grateful when Joe finally recognized what I had known for quite some time: Our marriage wasn't improving, no matter how hard we both tried. We needed some professional help. This time it was Joe who took the initiative. He selected a marriage counselor, Dr. John Vaccaro, a psychologist highly recommended by the chancery office of the Catholic archdiocese of New York. Not only did Joe arrange for us to meet him together, but this time he entered therapy with me. After several joint sessions we continued treatment separately. I liked Dr. Vaccaro; he had a warm manner and was nonjudgmental and easy to talk to, a far cry from my previous experience with clergy counseling.

The problems that Joe and I had before still existed, and the more I pressured him to communicate his feelings to me, the more he distanced himself. I had hoped that our new life on the East Coast, 3,000 miles away from my family, would make a difference, but things between us remained the same. With my mother out of the picture I had assumed that Joe would stop being so critical of her and that I wouldn't have to keep defending her; I was wrong.

One evening Joe and I saw an Italian film that had a profound and lasting effect on me. It was a documentary, *Mondo Cane,* with separate segments filmed all over the world. The one that remains sharp in my memory even today was filmed on Bikini atoll, where the United States had conducted atomic experiments. The camera focused on the efforts of a female sea turtle to dig a hole in which to lay her eggs. Totally disoriented by the devastating effect of radiation, her natural instinct for direction destroyed, instead of staying near the sea to deposit her eggs, she was moving inland toward contaminated sand and certain death. Her laboring steps were painfully slow as she struggled gallantly up a small sandy hill. Finally she stopped and dug her tail into the sand to make a nest for her eggs, unaware that it was too far from water and that her babies would all die.

As I watched this sad creature labor so diligently at her task, unaware of the futility of her efforts, I began to sob. That female sea turtle was me; the desolate landscape she inhabited my marriage, barren and infertile. It seemed that, like the sea turtle, I was moving blindly away from the life-enhancing sea depths toward desolation, with no hope of anything changing or growing.

When Joe, baffled, asked why I was in tears, I told him the sea turtle was me. I didn't understand then the symbolism she carried about my marriage, for I wasn't yet ready to see it. What I did experience was her struggle in a barren world in which she was slowly dying.

When Maria was settled in her preschool, I returned to what had given me comfort in the past—acting. When I first arrived in New York I had an inflated idea that because I had starred in a television series I would encounter no difficulties in getting work. I quickly learned that was a fantasy and that theater credits were what counted. Since the business contacts that I had had six years before had all moved to California, where the money and the work were, I had to begin all over again.

I auditioned for and was accepted into Lee Strasberg's class at the Actors' Studio. I was told that his name on my résumé would give me credibility, but more to the point, I wanted to learn everything I could about the theater, and I knew that he could teach me. Despite his diminutive size, Lee Strasberg was one of the most formidable human beings I've ever encountered. When he walked into that tiny upstairs room at the studio and strode down the aisle to his front-row seat, he seemed a giant. His fury could be annihilating, and, conversely, his compassion and incisiveness enriching. As I grew in confidence and improved in technique I was hired for jobs—first a few commercials, then some television shows, and finally a starring role in an independent movie.

In April 1964, Joe and I sold our Hollywood Hills home and bought a house in Greenwich, Connecticut, on Mackenzie Glen, a cul-de-sac leading off one of the main country roads. Our house stood on two and a half acres at the very end of the street. There were nine houses on the Glen and twelve children, so four-year-old Maria had plenty of playmates.

A few months after we moved, I was offered the role of Tiffany in the long-running Jean Kerr Broadway comedy *Mary, Mary*. I had to give the producers my answer in a few days, and with quite a few misgivings I decided that I would accept. Although Maria was in nursery school at the Convent of the Sacred Heart and we had a live-in housekeeper, I anticipated strong resistance from Joe. With a

The Mackenzie Glen house, Christmas Day 1964—our first Christmas there.
AUTHOR'S COLLECTION

great deal of trepidation I met him for dinner in the city and told him my news. He was not at all receptive and told me that I should turn down the offer. But unlike the episode with my mother in the hospital some years back, this time I held my ground, and on June 29, 1964, I realized what a thrill it was to *hear* the audience's laughter for the first time. I was finally acting on the Broadway stage.

After the initial excitement of the first few exhilarating weeks wore off, Joe no longer joined me for early suppers on matinee days. I came home at night to a dark house, with my husband long asleep, nestled into the permanent dip in the mattress made by the weight of his body, far on his side of the bed. There was no one to talk the evening over with, no one to share my thoughts. And as I lay in bed, waiting for sleep to come, I wondered if there was something about me, something that was missing that kept people from me, and if I was always going to feel so alone.

When *Mary, Mary* closed a year later, in June 1965, I was hired to play the role of Susan Ames Dunbar in the long-running and highly successful soap opera "The Secret Storm." This time, with the astute guidance of Dr. Vaccaro, Joe and I negotiated a mutual understanding and acceptance of my new job that accommodated both our needs.

Five months later I was driving into New York on an October evening. The weather had turned cold all of a sudden, and a light rain was beginning to fall. The traffic on the Merritt Parkway was particularly heavy and the roads threatened to become slippery and dangerous. I was meeting my mother in the city for dinner. She was staying overnight at the Ambassador Hotel before beginning a cross-country personal-appearance tour. I hadn't seen her for quite some time and this was going to be a special occasion, for I had happy news to share with her.

Both Joe and I had wanted more children, but after Maria's birth I

1965. Me as Susan Dunbar with James Vickery as Alan Dunbar in the long-running soap opera "The Secret Storm."
CBS/AUTHOR'S COLLECTION

hadn't been able to get pregnant again. While there were apparently no problems, I just didn't conceive and it had become one of those topics that Joe and I never discussed, each of us hoping, *Well, maybe this time . . .* But "maybe" never happened.

It's a good thing a person can't see into the future, I thought as I drove into New York, recalling the endless juggling of schedules that both Joe and I had to endure, and the bothersome daily monitoring of my temperature to determine when I would ovulate. What began, at first, as an improvised and playful game became, as the months wore on, a rehearsed and uninspired chore. After a while it just seemed hopeless. There was no longer any spontaneity between us, and our relationship was becoming more strained than ever. Instead of bringing us closer, as we had hoped, our mutual determination to conceive a child was only driving us further apart. It was Dr. John Queenan, a highly regarded obstetrician and gynecologist and a pioneer in the field of RH-factor pregnancies, who suggested the possibility that my Fallopian tubes might be blocked. I underwent a procedure to clear them and within a month I was pregnant.

Joe and I wanted to tell the world about our good news, but we remained cautious and decided to tell no one until I had carried past the first trimester. Now the three months were up. We hadn't as yet told Maria that she was going to have a little brother or sister because we didn't want her to be disappointed if anything happened. But that evening Joe and I both agreed to make an exception for my mother. I could hardly wait to give her the welcome news that I was going to be a mother again.

When I arrived at her hotel suite, Mary Coney answered the door. I loved this loyal and gentle woman, so indispensable to my mother and to everyone around her, and I hugged her thin little body and gave her a big kiss. We hadn't seen each other for three years. Then, as I started into the living room, Mary's voice stopped me. "Joe just arrived a few minutes ago. And Mr. Newton is here also." Although he lived in Boston, Ken Newton was my mother's frequent escort when she traveled to the East Coast.

I was surprised. "What's he doing here? I thought this was going to be family tonight. Mom told me she was only in town for one night and it was just going to be us."

Mary shrugged and shook her head. Always the faithful servant, she was an observer and very rarely commented. The intimate evening that I had hoped for, on this night of all nights, would include an outsider.

It was clear to me that the dinner with my mother was not to go according to my script. Nor did I make the entrance that I had fantasized about. My mother didn't rush to kiss me and tell me how wonderful I looked, instantly and intuitively knowing from my loose A-line dress the news I had to tell her. In fact, I didn't even have a chance to take my coat off because she already had hers on.

Instead, she greeted me with a polite, "Hello, dear. You're late. I'm afraid we're going to miss our dinner reservation." It was difficult to ignore the impatience in her tone.

"Hello, Mom." I kissed her. "It's good to see you." I wanted to ease the tension that I was now beginning to feel, but she had already gathered her things together and was moving toward the door. I greeted Ken, and Joe shot me a look. "Sorry I'm late," I explained, "but it couldn't be helped. The roads are wet and there's a lot of traffic."

"What seems to be the problem with Mom?" I whispered to Joe as we scurried out of the hotel into the drizzling rain and ran around the corner to Le Manoir.

"I really can't tell. She seemed fine, and then just before you arrived she got upset about being late. I don't know what's going on."

"Maybe tonight's not a good night to give her our news."

He didn't have time to answer, for we were already inside the restaurant. My mother and I stood close together waiting to be escorted to the table, conspicuously on display for the other diners who had noticed us.

With one well-manicured finger my mother pushed my bangs aside. "That's a new hairstyle, isn't it?"

I had recently had my hair cut with bangs. I liked the look, but suddenly I felt like a small child again, remembering how I used to hate it when she would lick her fingers and twist one of my curls into place. Her gesture annoyed me now, as it had annoyed me when I was little. I wanted to replace the bangs where they had been before, but I restrained myself.

"Yes, Mom, it is. Do you like it?"

"I liked it better the old way. It was more flattering."

As we were led to our table, I realized that she hadn't seemed to notice or offer any comment on my dress. That clue to my pregnancy was ignored. And any attempt to guide the conversation into a personal exchange where I could share my news was instantly diverted. It seemed the evening was to be exclusively about her, with no room for any life but hers. Even the news that Joe and I were leaving in a week for a vacation in Bermuda was met with apathy. That was going to be our first vacation together in quite a while.

My fantasy of a joyous reunion with my mother, of a private family evening sharing good news, was demolished. I wondered if Joe was feeling as left out as I was. I glanced to my left and saw him leaning toward my mother; her hand was resting on his arm, a touch of intimacy I had longed for and had yet to encounter.

After my initial high hopes were shattered, I was relieved when the evening ended. My mother and I kissed each other lightly on the cheek and said good-bye, parting like strangers on the rain-swept street.

Three days later I began to hemorrhage.

"How old are you, Mrs. Tinney?" The nurse standing in front of me was filling in her information sheet.

"I'm twenty-nine." Strange, it didn't sound like my voice. *What am I doing here in Greenwich Hospital? I hate this room. It's empty and I'm cold. I want to be back in my comfortable house, where I belong. Only a few hours ago I was sitting on my bedroom sofa, reading. What is happening inside my body? I shouldn't be having these horrible cramps. I'm pregnant. You don't have cramps when you're pregnant.*

"How many pregnancies have you had, Mrs. Tinney?"

"This is my second."

"Is this your first abortion?"

Her words cut through my pain like a knife. "What do you mean, abortion? I've never had an abortion . . . never. I wouldn't ever have one. Why do you ask me a question like that?" I began to cry.

"I'm very sorry, I didn't mean to upset you. Abortion is just the medical term. It says here, on your chart, that you're threatening miscarriage." She patted my arm.

I didn't want her to touch me. I moved away and climbed into the bed. Why was I so cold?

"Well, I'm not going to miscarry. I'm going to have this baby and we're going to be just fine." I wanted her to leave us alone, me and my baby.

"Of course you are. That's why you're here. Dr. Queenan's ordered complete bed rest."

I felt an overwhelming sense of fear and panic. *I'm having a miscarriage; that's what these cramps and the bleeding are all about. That's why I'm here, in the hospital.*

I had called Joe from home and he was already on his way to the hospital from the city. Now I dialed long distance to the hotel in Chicago where my mother was staying.

"Hello." It was Mary's voice on the other end.

"Mary, it's Judy. Is Mom there?" I heard my voice waver but I fought to hold it steady.

"No, she hasn't come back yet. I expect her around five."

"Would you tell her that I was just admitted to Greenwich Hospital threatening miscarriage and to please call me as soon as she gets in? I need to talk to her."

"Oh! I'm so sorry, Judy." Mary's sympathetic tone released the floodgates. I could no longer hold back the tears. "I'll tell her as soon as she comes in."

I closed my eyes and tried to rest. I was exhausted but I didn't want to sleep, I didn't want to surrender to unconsciousness. I had to stay awake, I had to stay aware of everything that was happening inside me, I had to remain the alert custodian of my baby. I willed myself to stop bleeding, willed the cramps to subside. By the sheer power of my mind I determined that I would carry my baby full-term. Nothing and no one could stop me.

When Joe arrived, Dr. Queenan assured both of us that they were doing everything they possibly could for me. He wanted me to have total rest, to stay hospitalized and under observation. All that any of us could do now was wait. Joe was tender and loving, gently reassuring me that everything was going to be fine. I was frightened and it was good to have him there, to rely on his positive attitude. I needed him now more than ever.

After Joe had left, the ring of the telephone broke the early-evening stillness of my room. I picked it up at once.

"Hello. Is that you, Mom?"

"Yes, Judy! I'm very sorry to hear that you're in the hospital. How are you feeling?"

"Frightened. The doctor says that I may be miscarrying. He wants me to stay here for observation."

"How far along are you?"

"Almost three months."

"Well, you know that's the critical time. I was three months along when I had my miscarriages."

Oh, God! I thought. *Not now, don't tell me that now. If you had miscarriages, I can, too. Tell me I'm going to be all right. Tell me my baby is just fine. Reassure me. Of all times in my life, now, as my mother, take care of me.*

"When I collapsed on the set of *Key to the City* and Clark Gable had to carry me to my dressing room, I thought it was because of the fog machine. I didn't know I was pregnant."

"What happened?" I felt compelled to ask. I didn't want to hear any of it, yet I couldn't help myself. I had to find out. I felt in some obscure way that if I knew about her experience I could learn more about mine. Maybe we could bond in this primitive fashion. I needed some connection to this woman who was my mother. Maybe I could find it in our mutual motherhood.

"I was rushed to Queen of the Angels Hospital. The doctors told me I was pregnant. At first I was thrilled, and then I was told that I had to stay in bed for two weeks. Finally the doctors told me that the baby would never be born alive. It was God's will. Just keep saying to yourself, 'Thy will be done, Lord, Thy will be done.' It helps."

That's ridiculous, I thought. *It's "my will be done," not His. I'm willing my baby to be well; I'm not going to hand it over in submission to God. I won't do it.*

I was not being helped by my mother, and I knew it. The bonding that I yearned for was not happening. Moreover, she hadn't even asked me how I was, if I was in pain, anything about me. Suddenly I wanted to get off the phone before I felt even more alone.

"Well! My doctor has told me we just have to wait and see."

"Then that's what you do. Follow his orders."

"Thanks, Mom. I will."

"Call me and let me know what happens, will you? I'm saying my prayers for all of you."

I began to live in a private inner world all my own, a primitive existence of survival in which there was no room for anyone but me and the child inside me. There was no world other than the one inside my body. It was as if I had crawled inside my own womb to hold and nurture my infant embryo with the very essence of my being. My concentration on keeping my child alive grew to such proportions that I was blind to everything, even to Joe's apprehension at the possibility of losing the child we had so longingly worked together to create. He remained the optimist, trying to keep my spirits high, unable to voice his own feelings and anxieties. What had been difficult for him, displaying his emotions, was now, under the circumstances, virtually impossible.

I was centered on my unborn baby. I mothered the child inside me with every fiber of my being. I talked to it inside my brain, I sang to it inside my heart, and I wrapped it in the soft, warm folds of my uterus and willed its life to continue. I gave my child all the mother love that I had never known and always hungered for.

Flowers and cards arrived from friends, business associates, and family; nothing came from my mother, not even a phone call. Then one evening Joe leaned over and pinned a relic to my nightgown.

"Ninney brought this to me today to give to you." Ninney was Maria's nickname for Joe's mother. "It's a relic of St. Gerard Magella, the patron saint of mothers. She sends her love and says that she's praying for you."

I was surprised. "What do you mean, she brought it to you? She came all the way to New York from Philadelphia?"

He nodded. "I called her when you went into the hospital."

"I know. She's called me several times to see how I was doing."

"She just showed up at my office today without calling first. I wasn't expecting her. She took a bus this morning from Philadelphia because she wanted you to have this. We had lunch together and she went back on the bus this afternoon."

I burst into tears. Marie Tinney and I had never been very close. She was not a demonstrative woman; in fact, quite the opposite. She was elderly now and the long trip must have been taxing for her, which made her immediate response and her thoughtfulness and supreme effort to console me all the more touching. And it made my own mother's silence and absence even more clear, acute, and painful to bear.

I couldn't fathom my mother's behavior. She didn't acknowledge me or my struggle to keep my child. If a woman discovers her motherhood in her connection with her own mother, then it seemed my mother had broken all connections. I felt excruciatingly abandoned by her.

After seven days the bleeding had subsided and the cramping was minimal, and I was released to go home and told to rest. The next day Joe gave me a surprise birthday party. It was November 6 and I was thirty years old.

Seven days later I was back in the hospital.

No matter how often John Queenan counseled me that the fetus was probably not alive, or, if alive, then damaged in some way, I would hear none of it. I stubbornly insisted on "one more day, please." In the end my child had to be separated from me with a scalpel. Our struggle together for his life was finally ended in an operating room.

"It was a boy, wasn't it, John?"

He looked away from me for a moment. Then he looked back.

"You'll have other babies, Judy."

But I knew that I wouldn't, just as I knew my baby had been a boy. I had wanted to name him Luke, but it was too late. This child had carried such hopes with him, hopes that neither Joe nor I was ever able to voice to each other. I know we had separately believed that this child would be the answer to our marriage, that he would make the difference. And now, with his death, I feared the death of my marriage as well; that, too, was in such fragile shape. It had taken such a long time for me to get pregnant. I knew we didn't have the courage to try again; there would be no other babies for me, ever again. I unpinned the relic from my nightgown and put it on the bedside table, knowing I had no further need for it.

When I began to write about this period in my life, I recalled that, at the time, I felt I had lost my mother along with my baby. Reason now tells me that that very primitive feeling was one I had often experienced before, one I can now identify as the very young child's belief that she can have only what her mother lets her have. In some very basic and inexplicable way, I felt I needed my mother to support me in order to keep my baby, and when she didn't call, no effort on my part could make my baby live.

Since it was my mother's silence that I remembered so clearly, it occurred to me that there might have been some written communication between the two of us during that time; perhaps I had had the courage to write what I didn't dare say. Indeed, I did find some letters that we had exchanged.

The first one I wrote three days after my birthday. In it I thanked her for the present that she had sent. I added that I hoped she wasn't ill because that would be the only excuse I could find for her not calling me or sending flowers while I was in the hospital. I was clearly unable to disguise my anger, for I added, "There is nothing further to report on the baby if you're interested. The doctor can't tell anything for another week."

Three weeks passed with no word from her. Then she returned my note enclosed in a letter, saying that she had been rereading it and she could find no "kind" words to express her reaction. She went on to say: "Years ago I gave up making 'excuses' for my behavior, especially to my children" because it seemed only to confuse rather than to satisfy. She said she had hoped, "foolishly, perhaps," that her children would one day come to accept her as she was, "an imperfect woman."

She added that when she didn't hear from me after our phone conversation, she assumed I was fine and that we had gone on our cruise. Initially when she heard that I was in the hospital with a threatened miscarriage she said her first thoughts were for Joe and me, and then came the upsetting thought that while I had chosen to hold back the good news of my pregnancy when we saw each other in New York, I had "preferred" to tell her the bad news of my possible miscarriage.

She closed by saying that the rift between us made her sad, and she alluded to that last night in New York, when we had seemed more like "polite strangers" than mother and daughter.

I wrote her back immediately, attempting to open up a dialogue between us:

> Contrary to your feelings of sadness at having to write the things you did in your letter, I am not sad. I'm happy because at least it's a communication between us and that is some kind of a beginning—not only as mother and daughter, but women, as you put it so succinctly, imperfect women struggling to keep our heads above water.

I explained that I had fully intended to tell her my good news, even referring to the dress I wore, but the circumstances of our evening together in New York had made it all but impossible to talk.

Then, addressing her silence following my phone call telling her that I was in the hospital, I went on to say:

> As a matter of fact, it never dawned on me that I wouldn't hear from you. When I didn't, I had a few million questions as to why. My only conclusion is that you didn't care enough to think of me. Do you know you have not *yet* asked me how I am or have I lost the baby or not?
>
> You say you can no longer allow your dearest darling to demand more than you have to give. I think you'll agree with me, as you've said many times yourself, I have never demanded anything from you, nor has Joe. Let's examine from my point of view what I was supposed to be demanding. Something that, up until now, I thought would be a natural impulse, to care enough to comfort someone in both physical and emotional pain, especially when that someone is your daughter. If you say you haven't got it to give, yes! I have to respect that, I have no other choice. But, I also cannot allow you to expect me to accept a painful realization and not voice my hurt at what I see to be true.
>
> As far as maturity in your children is concerned, living in the surroundings we did, I think we did indeed mature very quickly, learning to deal with life and ourselves, but also to accept you for you with all your imperfections, as you pointed out, and love you. And, in spite of what you might think, we do love you even though we have been hurt by your imperfections. And we will continue to love you. But maturity, Mom, is being able to communicate with each other, the good with the bad. I will always try to do that.

In her response to my letter, she said that it had been "stupid" to try to talk to me woman to woman when we were mother and daughter. She appealed to me to make peace, adding that "love between a parent and child can be beaten to death."

The implied suggestion that I might lose my mother's love was clear to me, and the thought was more than I could bear. Fearful of "beating her love to death" by any further communication on the subject, I "got off her back," as she had suggested, and made no further attempts to continue the argument. I kept quiet, as I had in the past, once more the submissive daughter.

As I reread these written exchanges of ours today, it strikes me that my mother and I were never able to communicate in any spontaneous way. What seemed the most direct and natural thing, to telephone, would have been unthinkable to me at the time. I was angry and hurt, but anger was a totally unacceptable emotion to display with my mother, especially if it was directed toward her.

It's also significant to me that I had actually made and kept a "scratch copy" of my letter. I rarely did that unless I wanted to draft my thoughts carefully before sending a letter. I was saying some dangerous things to my mother, things I'd never said before, things that weren't safe; I wanted to make sure I worded them correctly.

The fact that she didn't answer my note immediately and maintained her silence for three weeks is another example of the way in which she distanced herself, making herself inaccessible and unavailable to me. That was how she punished me as a small child; she wouldn't speak to me until I couldn't stand her silence another minute. When she finally spoke to me this time it wasn't directly by phone, but indirectly, by letter, risking nothing. It seems, when I then took a risk, hoping to open up a woman-to-woman communication, I was told I could have real communication with her only if she remained the mother, older and wiser, and I the child; like her mother and herself.

As soon as I had recovered from the miscarriage, I went back to work on "The Secret Storm." It was a relief to return to the familiar studio routine, one that I enjoyed and could once more lose myself in. The actors on the show had now become like a second family to me; I loved my work, and the public and professional recognition that I was receiving from it.

In our therapy sessions, Dr. Vaccaro and I had moved on from my marital problems and were now concentrating on resolving some of my conflicts over my mother, for she still continued to be the source of many of my arguments with Joe. He would bring up some character defect that he felt she had and I would feel obliged to defend her. The discussions were no-win for me, for if I agreed with him, I was disloyal to her. She and I had not seen each other for almost a year.

I hadn't yet summoned the courage to confront her about my father. Instead, I decided to enlist the help of her friend Ken Newton, whom Joe and I had gotten to know better. He was going to California on business and planned to see my mother. I gave him a copy of my birth certificate, which Joe had obtained from the Los Angeles County records a few years before. Much to my surprise, Ken agreed to ask my mother if I was her child by Clark Gable. Apparently the subject had come up before between them, and she had managed to cut him off. For my part, I must have been desperate to entrust this man whom I didn't know all that well with such a private and potentially volatile mission, but nevertheless I did.

After Ken got back from his trip, we met in New York and I'll never forget the feeling I had when he told me that my mother wouldn't answer his question, telling him it was none of his business. The look he directed toward me was one of loathing, and I felt like a traitor to my own flesh and blood. For Ken, the mission proved costly; my mother told him she never wanted to see him again.

"I've had your birth record removed from public access," he said as he handed me back my birth certificate. Then he gave me the name of someone in the L.A. County accessor's office who knew where it was located, should I want it for any reason. I assume that he removed my record so that only I could have access to it; anyone wanting it would have to go through me.

My mother never mentioned Ken's visit to me, nor did I ever discuss it with her; it was another of those undiscussed events that both of us knew about but neither of us acknowledged. Later, when she was traveling, she wrote that Ken had tried to contact her but that she was unavailable. She cautioned me to say that I didn't know how to reach her, should he get in touch with me.

A week before Labor Day 1966, my mother called with exciting news: She was going on an extended pleasure trip to India and Iran. This sudden decision surprised me. It was a change in lifestyle for her. In the past she had seemed content to remain in Los Angeles, retired from her career, and busy with her friends and active social life.

At that moment I made a quick decision myself. "I have a few days off from the show over Labor Day. I'm coming out for a visit," I told her. It was spontaneous. I had taken her, and myself, completely by surprise. She couldn't think of an excuse or a rejoinder fast enough, and I didn't want her to find one. I quickly added, "I haven't spent much time with you—just the two of us—for a very long time. Let's do it now before you go away." I meant it. I needed to see her, I needed to talk to her. I couldn't let her go away before I asked her if Clark Gable was my father.

"All right," she agreed. "Let me know when you're arriving and I'll meet you at the airport."

I felt the landing gear drop with a thud, and my heart dropped with it. My hands clenched the sides of my seat. *Relax, Judy. It's going to be all right.* But they were only words, without effect. I couldn't relax. I felt a slow-growing panic and it had nothing to do with the long five-hour cross-country flight.

I hadn't been in Los Angeles for four years. My home, my life, was now on the East Coast. But my mother and I had some unfinished business, and this time I was not going to be put off. I was going to get the truth from her, finally, once and for all. I could no longer tolerate living my life in secrecy and doubt.

Dr. Vaccaro's words resounded in my head: *Remember, Judy, you are entitled to know the truth, to know who your father is. It's your right.*

As I walked through the crowd and into the terminal I saw her instantly. You couldn't miss her. She didn't blend into her surroundings. She stood out. I had grown up observing my mother's effect on a crowd. It was instantaneous and always effortless. She just "was." Yet something about her kept others at a distance; she was seldom intruded upon.

That night she had dressed the part of the star. She looked beautiful in pale blue patterned silk from head to toe. Her hair was hidden, wrapped into a turban of the same silk as her dress. Two wisps of curls caressed her cheekbones. A double strand of pearls hung around her neck and she wore a large freshwater-pearl-and-diamond ring.

Her presence in that ugly, stark terminal was striking, almost overwhelming, and probably calculated to have just that effect. I stopped short, and for a moment I wished that I hadn't come, that I could retreat to Connecticut and avoid what I knew lay ahead of me. That my mother had dressed for her role was obvious at a glance and I had forgotten what that was like, what it usually meant for me when she was playing the movie star. She could be very frightening. I had seen her intimidate producers and network executives and advertising agencies, and she had always frightened a little girl who might ask questions that she didn't want to answer. It had worked in the past.

She was going to be a formidable opponent to my intentions. Had she guessed the purpose of my trip? The next few hours would tell. It wouldn't surprise me if she did know. She was often intuitive, at least on that one subject. And she had always successfully staved off my questions. I smiled and waved, walking toward her.

"Let me look at you," she said, as she pulled away from my embrace and stepped back from me. "You look tired." She gave me an appraising look that didn't miss much. "You've still got your television makeup on."

I laughed. "Yes, Mom, I am tired. It's been a long day. I didn't have time to take the makeup off after the show. Joe picked me up at the studio and drove me out to Kennedy."

She reached over and kissed me. "It's good to have you home."

I put my arm around her waist as we turned to go. "It's good to be home." And it was.

Directly behind us a porter stood by an electric cart. "We're going to ride in style," my mother announced, as she climbed onto the seat and patted the seat opposite her. I welcomed the luxury of the transportation, but I felt silly riding while everyone else was walking. My mother was enjoying the attention we were getting. She smiled like a queen riding in her carriage among the peasants. The stares that greeted us as we drove by embarrassed me.

The porter finally stopped the cart, and my mother stepped off, right in front of a large Rolls-Royce parked at the curb. I couldn't stop staring at the sable-colored Rolls with the initials *LYL* in red on the door. A beautiful car, very impressive, and one I'd never seen before.

On the way home from the airport my mother talked about her upcoming trip. She seemed very excited about her adventure and was so absorbed in her plans that she was unaware I was only half-listening to what she was saying. Distracted, I sank back against the soft beige-leather seat. *I'm never going to be able to do this,* I thought. *How am I going to find the right way to ask her? Just come right out and say, 'Mom, was my father Clark Gable?' What if she says no? What if she refuses to answer me? What, then? What will I say to her then?*

"Judy? Are you listening to me?" Her voice cut into my thoughts.

"Sorry, Mom. What were you saying?"

"I asked you how long you can stay."

"I have to go back early on Wednesday morning. I've got an afternoon rehearsal for Thursday's show. But that gives us five days together."

Maybe she'll ask me now what I'm doing here, why I came out. Maybe then I can tell her that I came to find out who my father is. Please let it be now. I don't think I can stand this waiting.

"That's not a very long time. There are a lot of people who are dying to see you. Your cousin B.J. has been calling every day for a week asking me when you're arriving. And Mama, of course. And Georgie and Ricardo. But still, five days is better than nothing, isn't it?"

I could have said "I came out to see you. We have to talk." It was a perfect opening. But I didn't. I wondered if she knew. *She must.*

She's never going to give me an opening, I told myself, *not after all these years.* This was going to be harder than I thought.

At the house, as I started up the front stairs to my old bedroom, my mother stopped me. "I've put you in the oval apartment. You'll have more privacy there."

Why, I wondered, wasn't she putting me in my old bedroom on the second floor? Was she trying to isolate me completely from her?

I turned and, looking across the marble foyer into the dining room, saw that what had once been a solid wall was now two large, paneled folding doors leading to an oval-shaped living room, bedroom, and bath. It was the apartment she had converted for Peter so he could entertain his friends and practice his music without disturbing everyone.

"It works nicely, doesn't it?" She had seen the look of surprise on my face.

"Yes, Mom, it does. It looks as if the house was originally designed that way."

I gazed at her, standing at the bottom of the stairs, alone in the middle of the foyer. Suddenly she looked small and vulnerable, no longer the powerful movie star who frightened people. She was all alone in this beautiful home. The rest of her family had left long ago. Tom had gone ten years before, although he had returned to California and was living in the Ojai house. I had gone to work in New York nine years ago. Peter had moved out and was living in northern California with his wife, Diana. His new rock band, Moby Grape, was now gaining in popularity and he was appearing in concerts all over the country. Christopher was on location pursuing his career in motion pictures.

I felt a strong sense of sorrow for this woman standing in the front hall of her empty home. Once, many years ago, there had been so many people and so many dreams. Now there was only Mom and a housekeeper. What had happened to the plans, to the family that had lived there? Where did all the dreams go? Everything sacrificed for work and career. It all seemed very sad, and as we walked up the marble steps into the dining room to have dinner, I hugged my mother tightly.

After dinner we settled down on the comfortable peach-colored couch in her bedroom. *This is the perfect time for our talk,* I thought to myself. Mary Coney had joined us at dinner, so there was no opportunity then. Now we were alone again. But before I could say anything my mother had reached for the controls and turned on the television set.

"Mom, I came out here for a special reason. There are some things I want to talk to you about." At last, I got it out. I had been rehearsing it silently all through dinner, and I had finally said it.

"Not now, Judy. Let's watch this show, all right?" She turned the volume up a little louder.

I wasn't about to compete with a television set. I had traveled 3,000 miles and waited thirty-one years to ask this question. I could wait a little longer. Now that I knew she was avoiding the inevitable, part of me wanted to avoid it, too.

It was midnight before the show finally ended. As my mother turned off the set, she said, "I'm tired, and I know you must be exhausted. I'm going to get ready for bed."

She was right. I was exhausted. I had been up for eighteen hours. Maybe this was not the right time; maybe it would be wiser to wait until tomorrow, when we were both rested and could think more clearly.

"What's your schedule like tomorrow?" I asked.

"I have packing to do. Then I have some fittings at the dressmaker, and some other appointments in the afternoon."

"It sounds like you're going to be very busy. I'm afraid I won't have any time with you. I made this trip because I wanted to see you. There are some things that I want to talk to you about. Important things."

She cut me off. "Not tonight. I'm too tired to think."

"All right, Mom. Good night. I'll see you in the morning."

I undressed, got into a nightgown and robe, and took off my makeup, relieved that I could delay the confrontation a few hours more. I rehearsed in my mind what I would say and how I would say it, but the more I thought about it, the more anxious I became.

As I stood looking at my reflection in the bathroom mirror, I told myself, *You've been tricked again into avoiding the issue. If you don't get it done now, tonight, she's going to find more excuses, and so are you. What are you afraid of, Judy? All she can say is, "I'm not going to tell you." At least you will have tried. Don't give up now, and don't go to bed tonight until you have gotten the truth out of her. That's why you're here, and that's the only reason. Do it now.*

I went back to her bedroom through the darkened stillness of the house. She seemed shocked to see me standing in the doorway to her dressing room.

"What is it? Did you forget something?"

"No, Mom. I'm not tired. I guess I'm still wired from the trip. I just want to spend a little more time with you. It's so long since we've seen each other." I didn't know what else to say. She looked at me for a long moment and then went back to combing her hair. Neither of us said a word; the room was very still. Finally she turned and looked at me.

"I'm not feeling very well."

"What's the matter?"

She got up and went past me. "Nothing." She shut the bathroom door behind her, leaving me standing alone. I could hear the water running and I decided to wait and see if there was anything I could do for her. After a short while I heard the sounds of vomiting.

I knocked gently on the door. "Mom, can I help you?"

"I'm fine." Her voice was muffled and weak.

I opened the door and found her kneeling over the toilet bowl, her body doubled over, regurgitating. I knelt beside her, gathering her hair in my hands and holding it away from her face. Finally she stopped retching and slumped against me, then looked up at me.

"I don't want you to see me like this."

She was pale, with dark shadows under her eyes; her skin without makeup was translucent. She looked very frail and delicate, and seemed embarrassed that I saw her so naked and vulnerable.

"I'm your daughter, Mom. It doesn't matter to me what you look like. It's okay." I helped her up. She was very shaky.

"I had my shots for my trip today. That's what's making me sick."

I ran some cold water over a washcloth, my back to her. I was glad I couldn't see her face. We both knew her sudden illness had nothing to do with getting shots and everything to do with my arrival. She was frightened, so frightened that it made her physically ill. The inner strength that I had gained from my years in therapy must have seemed very intimidating to her. It was obvious that there was a purpose to my trip and that this time I wasn't going to be deterred. Our relationship had shifted and I was no longer compliant. But my heart went out to her. She needed to keep her dignity.

"That's all right, Mom. Let me help you."

I washed her face with the cold washcloth. And she let me do it, neither of us speaking. I helped her up and left the bathroom. She finally came out and lay down on the couch, and I covered her with an afghan. Her color was a little better, but she still looked drained.

"Are you comfortable, Mom?" She nodded. "I need to talk. Do you feel up to it?" I had already made up my mind that no matter what she answered, I was still going to pursue my questions.

"I'm very tired. What is it that you want to talk about?"

"I want to talk about us."

Her eyes took on a questioning look, as if she didn't understand what I meant.

"What about *us*? What do you want to know?"

"I want to know who my father was."

Her expression didn't change. "Why? This is the eighth time you've asked me this. You've gone this far without knowing. What do you want to know for?"

I didn't remember ever asking her that question directly even once, much less eight times. Perhaps she was referring to my early childhood questions when I thought I was adopted and asked about my birth parents. I had also never told her directly that I knew she was my biological mother; it seemed to be an unspoken understanding between us. But now was not the time to go into what she meant; nothing was going to divert my attention from getting an answer now.

"Because it's very important to me to know. I've been told that my father was Clark Gable."

Still no change in her expression. "How would you feel if he was Clark Gable? What would you think about that?"

"It would make me very happy. From what I understand, and from what everybody tells me, he was a wonderful man." *Is she going to tell me, or isn't she?*

A resigned expression came over her face. She looked at me for a long moment. "Well, he was your father."

A feeling of utter relief went through me. It was as if I had been holding my breath for the past several hours and suddenly I could breathe again. Finally all doubts were gone, I had a name and a face and an identity to the other missing half of myself. I had known that my mother was my birth mother for years, even though we had never discussed it, but the mystery of my father was finally solved. Now I knew definitively once and for all that I was really Clark Gable's daughter. I almost laughed with relief. It had been such a long and difficult journey to get to this moment. And now, finally, after all these years, I was past it, on the other side—a whole person.

"I want to hear everything, from the very beginning."

She closed her eyes and let out a sigh. I felt her relief, in conjunction with my own.

"What was he like, Mom?"

"Clark?" She opened her eyes. "He was darling. Sweet and very gentle. He had a good sense of humor, he made me laugh. He was a real man. Everybody loved him, except Bill Wellman—they didn't like each other very much." She stopped.

Oh, God, I thought, *don't let her stop now; she's just started.* There was so much that I wanted to know. I wanted to hear it all in her words, her story. If I could somehow understand how she felt, then it would make my existence, my birth, everything about me more real. I hadn't felt real before, only a part of someone's made-up story. It was important for me to live in *her* mind now, not in mine. I felt

February 7, 1935—that is the dateline on this photograph of my mother and father taken when they were filming Call of the Wild. *The caption stated: "The much bewhiskered, dark-complexioned gentleman discovered lunching in a Seattle, Washington, hotel recently has been identified as Clark Gable, film star. And his pretty girl companion has been identified as Loretta Young, equally noted film star."*

UPI/BETTMANN

almost numb with fatigue, yet I distanced myself from my own feelings. There was no time for joy that Clark Gable was my father. I could think about that later. At the moment I was focused on getting information. I waited for her to return from where she had drifted off in her thoughts, to come back from 1935.

"We fell in love on location, while we were making *Call of the Wild.* He was married, so when I discovered I was pregnant with you, I was frantic and terrified. It would have ruined both our careers, a scandal like that. We would never have worked in films again. I was so frightened I didn't know what to do. I was Catholic and I couldn't have an abortion.

"Mama and I decided that Clark had to be told, but when I told him, he turned to Mama and he said, 'I thought she knew how to take care of herself. She's been a married woman, hasn't she?' " Her voice had an angry edge to it.

"How did Grandma treat you when she learned you were pregnant?"

"She was upset at first, but then she was very understanding and supportive. Clark separated from Ria after that and I started work right away on another picture, *The Crusades*."

I couldn't believe it when my mother revealed that she was three months pregnant with me when she filmed The Crusades in 1935.
THE BETTMANN ARCHIVE

"Did he try to see you?" I didn't want my father to abandon her.

"Oh! All the time. Constantly. He'd call the house. But I was always afraid someone would be listening. I'd ask him not to call. I was afraid all the time. Then we set up signals so I would know it was him but no one else would know. He even came on the set of *The Crusades* to see me."

"Did you know he was coming?"

"No. It was a surprise. I was so embarrassed. I just wanted him to go away. I was afraid everyone would guess. I thought people could tell just by looking at the two of us. Rumors were already going around about us. Ria was calling the house trying to talk to me and I wouldn't take her calls. Photographers wanted to take our picture together and I wouldn't let them. I was so frightened. Every time he came near me or tried to see me, I kept saying, 'Go away. Go away.' "

"Why didn't you want to see him? Weren't you in love with him? You were carrying his baby. Wasn't he in love with you?" It didn't make sense to me. He had separated from Ria. Wasn't that some kind of victory for her? Why did she keep pushing him away?

"We were very much in love and I did want to see him. I kept him away because I was so frightened of the scandal ruining our careers and our lives." Her voice began to rise. "You don't understand, Judy, those were different times then. I was unmarried and pregnant—that was the worst possible thing that could happen to a movie star. Illegitimacy wasn't accepted then. I couldn't risk anyone seeing us together."

I could see she was getting impatient with me. I didn't want her to stop, and she could, at any time. I cautioned myself to listen more carefully and not ask so many questions. I might never again have her so available to me. "Go on, Mom," I urged her. "I'm sorry for interrupting."

"When I was about five months pregnant I began to show, so Mama and I went to Europe. The studio owed me some vacation time and I thought if I left town the gossip would die down. It didn't. When I came back a few months later Clark told me that he had filed papers to legally separate from Ria. He thought that would make me feel better. It didn't. Finally he said, 'What do you want me to do?' I could only cry and so he said he would go away on a trip to South America. I told him to go. I thought maybe if he were out of town, all the gossip would die down. I was frantic. I didn't know what else to do."

"How pregnant were you by then?"

"About seven months. Ria knew I was back in town and she kept calling, telling Mama that if I just showed myself to the press all the rumors would stop. I couldn't show myself. I was too big."

She told me about the Venice house and how she didn't dare to go outside except at night. Her sisters Polly Ann and Sally visited her and they devised a way to help her get the exercise she needed by attaching a rope to the back of the car so she would hold onto it. Sally would drive very slowly while my mother walked along with Polly Ann for company. If there was any chance of her being recognized, the car was there for a quick getaway.

As I sat beside her on the couch, watching her remember those days when she was carrying me, my heart went out to her. I felt her isolation. I wanted to know what it was like for her because I was part of her, inside her, during that time. What she felt I felt, what she experienced I experienced; we were one then. And we were one now, reliving the experience together.

"The rumors got so bad that there were stories going around town that I had been in an accident and my face was scarred. But mostly they were saying that I was pregnant with Clark's child. Ria wouldn't stop calling and insisting that I hold a press conference, so Mama and I had to do something."

She told me about the rigged interview with Dorothy Manners. The stories and the manipulations of people that my mother and grandmother pulled off in order to keep my birth a secret amazed me. What was even more intriguing was their total success.

"After you were born I went back to work and no one mentioned it again."

"You mean no one challenged you?"

"No. No one dared. Isn't that incredible?"

It's unbelievable, I thought to myself.

She went on with her story. "The morning you were born, the milkman was making a delivery to the Venice house. He rang the doorbell just as you were opening your mouth to let out your first cry. I didn't want him to know that there was a baby in the house and so I put my hand over your mouth."

"Did Dr. Walter Holleran deliver me?" I remembered his name on my birth certificate.

"Yes. And he gave me no medication at all."

"Where was my father when I was born?" I longed to hear more about him.

"He had come back from South America and was staying at the Waldorf in New York. He later told me that he received an unsigned telegram the day you were born saying 'Beautiful blue-eyed blond baby girl born eight-fifteen this morning.' He tore it up into little pieces and flushed it down the toilet for fear someone would find it. To this day I don't know who sent it. I certainly didn't."

"When he came home, did he try to see me?" I held my breath and silently prayed that he had wanted me.

"Yes, on more than several occasions. He came straight to me and said, 'Well! Where is she? I want to see her.' I lied to him. I told him that I had sent you out of town."

"Where was I?"

"With your nurse, Frenchy, at the Venice house. I came to visit several times a week. You were surrounded by people who doted on you. You had lots of attention. You were always picked up and held."

I didn't believe her idealized view of my early months of life, but I didn't tell her that. "Remember when I was fifteen and you brought my father home to meet me? Was that the first time he had ever seen me?"

"No, of course not. And I was always trying to get you to come to the set when we were working together, but you never wanted to come.

"He saw you twice after you were born. I went to a big party one night and he was there. I looked at him across the room and felt guilty that I had lied to him. After all, you were his child, too. When

I asked him if he wanted to see you, he was angry with me and replied, 'Do you mean to tell me that she's been here in town all this time?' I admitted that, yes, that was true. He said, 'Yes! I want to see her.'

"We still had to be very careful that nobody saw us. So we set up elaborate arrangements and changed cars several times before we got to the Venice house, in case anyone was following us.

"You were sleeping in a dresser drawer. He reached into his pocket and took out a thick wad of bills. He handed me four hundred dollars and said, 'The least you can do is buy her a decent bed.' And that was the only money he ever gave me for you."

I was surprised at the anger in her voice and the hardness in her eyes. The thought crossed my mind that perhaps she had expected him to support me financially.

"I even had my lawyer, George Breslin, open up a bank account for you in San Francisco—just in case he might want to contribute something. Nothing was ever put in it." She still seemed angry with him, even after all these years. I certainly wasn't my mother's little "money-maker."

"What did he think of me?" I wanted to hear more about me and my father.

"He loved you. He couldn't keep his hands off you. He just kept holding you; he couldn't stop."

"Was that the only time he saw me?"

"No. You stayed at the Venice house for six months, and he saw you one more time before I sent you away to St. Elizabeth's in San Francisco for nine months."

"What was St. Elizabeth's?"

"It was a home run by nuns, the Daughters of Charity, for unwed mothers and their babies. I had to get you out of town. I was afraid someone would discover where you were. You had lots of company. There were other children to play with there. I traveled to see you several times a week. You were well taken care of and given a lot of attention."

My mind was spinning. Had my mother given me up for adoption and then changed her mind? How old was I when I was sent away?

What was she thinking at the time, and what was my life like there?

"How did you find this place?"

"Through the Paulist fathers. You were there for nine months. And then I told Louella Parsons that I adopted you and I brought you to the Sunset House."

"Was it an orphanage?"

"Yes. Some of the babies were adopted. You were nineteen months when I brought you home. I picked Louella because she was a friend and I knew that she wouldn't ask too many questions. I told her that I had adopted two little girls and that I couldn't tell her where I got them. Three weeks later I gave out another story that I had to give one of the little girls back to her mother. I wanted to confuse the press as much as I could. I changed your age from nineteen months to twenty-two months."

"And Louella believed your story?"

"If she didn't, she never let me know. She was always very generous to me and I was forever grateful to her for not asking any questions."

She closed her eyes. She looked exhausted; the shadows under her eyes were now very dark. I reached for her hand and it felt ice cold. I sat holding her hand and a tiredness came over me so suddenly that it surprised me. My bones began to ache, my head felt light, and my eyes stung from lack of sleep. The early-morning light was beginning to seep through the woven draperies drawn across the windows. A new day was dawning and I hadn't been to bed yet. There were still many unanswered questions, but they would have to wait. I touched my mother's cheek gently with my hand.

"Mom, are you falling asleep?"

"Almost." Her voice was so low I could barely hear her.

I leaned down and kissed her. "I love you very much, Mom. Thank you for tonight."

When I finally got into bed I cried myself to sleep. I cried for the father that I never knew, for the mother who was so frightened, and, most of all, for the child who was abandoned.

My mother left shortly thereafter on her trip and was out of the country for nearly a year. It wasn't until I returned to Connecticut and shared everything I had learned with Joe that I realized that several months of my early life remained unaccounted for—from the time I lived in the Venice house and St. Elizabeth's until I joined my mother in the Sunset house at nineteen months. I suspect my mother doesn't remember all the details accurately herself; in any case, these months will always remain a mystery.

My mother and I corresponded fairly regularly that year and I had confided to her my feelings about my marriage. In her birthday letter to me from Rome where she was visiting friends she commiserated with me, saying that if she'd known how unhappy I was going to be on my thirty-second birthday, "I might have put a pillow over your face and not let you take that second breath, in the hope of saving you from it." She told me that as much as she wanted to protect me she knew that in the end it was in God's hands.

Later on in her letter she wrote of her unhappiness over my birth, but as if to console me, she said I had been "a special gift from God." Encouraging me, she said to "let God do the work," that she couldn't help me, that only God could do that, and in order to have His help I should do nothing.

I too believed that God *would* do the work, that miraculously He would lift my unhappiness from me and that I would be rewarded for my perseverance. Unable yet to define myself, I believed like my mother that I must be true to God, first, before myself. I could depend only on Him because my own decisions wouldn't be the right ones. I believed that my marriage was a sacrament and that it couldn't be dissolved in the eyes of the Church. And although I was terribly unhappy, I still wanted my daughter to have what I didn't—a mother and a father. And so I did nothing and continued to search for answers in my therapy, my Church, and the writings of women who addressed some of the same emotions that I was feeling. It was comforting to know that I wasn't the only woman in her thirties asking herself: "Is this all there is?"

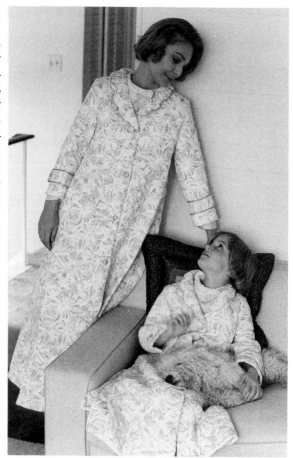

Joe was shocked and disappointed when the company he had joined, against my better judgment, went into bankruptcy in August 1968. Even though I had had trepidations about the firm, I was surprisingly unprepared for the abrupt termination of his job, which produced high anxiety in the two of us. Now we were both unemployed, for in June my character had been written out of the show. Although I was told that in the fall a new story line was planned and a contract would await me at that time, I had heard nothing for a while. When the offer finally came, I accepted gladly. Joe had worked a brief ten weeks for CBS during the election coverage, but the strain of his ongoing unemployment was almost more than either of us could bear. Now at least one of us would be working. As the year wore on and a new one began, Joe remained out of work with no future prospects on the horizon, and our arguments escalated.

One evening in the fall of 1969 I arrived home from work and, after fixing myself a drink, joined Joe in the living room. He was waiting for me, a martini in hand.

"I saw your mother today," he announced. "I was in the city." My mother had taken an apartment on Central Park South the previous year, although she was about to move back to Los Angeles and had sublet her apartment to her godchild, Marlo Thomas. She and Tom had just recently gotten a divorce after having previously divided up their community property.

"I brought home a plant that she wanted you to have."

"That was nice of her."

"You won't think what else I have to tell you is very nice." Joe had that familiar look on his face. In recent years, any discussions he and I had about my mother held the potential for being incendiary, so I tended to choose my words carefully to avoid an unpleasant confrontation.

Maybe if I changed the subject and pretended I didn't hear what he said there wouldn't be an argument. "When is she leaving for California?"

But he persevered. "I'm not supposed to tell you what she told me today. She doesn't want you to know."

"Then perhaps you shouldn't."

"No. I think it's something you have to know."

"All right, Joe. Since you seem so intent on telling me, what is it?"

"She has given her emerald earrings to Antoine Marderosian to sell for her." Antoine, a jeweler, was the husband of Georgiana and Ricardo Montalban's oldest daughter, Laura.

"When did she do this?" I was very surprised. Over the last few years my mother had made a point of telling me that she was willing me her emerald earrings, the ones Tom had given her one Christmas.

"A few days ago."

"Why are you telling me this?"

"Because if anything happened to her or to me, you wouldn't know where they are, and we both know how many times she's promised them to you."

"And now she's going to sell them?"

"That's what she told me. She's selling her earrings and she doesn't want you to know about it."

She had promised, as recently as a few months before, that the emerald earrings would be mine and that she'd never sell them. Bad enough that she had broken her promise, but to make matters worse she had sworn my husband to secrecy—and in some curious fashion he seemed to be enjoying it.

"I guess she doesn't care as much for you as she says she does, huh?" Joe said.

Suddenly I wanted to hurl my glass through the window, and it took every ounce of self-control not to. When the impulse passed I turned swiftly, set the glass on the nearest table, walked down the front stairs and out of the house.

I began to run up Mackenzie Glen. I wanted to get far away. My breath came in short, labored spurts, my lungs and chest aching from my effort, my legs cramping from the force of my speed, but still I kept running. I didn't know where I was going and I didn't care. All that mattered was that it was far, far away from everyone and everything.

I remember how betrayed I felt then. It didn't matter to me whether or not she gave me the emeralds. What mattered was that she had gone out of her way to promise me something, not once but many times, and then deliberately took it away while colluding with my husband to deceive me by not telling me what she had done. That was what hurt so much. Once more her actions allowed Joe to tell me how she could withdraw her love on a whim, all part of the endless arguments we had about my mother. This time she had proved him right, and he was enjoying his victory at my expense.

As the year wore on, Joe was drinking heavily. The tenuously delicate threads of our marriage unraveled completely until there was nothing left. Joe had already left therapy without my knowledge and there was no hope of reconciliation. Each battle left both of us exhausted and debilitated, and by October we were occupying separate bedrooms.

In November I retained a lawyer and told Joe I wanted a divorce. I wasn't at all surprised when he told me that he would never agree to a divorce; there had never been one in his family. He told me I could leave if I wanted to, but he would keep the house and Maria, which, of course, he knew I'd never agree to. He pointed out that both my mother and grandmother had divorced their husbands and he wasn't going to allow that to happen to him. We were both stuck in a bad marriage.

Finally, in early December, after I had resorted to enlisting the assistance of a priest friend of ours, a doctor, and Joe's sister and brother-in-law, Joe left our Mackenzie Glen home.

The next three years were fraught with hostile lawyers, legal battles, and court appearances. Joe remained uncooperative throughout, contesting the divorce and all efforts to settle our differences amicably, finally pushing the proceedings to a court trial with one party forced to prove cause.

In January 1970, right after Joe left, my mother visited me. I had written long letters to both her and Grandma, explaining the reasons for the separation and pending divorce. I never received an answer from my grandmother. My mother was sympathetic but cautioned me to go slowly and to pray for strength. I got the very definite feeling that she expected me to remain married, although she never explicitly said so.

By this time, Joe, on his lawyer's advice, had informed our creditors that he was no longer financially responsible for any bills. Financially overwhelmed, I was frightened for my future and for Maria's. I asked my mother for a loan to cover some outstanding bills. My part on the show was secure and I promised her that I would make regular monthly payments, including interest at the current bank rate, but she refused, saying she couldn't afford a loan at the time.

(What she didn't know, and I never told her, was that I knew she had received a check for $25,000 a few days before. It was the repayment of a loan she'd made previously to her limousine driver so that he could start his own company.) As it turned out, I was fully able to handle everything without help. I had simply panicked. Only several years later, when my childhood nurse, Margaret Ash, visited me did I learn that my mother had told her that she had no intention of "financing a divorce."

In midwinter of 1970 I received a very welcome call from an old childhood friend. Jill Schary had moved to New York with her second husband, Jeremiah Robinson, and her two children, Jeremy and Johanna Zimmer. We had been writing long, rambling letters to each other all about our present lives and feelings, and our correspondence had renewed our friendship. I accepted her invitation to spend a night in her new home in Greenwich Village.

When I arrived I was delighted to find Jill's parents, Dore and Miriam Schary, waiting for me, but my pleasure soon turned to profound sadness. Dore looked nothing like the strong and vital studio mogul of my memory. Instead, he now appeared beaten; none of the power and regal bearing that my child's mind attributed to him existed in the old man sitting before me in Jill's cozy living room. I soon learned the cause of his distress; the Broadway show he had recently produced had closed right after opening. His disappointment and disillusionment showed in his speech and demeanor. I wanted him to be the man I remembered; I wanted something of my old life to remain the same.

Miriam, his beautiful and multi-talented wife, now sat in her armchair, silently knitting. Her eyes were cast down most of the evening as she concentrated on her work, saying little. I thought of the many hours we'd spent together in her intimate studio, talking about every subject under the sun, and I wondered what had happened over the years to so change these two dear and dynamic people.

And Jill, my childhood chum, regaled me long into the night with intimate and detailed Technicolor tales about her tempestuous marriage to alcoholic Jeremiah, and her own addiction to speed and other drugs. She was working on a new book and was very excited about it. I was a rapt audience as she proudly showed me reams and reams of manuscript detailing their self-destructive, tortured, co-dependent relationship.

My own life and marital problems seemed minor, diminished by the drama and scope of hers. When she left me in the early-morning hours to go to bed, I felt numb. I lay there in the dark remembering what used to be and comparing it with what was now, and suddenly I couldn't stay there one more minute. I dressed quickly, wrote a short note to Jill, making up a lame excuse about having to be home early for some meeting, and drove to Greenwich, leaving disillusionment behind me.

The year 1971 was a time for more legal motions and sessions in family court, determining visitation rights. The result was that Maria, who was eleven, was to spend every other weekend with her father, and two weeks separately with each of us during the summer.

One evening in May, Maria and I were driving back to Connecticut after having dinner with my mother in New York City. We had visited her once the previous year in California, but it had been some time since Maria had seen her.

"Gaggy's getting old," Maria said to me, out of the blue.

I laughed. "We're all getting old."

She was silent for a while and then she said, "Is Gaggy rich?"

"She's supposed to be," I said. "I'd be very surprised if she wasn't."

Maria was quiet for a while and then she asked me, "Is Tom Lewis rich?"

In unison we both said, "He got a lot of Gaggy's money." The topic had been discussed around Maria, since everyone in the family felt that Tom had taken unfair financial advantage of my mother.

"I don't think that was very nice of him, Mommy," Maria added.

"Well, I don't think they were very happy together, Maria. But a husband should want to take care of his wife, even so."

"And his child," Maria added quickly.

I said nothing. She thought Tom was my father; I didn't know how to tell her he wasn't. I wasn't sure what she would think, so I avoided the subject.

Suddenly, out of the blue, Maria said, "I want to see him."

"If it's important to you, I'll see to it that you do."

"He mustn't care very much about me. He never calls or tries to see me. But I want to see him because he's my grandfather and I haven't seen him since I was two, and I'm already eleven. What did he say when I said 'I don't like that man'?"

"I don't remember, Maria. It was so long ago."

"He mustn't care very much for me, Mom. He never calls or writes to me." Her voice was poignant. There was such a tone of longing, and with it the suggestion that in some way she might be responsible for Tom's staying away because she had said she didn't like him. I couldn't allow her to think those thoughts; she was having a difficult enough time dividing her time between her parents. I decided to share my secret with my daughter and tell her the truth.

"Maria, Tom Lewis isn't my father, he's my stepfather."

As I glanced to my side I could see her large blue eyes get larger. She leaned forward in the seat. "Your stepfather? I didn't know that. Then who's your father?"

I couldn't say it. It was too risky and I was too frightened of her reaction. "He's dead now, but he was a wonderful man."

She didn't back down. "If Tom Lewis is your stepfather, then I don't want to see him. What was your father's name?"

"I'll tell you that when you're a little older. He was a wonderful man, but he's dead now." My hands were shaking on the wheel. This is not at all how I'd planned to tell my daughter about my father, not in a moving car on the Merritt Parkway, where I couldn't see her face in the darkness to gauge her reactions.

"Why won't you tell me his name?"

I took a deep breath. "Clark Gable." There. I'd finally said it, after all those years; it was no longer a secret that I had to keep from her.

I heard her gasp. "Clark Gable is my grandfather?" I could see she was delighted. She had hung his poster in her room after I took her to see *Gone with the Wind.*

"Yes, Maria." Thank God, I was so relieved.

"Why did Gaggy divorce him to marry Tom Lewis?"

"Clark Gable and Gaggy loved each other very much, but they were never married."

"You were a love child?" My dearest child in all her wisdom had just given me the greatest gift of unconditional love and acceptance I had ever received.

Tears filled my eyes as I whispered, "Yes, Maria."

We drove in silence for a while until I could no longer stand it. I had to ask.

"Does that bother you, Maria?"

"No, Mom, not at all," she answered simply. "That's probably why Tom Lewis was so mean to you. Did he know?"

"I don't think he was ever told, but I was there when he married Gaggy and I think you're right. He must have been very jealous."

"Why didn't Clark Gable and Gaggy get married?"

"Well, people looked on that kind of thing in those days differently than they do now, and they were both big stars and important people and I think they were too frightened. Gaggy told everyone I was adopted."

"Who knows? Does Dad know?"

"Yes, he does."

"Do Peter and Christopher?"

"I've never discussed it with them, but I'm sure they do."

"That means I'm related to John Clark Gable. You have his picture on your desk."

"Yes, I guess you are. You'd be his half-niece. I was the only child my father knew while he was alive. He died before his son was born."

"His wife must have been very sad."

1971. Maria, a twelve-year-old equestrienne, is shown here with a friend's pony and me.

"You were his only grandchild, Maria."

"How many wives did my grandfather have?"

"Five. This is just between the two of us, Maria. It's nobody's business but ours, okay?"

She nodded. "Okay, Mom."

Reaching over, I touched her face with my hand. "I'm so glad I've told you, Maria. I've wanted to for such a long time, ever since I found out myself a few years ago."

She smiled. "I'm glad you did, too, Mom."

In December I was a key witness at a hearing of the Tribunal in the Catholic archdiocese of Brooklyn. Joe had requested an annulment of our marriage in the Church. At first I was shocked and very hurt; I never considered there could be even a remote possibility of that; nevertheless, I cooperated with the required procedures. If I could be free to marry again in the Church, I wanted that chance.

Although this hearing preceded my divorce trial by a year, in many ways it was far more traumatic. I was questioned at great length about the most intimate details of my life by a group of priests in judges' robes sitting on a high dais. My marriage was subsequently annulled on the grounds of psychological incompatibility.

In April 1972, CBS, which had bought "The Secret Storm," notified me that my part was being written out. I was now unemployed. When I called to tell my mother the bad news, she was sympathetic and suggested that perhaps I could take in some boarders to help cover the mortgage payments. Although highly impractical and hardly cost-effective—Greenwich was not like downtown Los Angeles in the early 1900s—it seemed a logical suggestion to her, since that was what her own mother did in lean times in order to survive.

I did not, however, follow in my grandmother's footsteps and turn my home into a boardinghouse. I rented it instead, and Maria and I, along with our dog, went to California for the summer. Grandma had invited us to stay with her since my mother said she didn't have enough room for us in her house. We arrived in Los Angeles to find that we had been forgotten. When we arrived by taxi at Grandma's apartment complex and still there was no one to greet us, I asked Maria to stay with the luggage while I took the dog for a quick walk. The apartment on Spalding Drive, where my marriage had begun, was only a block away. I wanted to see it once more.

When I returned, Maria was still where I left her, but now, as I walked toward her, I saw a man beside her, his arm placed protectively around her shoulders. There was something very familiar about him, and then I saw it was Russ Hughes. I broke into a run toward my old love and good friend. Mary Coney had told him we were coming. Russ was there for us that summer; my mother was not.

Indeed, that summer stands out in my mind because of her absence. She distanced herself, never calling, and with the exception of two occasions when we were invited to dinner, we never saw her. I couldn't understand her behavior, nor could I explain it to Maria. I thought that perhaps she disapproved of me because of the divorce or was afraid that I would ask her for help. In desperation, I asked my grandmother why my mother was behaving in such an unfriendly manner. All she could say was, "I just don't understand your mother, dear, I don't understand her at all."

Yet when I called my mother to say good-bye and tell her I was going back to Connecticut, she started to cry, saying, "I don't know why I haven't seen you this trip, I don't understand."

Neither did I.

On September 7, 1972, I was the first witness in our divorce trial in Stamford, Connecticut. When we broke for recess, I was feeling demoralized and humiliated; I told my lawyer that I would agree to meet Joe's demand of $25,000—for the divorce and my freedom.

My divorce was granted. I was no longer Mrs. Joseph Lewis Tinney. With no job, my financial situation was precarious and I couldn't pay Joe. His lawyers were serving me with subpoenas to appear again in court, when an old childhood friend came to my aid and loaned me the money. I had no choice but to sell the Mackenzie Glen house.

In the summer of 1973 Maria and I returned to California. It wasn't possible to remain in the East, even though I wanted to, without the security of a steady job. So I returned to a familiar place, one that had been home to me in the past. Coming home meant having my family nearby, something that I felt the need of, especially now that I was a single parent. Even after my mother's indifference the previous year I still hoped for a relationship. I wanted to provide Maria with as large and supportive a family structure as I possibly could, and for that I turned to my own family. I couldn't really foresee what I was returning to; I knew only that Los Angeles seemed the natural place to go.

13 MOTHER'S DAY 1986

My return to California in the early 1970s marked the beginning of a period filled with losses and major life changes. I was no longer in therapy, but the years that I had spent with Dr. Vaccaro had helped me to understand more about how I had led my life, or rather, how I had let it lead me. I wanted to change that, to have more direction and to resolve the distance between my mother and myself, so I worked harder at our tenuous connection to each other.

Those first few years back in California were extremely difficult ones. I was still mourning the loss of my dream and didn't have another one to replace it. My life as a single mother and breadwinner did not come easy. Nor did the shifts in my career. I found I had to begin, once more, all over again like any newcomer. My New York career meant nothing in film-oriented Hollywood.

However, I had great support from my friends, among them Russ Hughes and his wife, Nancy, and their children, Kevin, Gary, and Christy. They included Maria and me in their busy lives, and their house became a second home.

I enrolled Maria in Notre Dame Academy, an all-girls' Catholic high school, and a year later moved from a small rented house in Westwood to a two-bedroom apartment across the street from Beverly Hills High School, where Maria finished her junior and senior years.

Finally, in 1975 I landed a year's work as Barbara Vining in "General Hospital," ABC's popular daytime series. The story line caught

1975. Maria and me in the living room of our Beverly Hills apartment.
AUTHOR'S COLLECTION

1977. Maria's high-school graduation party. Left to right: my mother, my grandmother, Maria, and me in the living room of my mother's Beverly Hills home.
AUTHOR'S COLLECTION

on with the viewers and I was thrilled to be acting in daytime serials once again.

On July 26, 1976, Maria and I attended my brother Christopher's wedding to Linda Corkran in Santa Barbara, where we saw Tom Lewis for the first time in many years. He was living in the Ojai house and had joined the Jesus Movement, then extremely popular in California. He had become friends with Kathryn Kuhlman, a charismatic preacher. The years had not been kind to Tom; he had aged badly; his once-handsome face was weathered and puffy, with deep, furrowed lines, and his beautiful thick head of hair, once black, was now snow-white.

When he saw Maria and me at the reception he rushed over, threw his arms around me, and began to cry. "I did the best I could, Judy, the very best I could. At least I saw that you had a good education." His wave of emotion passed as swiftly as it had begun, and he continued past us as if nothing had happened.

He and my mother were cordial to each other that day but kept their distance. They had had little contact with each other over the years, and she was embarrassed by his appearances on Kathryn Kuhlman's television show.

The following June, Maria graduated. Grandma and my mother were there, and Joe flew out for the ceremonies and the party that I gave Maria at my mother's house in Beverly Hills. Maria had been able to spend some time with my mother and they were fairly comfortable in each other's company. I was pleased that Maria was getting to know her grandmother, her only living grandparent. I wanted her to feel loved by my family as well as by Joe's.

In the years that Maria and I lived together in California, she had spent her summer vacations and most of her holidays with her father in New York. Now it was time for college, and since her father

1975. A cast party to celebrate the thirteenth anniversary of ABC's popular daytime soap opera "General Hospital." I am on the right in the back. Back row, left to right: Deanna Lund, Don Matheson, Denise Alexander, Michael Gregory, John Beradino, Emily McLaughlin, Rachel Ames, Richard Dean Anderson, Bobbi Jordan, me, Valerie Starett, Craig Huebing, producer Tom Donovan, director Ken Herman. Front row: unknown, Stacy Baldwin, Patsy Rahn, unknown.

was paying her tuition on the condition that she be on the East Coast, she chose Villanova, a Catholic university in a suburb of Philadelphia, her father's hometown.

When the time came, I accompanied Maria to Philadelphia. I wanted to see where she was going to spend the next four years and help her get settled. We stayed with friends who introduced Maria to Danny Dagit, the young man she would later marry.

When I left Maria at college, I dreaded returning to California and my empty apartment, so I had made plans to stay in New York for a while with a friend, Jackie Smith, vice-president of ABC daytime.

As a result of that trip my life changed radically. When I suggested that Jackie hire Gloria Monty, my director on "The Secret Storm," to produce "General Hospital," I had no inkling when she moved to California as G.H.'s new producer that in January I would be working as Gloria's assistant.

*1978. An anniversary
celebration for
"General Hospital"
at the Beverly Hills
Hotel. Left to right:
actress Brooke Bundy;
producer Gloria
Monty; and me,
Gloria's assistant at
the time.*

PHOTO BY FRANK EDWARDS

The transition from being in front of the camera to behind it was difficult at best, but in that year I gained significant knowledge and valuable firsthand experience in producing a network daytime series that quickly became number one in the ratings.

By the end of 1979 I found myself in my mid-forties, evaluating the past ten years of my life, and wondering what I was going to do with the rest of it. With Maria away at school in the East I was now a long-distance parent and I missed my full-time role as mother. My role of producer's assistant had ended and the role of actress just wasn't happening. I now fell back on the one role I was most familiar with, one I had played all my life—that of daughter. With each disappointment I drew closer to my mother and she responded and appeared pleased with our frequent dinners and social engagements. I even discussed my idea of writing a book about our family. I told her of my early efforts, some ten years before, after Joe and I had separated. At the time I was writing a weekly column for the Westport *Town Crier* and I had some preliminary meetings with a newspaper editor there. I tape-recorded our sessions as a way of remembering important incidents, never mentioning, however, that my father was Clark Gable. Now, as we talked, my mother and I both envisioned a generational saga of strong women.

As I look back on those exchanges I can see that my mother viewed the book as a charming story glorifying her as the beautiful Hollywood star who adopted a little girl and lavished attention on her. That wasn't my view. I wanted to tell *my* story, and it would include who my father was. But I knew that in order to ensure my mother's love, I had to preserve the lie.

I wrote in my journal the last day of 1979:

> The end of a decade, ten years ago was the end of my marriage, my work, my home, my life on the East Coast. Endings and beginnings, a new life here in California and a new relationship with my mother, a new home; mine, ten years of struggle.
>
> Now, what next in the '80s? What do I want for me? Marriage? Yes, for the first time in ten years, just this last year, I could think about sharing my life again with a man. Hard work in a career? Money? Success? Yes, all of that. I'll have to go out and get it, produce a special, write the book, or act in a series, or all of those things. That's what I want for me in the '80s.

I didn't produce a special, but in May 1980 I moved back to New York to produce "Texas," a new daytime soap for Procter & Gamble. My stint with Gloria Monty was about to pay off. It was a wonderful career advancement and I was excited about the job and the fact that I would be closer to Maria, now in her junior year at Villanova.

The ensuing two years of my life working on "Texas" seems like a tape on fast forward, much like the tape machines I sat in front of daily. The events of my life played swiftly, seemingly with no time to analyze what was happening. The show was everything; whatever was happening in my own life I dismissed, and continued creating more shows.

It seemed there was never enough time: no time to contemplate my personal, spiritual, or even my professional life, only time to tape and edit "Texas" five days a week, fifty weeks a year, and always to read, read, and read more scripts, more story projections, more outlines.

In July 1980, two months after I had moved east, I had dinner with Russ Hughes, who was in New York on business. He didn't look well and complained that he didn't have any appetite. At my suggestion he promised to have a thorough physical when he got home and to phone me with the results. We kissed each other good-bye; I headed home to my apartment and he went to the airport. It was the last time I would ever see him.

A few weeks later he reached me at the studio. He was calling from the hospital and his voice was light.

"Well, I've just gone through a battery of tests and I promised you I'd let you know when I got the results. Everything is fine. I've got a clean bill of health. There's still one more test, something about the liver, but I don't anticipate any problems. Now, will you stop worrying?"

I thanked him for calling and told him how relieved I was, but insisted he call me with the results of the final test. When a few days passed and I didn't hear from him, I called the hospital, only to learn that he had been discharged that morning. I reached Russ at home and scolded him for not telling me he was being discharged. I asked him how the liver test had gone and he assured me that everything had gone well.

I learned the truth from my lawyer, and also Russ's, Robert Tourtelot, during the last week in August when he called me from California about my contract. He seemed distracted and finally he blurted it out: "Judy, I have some bad news, and I know no other way to tell you than straight out. Russ has an inoperable tumor in the pancreas and it's spreading to the liver. The first doctor gave him three months to live. The cancer specialist who is treating him twice a week with chemotherapy is more hopeful."

"How is he, Bob? Have you seen him?" My voice seemed to come from a great distance. I was unable to take all this in.

"Yes." He hesitated. "Today in my office."

"How is he? How is he taking this?"

"He's in good spirits, Judy. But he's very tired and he looks gray. His left arm is swollen. He didn't sit still very long. He kept moving around. He said it helped him."

I wondered why he had lied to me. "Did he mention me, Bob?"

There was a long pause before he spoke. "Yes. I told him that I thought you should know and I wanted to tell you, and he said that it was okay with him."

I started to cry. "I wish he'd told me himself."

"He couldn't, Judy. He doesn't want anyone to know. He's told his children and his family and that's all. He was forced to tell me because I'm his lawyer." Bob's voice cracked.

Russ and I finally talked to each other a few days later. He told me that he had lied because he hadn't wanted to upset me and that he didn't want any pity. He asked me not to tell anyone, especially not Maria, saying, "You know how upset she can get sometimes."

But in the end he left it up to me. I told her because I wanted her to have some time to say good-bye if he should die. I hadn't had a chance to say good-bye to my own father, and I wanted to give my daughter every opportunity to tell Russ, who had been like a father to her, how much he had meant to her. They wrote to each other and talked on the phone and, although it was difficult for her, she never let on to him that she knew he was dying.

Russ's brother Patrick called late in the evening Monday, September 29. Russ had been taken to the hospital and the doctor had given him a week to two weeks to live. I told Patrick that Maria and I would go to California that weekend. At two the next afternoon my mother called me at the studio. She was crying.

"Russ died early this morning. Bob Tourtelot just called to tell me. He offered to call you, but I told him I wanted to tell you myself. I know this is an awful shock, Judy. Just go in the bathroom, close the door where no one can see you, and have a good cry for yourself."

Four days later Maria and I arrived at Russ and Nancy's house in Mandeville Canyon. During the course of that afternoon we relived with Nancy Russ's last days and his funeral at St. Martin of Tours Church, which had been packed with hundreds of his friends, relatives, and business associates. My mother told me that Grandma had been impressed by the crowd. It didn't surprise me, for Russ drew people to him.

The house was full of his presence: His clothes still hung in the closets, and his riding boots stood beside his favorite chair, where he'd placed them after winning fourth prize in a Santa Barbara horse show. It wasn't until the next day when Patrick took us to Holy Cross Cemetery on the way to the airport that I fully realized that Russ was gone. I knew that I would never see him again, but I would always carry him in my heart and see him in my mind's eye standing beside my young daughter, his arm protectively around her.

When Maria graduated from Villanova University in June 1981, I paid my mother's expenses to attend her graduation. It made me very happy to be able to do something for my mother, and I wanted to share with her, firsthand, my pride in my daughter's accomplishment. Maria was the first woman in my mother's family to earn a college degree. I also wanted her to meet the man in Maria's life — Danny Dagit. From the moment they met, he had been her steady boyfriend. There was never anyone else for Maria but Danny. Philadelphia was now her home and there was no question that she was going to remain there after graduation.

*J*une 1981. Maria's graduation from Villanova University in Pennsylvania. Top: me, Joe Tinney, Maria, and my mother. Bottom: Danny Dagit (Maria's husband-to-be), my mother, and Maria.

"Texas" wasn't faring very well in the ratings wars. Traditionally it takes a year or two for a new soap to develop a devoted audience, but, from the outset, "Texas" had the unfortunate luck to be scheduled opposite the two most popular and highest-rated soaps on the air, "General Hospital" and "Guiding Light." In December 1982 the show was canceled and once again I found myself unemployed.

The previous two years had been so rich in activity and so empowering that to be suddenly without my identity as a producer left me with no identity at all. Each month that went by without another job offer became more and more difficult. I had lost my role as a wife long ago. Now Maria was a grown woman, and although I would always be her mother, my active mothering days had ended, too. I had changed careers and no longer was an actress, and now I was no longer a producer either. At forty-seven, I felt that I had somehow failed.

Then in late March 1983 I received a call in New York from my mother, telling me that an unauthorized biography was being written about her. She had just received a letter from the authors asking permission to interview her, which she refused.

"I'm telling you this because they're going to write their book anyway, without my permission. Maybe now it's time for you to write yours."

I couldn't believe what I was hearing. This was the first time she had ever given me her unqualified permission and support, and I didn't hesitate to put the necessary wheels in motion. The timing couldn't have been better. I immediately called an old trusted friend, John Dodds, an editor whose gifts I greatly admired. He got very excited when we met the next day and I outlined my ideas, and he set up a meeting the following day with Lynn Nesbit, a highly respected literary agent at International Creative Management who had represented my friend Jill Schary Robinson for her best-selling autobiographical novel, *Bedtime Story,* and also a more recent book, *Perdido.* I wrote a letter to my mother, telling her my good news, that I was well on my way to consummating a book deal and that

John Dodds had intimated I would probably be given an advance to write it. I was very excited about this new venture.

A week later, on April 2, 1984, my mother answered my letter expressing congratulations but cautioning me against revealing "the area of my bloodline." She indicated that she would be "mortally offended" if I even discussed the truth with any editor, lest he or she do "as they pleased" with the information. She felt that I would be "pressured beyond belief" regarding this issue, and she warned me to be prepared to drop the project if necessary. She told me that she would pray that I find some "inspired" way to handle that topic and suggested that I discuss the matter with Father John Fitzgerald.

There was no way that I would discuss anything with Father Fitzgerald, the priest who had baptized me, signed my phony baptismal certificate, and failed to return my phone calls before I was married. But there was also no way that I wanted to risk offending my mother. She had an uncanny knack for using just the right word (typically, written, not spoken) like *mortally* to communicate her subliminal messages to me. I had learned at an early age to be attuned to these words, and I knew that it would be the death of our relationship if I wrote the true story. I had struggled too long and too hard to gain what I now considered a friendship with her to compromise it.

Yet her suggestion that I continue living the lie, denying my father and evading the truth of my heritage, was preposterous. The whole purpose of telling my story was to claim my father and my identity, but as my mother's letter indicated, I couldn't do that without losing her. Embarrassed, I told both John Dodds and Lynn Nesbit that I didn't have my mother's cooperation and that without it I didn't feel free to write the book.

Several years later my mother and I discussed this episode. Her words to me, as closely as I can recall them, were: "The thing that makes your life story interesting and makes people want to read it is that I am a movie star and your father was a movie star, Clark Gable. No one would be interested in the book if your father was the milkman."

This belaboring of the obvious was amazing to me. Of course I knew that was the draw of the story, but the heart of it lay else-where. And she had no concept of my entitlement to claim my fa-ther. It didn't matter to me what he did for a living. I had innocently lived a lie for most of my life and I had the right to acknowledge my father. At the time I posed a question to her. "Let me ask you this, Mom," I said. "If you were me, would you write *your* book and leave out or evade who your father was?" The only way I could make her see that I had rights was to put her in my place; if she was honest with herself, then she would know my feelings.

"No," she answered, "I wouldn't."

To which I replied, "I didn't think so. And neither would I." Her answer was what I had hoped for. Writing my story truthfully ap-peared to be the one area in which I held any power over my mother. I wasn't ready yet to give that up and I told her so indirectly, the way that she had taught me, the way we usually communicated our anger toward each other.

The months went by and I remained in New York with no job pros-pects. Financial worries and loneliness brought me close to despair. I was living on savings and unemployment benefits, hoping to get another assignment, but when no new position presented itself I turned inward and regressed, examining my life, looking for the pos-sible wrong turns I'd made. With so much time alone I began to ask myself the questions I hadn't had time for in the past. Struggling to regain my emotional equilibrium, I turned to my Church, searching for answers, but none was forthcoming.

I sublet my apartment for the summer and returned to Los Ange-les. Since my condominium was occupied by a tenant, I stayed with my mother. I visited my grandmother, whom I hadn't seen for quite a while, and was surprised to see how fragile she had become. I had been warned that she was declining, but I now saw firsthand just how much she had aged.

Five years before, at ninety, she had begun to have tiny strokes, not serious enough to incapacitate her totally, but enough to diminish her memory and her ability to work. Ever since Grandma had become too ill to take care of herself, she had been living with Polly Ann, who had also nursed her husband, Carter, through a lingering terminal illness. Polly had always been the caretaker in the family. But my mother was a tremendous help to her older sister; her life was now organized to spend half the week at Polly Ann's house, where they shared the task of making Grandma comfortable and worry free. I marveled at my mother's unselfish devotion to her mother in those last years; it further confirmed the strong bond that existed between the two women. Grandma became my mother's first priority and she was totally dependable in her care and love. I was amazed at times at her patience, for Grandma could be very difficult and demanding.

It was very sad to see a woman who had been so vital deteriorate so rapidly, and Grandma hated it as much as her family did. She cried a great deal, which was most unlike her, and toward the end she even became disoriented, not knowing where she was or who we were. But to the end she retained her intense sense of beauty, her joy in nature, and her love of God.

That fall I returned to New York to work on a pilot. When that was completed in December I returned to California. Since my condominium was still leased, I moved back into my mother's house, but not for long. In early February 1984, I again returned to New York, this time to work as an associate writer on the daytime soap "Search for Tomorrow." I was very hopeful about this new endeavor. I had the necessary training and the background, but, unfortunately, after six weeks, my option wasn't picked up and I was once more unemployed. This last disappointment was hard to bear. I hurried back to California and my mother's house, struggling not to feel utterly defeated. Ironically, a year later I won a Writers Guild award for my work on "Search for Tomorrow."

My recollection of the eight-month period that I lived in my mother's house was that I was nonproductive and living off my mother's generosity, even though I was paying my own expenses beyond room and board. Yet when I went over my personal and business journals in preparation for this chapter, I got a totally different picture. Aside from attending business meetings with network executives and other industry people, I had written two scripts for two separate daytime soaps on speculation and gotten paid for them and I was also hired by Group W to develop an idea for a Gothic supernatural soap. But the fact that none of these projects came to fruition furthered my sense of failure. It was as if the four-year-old had come home, instead of the adult woman who had been self-supporting and raised a child successfully. I had to ask myself how I could have thought so little of myself then. Why did I give myself so little credit for my efforts?

Finally it began to make some sense to me. My mother's house wasn't the sanctuary I imagined, but in reality a "charged nest." Once again my mother tried to convince me that I was unable to compete in the rough-and-tumble world of show business, and she consistently encouraged me to seek secretarial work and even enlisted her friends to arrange secretarial interviews for me. She was once more writing the script for me, casting me as the secretary, even as I was struggling to write my own script, with success in the creative arts as my goal.

On October 10, 1984, my grandmother died at the age of ninety-six. She had had another stroke and, after several days in a coma, she died quietly in her sleep. The heart of the family was gone. Without Grandma's healing interventions her family changed and would never again be the same.

The day after Grandma died I moved from my mother's house, back into my own condominium. By now I was burned out professionally and personally. In desperation I sought out a therapist and together we began the year 1985 with a slow and meticulous sorting through the history of my life. In order to become whole again, I had to go back and find the parts of my self that had gotten lost. To

1985. Maria and me during her summer trip to California.

support myself I took a sales position in a Beverly Hills boutique. It was a first-aid station for me: a place to go and something to do to keep my mind active and to make the days pass swiftly.

In early July, Maria and Danny told me they were getting married. Since I couldn't be there to share in the plans for Maria's wedding, she came to California to be with me. We had a wonderful two weeks together that summer. It had been many years since she had been home, and everyone wanted to see her. She was just beginning to plan her wedding.

It was clear to me that Danny was good for her, for Maria was very happy. Danny's family had always welcomed her and together she and Danny had built a network of loving young friends. Danny was associated with a well-known and reputable real estate firm and beginning to climb the corporate ladder. He had even bought what was to be their first house. There was no doubt in my mind that Maria would have a secure and peaceful life, all the things I had hoped she might have.

As the months passed and I began to understand a little more about how I had viewed my life, and the ways I had dealt with it, I was faced with the question of what I wanted to do with my future. I was nearing fifty and was free to choose a new direction. The one that had been written for me, the one that said "And they lived happily ever after," had ended. It was time for me to write a new one.

I had always wanted to study psychology, and the idea that I could go to college, get a degree, and begin a new career intrigued me. With the encouragement of my therapist, I researched which university programs offered credits for life experience and good student loans. Antioch University had what I wanted: credit for life experience, a master's program in clinical psychology that followed the state requirements for a marriage-family-child-counselor license, *and* financial aid, for which I qualified. I enrolled in September 1985, signing up as a full-time student.

According to my preliminary timetable, if I went to school full-time I could get my bachelor's degree in a year and my master's in two. It would probably take two more years to complete the 3,000 internship hours required before taking my state licensing exams, but in five years' time I could have a new and rewarding career for myself.

Although I had left the boutique for a better-paying office manager's position, I found I still needed financial help and, for the first time since my divorce, I went to my mother. When I told her that I wished I didn't have to ask for her help, she replied that she was fed up being asked for money, adding, "And that goes way back before you kids were born."

However, she agreed to give me the tuition for the first quarter, saying that she'd let me know what she could do when it came time for the next quarter. She also added that she didn't think that I could work and go to school at the same time. Fortunately, I proved her wrong. When I thanked her, she said that if she were in my shoes she would have asked for help, too, but somehow it didn't make me feel any better.

It was around this time that my mother had a discussion with me about my grandmother's will. Grandma had left her entire estate to her five children to be divided equally. One day my mother casually mentioned that my uncle Jack had brought to her attention the fact that the wording in the will referred to any children of my grandmother's beneficiaries as "issues." "That would indicate that you are my natural child," she informed me.

"But I *am* your natural child," I replied.

"Yes, but I wasn't married to your father. Your birth was a mortal sin. You know it and I know it. I instructed Jack to change the wording in the will from *issue* to *child*. I just thought you should know."

I was so stunned by this information I didn't know what to say. I knew that Grandma hadn't named any of her grandchildren in her will, so it was a surprise to hear that I might be mentioned at all. Now I wondered if my grandmother might have intended to legitimize me subtly by her use of the word *issue* or whether that was just the usual legal terminology in wills. Overriding all these feelings was the most familiar one of all, being hidden and denied yet one more time; this time I was told that my birth was a mortal sin. I reverted to my infant conditioning, the child who can't have anything unless her mother gives it to her, and cannot feel anything but gratitude for being kept. So I thanked my mother for telling me and said nothing more.

Maria spent New Year's with me, her last visit to California before her wedding in April. I planned a bridal shower for her the first week in January. All of my family, except for my mother, had already sent their regrets for the wedding, so the shower would be the only party in California for Maria, and I wanted it to be very special. At the last minute my mother received an invitation to spend Christmas and New Year's in Mexico, so she called me to say that she wouldn't be back in time for the shower. Because Maria and I both wanted her to be there, we changed the date to coincide with her return.

It was at Maria's shower that my mother made her surprising announcement. We were alone together in the dining room when she said, "I may not be going to Maria's wedding."

"Why not?" I asked. I thought she was kidding.

"I just might not go, that's all," she said casually.

I glanced out into the living room to make sure Maria couldn't hear this. I didn't want to hear it myself. Quite suddenly I began to feel a little sick.

"I don't understand, Mom. Why wouldn't you want to go to Maria's wedding? What could possibly keep you away?"

She gave a small shrug of her shoulders. "We'll talk about it later. Now's not the time." She walked past me into the living room to join the others, leaving me standing alone.

It didn't make any sense to me that my mother wouldn't go to Maria's wedding. I glanced over at her, sitting on the couch, holding the rapt attention of everyone at that end of the room as she described how she had left an ABC movie produced by Aaron Spelling because she didn't approve of the way her character had been written. She confided to a friend of mine with a smile, "I am known as the Iron Butterfly, you know. I get what I want." My friend was entranced. I wondered if maybe my mother had expected me to make more of a fuss over her, beg her to come. Maybe she was feeling left out and wanted more attention. Then I decided not to worry about it. She probably didn't mean what she had said. It was a momentary whim. I purposely didn't mention it to Maria.

About a month later, Maria called me, very upset. "Mom, I just went through the most horrible conversation with a nosy reporter for *The New York Times*."

What, now? I thought. "What about, Maria?"

"I gave the paper the information for my engagement announcement and Gaggy's name must have alerted this reporter. Anyway, he called me and was asking all kinds of questions. He wanted to know who my grandfather was."

"What did you tell him?"

"I had to lie and tell him Tom Lewis. I didn't know what else to say." She sounded very angry, for which I didn't blame her. "I knew he was looking for some news and I wasn't going to give it to him."

"You did the right thing, Maria. It's just a damned shame that Tom Lewis gets the credit. He doesn't deserve it." I saw that this would never end. Now the lie that started with my birth was affecting the second generation; my daughter was experiencing discomfort and frustration about her lineage, and was forced to keep it a secret.

In early March Mary Coney had surgery for cancer. When I walked into the hospital room at St. John's Hospital in Santa Monica, I found my mother sitting by Mary's bedside. Mary was sleeping, a tiny vulnerable figure with tubes in her arms, surrounded by ugly steel machinery. Mom glanced up and motioned for me to sit down beside her.

"It was a long procedure," she said, "but the doctor told me the operation went well." We were whispering.

"What's the prognosis?" I was hoping for the best, but somehow knew better.

"It's not good. Poor little thing, after her last illness she swore she wasn't going to have anything more to do with doctors, and now this."

In the stillness of that stark atmosphere, time seemed suspended. I vaguely heard my mother's voice explaining medical terms and procedures as I watched Mary sleep. That still, small body lying in its criblike hospital bed seemed almost inanimate, in keeping with her sterile surroundings. The word *terminal* echoed in my thoughts. Had my mother voiced it, or had I imagined it?

"The doctors have prescribed postoperative chemotherapy."

That's a good sign, I thought. They wouldn't suggest such drastic measures if there wasn't some hope of remission.

Again silence; the only sound being Mary's deep breathing. Then my mother spoke. "I don't think I'll be going to Maria's wedding."

So it wasn't just a whim. She had really meant it. She was looking straight ahead; she didn't even turn to see my reaction. It took a moment for me to gather my thoughts, and before I could say anything she spoke again.

"Did you hear what I said?" Her voice had an edge to it as she turned to look at me.

"Yes, Mom. I heard you." We were facing each other now.

"Well, what do you think I should do?"

"I think you should go to the wedding. However, it's entirely up to you. You do what you want to do." I still couldn't understand why she wouldn't want to go to her granddaughter's wedding. I was hurt, angry, and confused.

The room was again filled with silence; even Mary's breathing seemed to lighten, hesitating, awaiting a decision.

"Mary will need someone to take care of her when she gets home." Yes! I thought, the perfect excuse. "When is Maria's wedding?" she went on.

So she'd already forgotten the date. The invitations had been mailed long ago and she had already received hers. "On April 4, about a month from now," I said.

She turned away from me. I could barely contain myself, my disappointment was so intense. *Make your decision, dammit!* I told her inwardly. *Tell me you wouldn't think of missing the most important day in your granddaughter's life. It can't be that hard to say.* But neither of us spoke.

Mary began to stir. She moaned and turned toward us, opening her eyes. Without a backward glance Mom got up and moved across the room to stand by the bed, her decision still hanging fire.

I didn't have to wait too many days for an answer. Maria's phone call told me what my mother had decided.

"Mom, I'm humiliated. I just got a letter from Gaggy. She's not coming to the wedding. She says she has to stay home and take care of Mary. What am I going to tell Danny and his family? What am I going to tell my friends?"

She was very hurt and I couldn't blame her. How could I possibly explain to my daughter what I didn't understand myself?

"She came to my college graduation. Why can't she come to my wedding? I don't understand."

Neither did I, but I struggled to make some sense of my mother's behavior, for Maria's sake. "Mary is critically ill and just recently out of the hospital. Maybe she feels she should be with her."

Always the realist, my practical daughter retorted, "Mom, she could hire a nurse for the weekend. I'm her only granddaugher. She's the only grandmother I have. She should want to be here for the wedding."

Yes! She should, I thought, *but apparently she doesn't.*

As if reading my mind, Maria said, "Now that I recall, you paid for her trip to Philadelphia when I graduated from Villanova, didn't you?"

She wouldn't have come otherwise, would she? "Yes. I paid for her trip, Maria. But when she traded in my coach ticket for first class, she paid the difference herself."

"I didn't know that, Mom. You never told me."

"She told me Grandma had cautioned her that she couldn't fly coach. What would people think? But I paid for her hotel—for everything, Maria, everything except her first-class fare."

"What can I tell people, Mom?" Maria asked. "They're not going to understand."

No, I thought, *if we don't understand, how are total strangers expected to? It's unnatural for a grandmother not to want to come to her only grand-daughter's wedding.* I was very angry at my mother's blatant indifference to Maria's feelings, her rejecting attitude.

"Maria, just tell the people the truth. Tell everyone that she's not coming because it's your day. You'll be the star and she won't be." I knew in my heart that that was really why she had decided not to make the trip.

There was a gasp on the other end of the phone. "I couldn't say that, Mom."

"No, honey, I guess you can't. You have to be charitable, even though she hasn't been toward you. Just give everyone the same excuse that she gave you in the letter. Tell everyone that she had to stay home and nurse Mary. People should accept that and they probably won't ask any more questions."

"What if they do ask?"

"Then do what I've always done all my life when a tough question about my mother came up—ignore it and change the subject. They'll get the message." It was a lousy solution, but the only one I could come up with at the moment.

The upset that my mother's decision was causing Maria made me very angry. It reminded me of the important times in my life that my mother wasn't present for me. Because she was a celebrity, her absence would be noticed by everyone, questions would be asked, and Maria would have to explain. I felt it was unkind and unfair of my mother to treat Maria this way and I confronted her with my feelings. At first she insisted that Mary Coney needed her constant attention, that Mary couldn't be left for any length of time. I suggested that a practical nurse could be hired for the few days that she would be in Philadelphia and that I was sure Mary's insurance would cover that expense. But still she held firm to her decision, so I challenged her.

"What's the real reason you're not going, Mom? I know it's not just Mary. It's something else. What is it?"

She exploded. "If you must know, by the time I buy a new dress and pay for the plane fare I'll be spending thousands of dollars. It's too much money."

This time I didn't have the money to pick up the bill if she was too cheap to spend what it would cost for the trip, so the subject was dropped. We ended on a cool note. I was still very upset with her, and it was quite obvious she was with me.

My mother called a few weeks later. We hadn't spoken since our confrontation about the wedding. Now her voice was cold and businesslike, and she got right to the point.

"I've just received a letter from Liz Smith. She says rumors are flying all over New York that you are writing a tell-all book." Liz Smith, then a columnist for the *New York Post*, was an admirer and friend of my mother's. "Is this true?"

I didn't have the slightest idea what she was talking about. The last discussion I'd had with anyone about a book was in 1983, three years before, when I had told John Dodds that I couldn't write it. John was dead now. I was sure the rumor hadn't come from Lynn Nesbit, and I was equally sure that Liz Smith knew the source.

"Does Liz say where she got this information?"

My mother didn't answer but repeated her question. "Are you writing a tell-all book, Judy?"

"At the present moment, no, I am not writing a book." It was the truth. I purposely qualified it because I wanted her to know that I still reserved the right to write one in the future if I chose to.

"What do you want me to tell Liz Smith? I have to give her some kind of an answer." Her voice had an edge to it; I knew she was very angry. But, then, so was I.

"Tell her anything you want. It doesn't matter to me what you tell her."

Again a long silence followed by a terse, "Good-bye, Judy," as she hung up.

A few days later Liz Smith called me. She told me the rumor about the book and said she wanted to hear my side. When I asked her about the source she wouldn't tell me, but she did say the item would be announced by another columnist.

I told her what I had told my mother: "Liz, at this time I am not writing a book."

"That means that you will write one," she immediately responded.

"It merely means that I'm leaving my options open for the future."

A few days later the phone rang early in the morning. It was my aunt Polly Ann and she was very upset. A New York friend of hers had just called. There was an item in Cindy Adams's column in the *New York Post* that I was writing a tell-all book entitled *The Virgin Mary*.

I'd never heard of Cindy Adams and told Polly Ann that, assuring her that I was not writing anything.

"Then I won't even dignify this with a call to your mother," she replied. "There's no reason she has to know." It was obvious that my mother hadn't told her about our conversation.

It's not going to be possible to keep this from her, I thought; *her phone's probably ringing off the hook right now.* But I didn't voice this to my aunt. I just reassured her that I knew nothing.

Polly Ann's call was followed instantly by one from my mother's best friend, Josie Wayne. The news was traveling fast. Mal Milland, Ray Milland's wife, had just called Josie. "I told Mal I was sure it wasn't true, and that you would tell me the truth if I asked you," Josie explained.

"You're right, Josie, it isn't true. I don't know who Cindy Adams is, and I'm not writing a tell-all book." I was beginning to feel as if I were on the witness stand being cross-examined for a crime I didn't commit.

It wasn't long before the phone rang again. An old and good friend, Susan Kohner Weitz, was calling from New York. She knew the item wasn't true, she didn't have to ask, but she insisted that I defend myself by demanding a retraction. Even when I pointed out that a retraction would simply invite more publicity, she continued to suggest that I pursue my defense with a lawsuit. I reminded her that a sacrosanct rule that I grew up with was to ignore this kind of untrue item. For a Hollywood family, invasion of privacy from the press came with the territory and it had to be tolerated.

Susan's insistence prompted me to send an urgent message to my agent, Marie Stroud, who was vacationing in the Bahamas; maybe there was some recourse available to me that I hadn't considered.

There were more calls that day, mostly from friends on the East Coast, including Bunky Hearst. But the phone call that I was expecting from my mother never came. I was surprised and somewhat relieved. I presumed that she had accepted my earlier denial of the rumor and regarded the newspaper item as false. I should have known better.

When Marie Stroud returned my call late in the evening she told me that she would get in touch with Cindy Adams. Marie agreed with me that it was important to deny the story. We both knew that a retraction was too much to hope for, but I wanted my disapproval to go on record. Cindy Adams never returned or acknowledged Marie's calls or letters, but no one could say that we didn't try.

Maria was married at six in the evening on April 4 at St. John Vienney Catholic Church in Gladwyne, Pennsylvania. When she walked down the aisle on her father's arm she glowed with happiness. As she slipped the wedding ring on Danny's finger she said "Gotcha!" in a loud voice, bringing down the house.

Maria and I stood together in the coatroom of the Philadelphia Horticulture Center, where her reception was held, while I helped her change out of her wedding gown and into her pink-linen suit. Her bridesmaids surrounded us, and her new mother-in-law, Sue Dagit, sat nearby. I wanted everyone to disappear and leave the two

April 4, 1986. Maria is truly glowing as she enters her wedding reception with her husband, Daniel Dagit.

RICHARD REUSS/ AUTHOR'S COLLECTION

of us alone; there were too many distractions and so much that I wanted to say. I wanted my little girl back again all to myself, just for a brief moment. It was so hard to say good-bye, to let her go. Brushing a strand of hair away from her eyes, I looked into her glowing face. "I love you very much, sweetheart."

She smiled at me. "I love you, too, Mom."

We kissed and held each other for a moment. Then she moved out of my arms, away from me into the hallway where her husband, Danny, her father, and all her friends were waiting.

As I watched from the back of the crowd, she lingered, as her father had so many years before her, saying her good-byes. *She's very like him,* I thought. She kissed her friends and hugged her father, whispering in his ear for a moment. I heard him say, "We're crying a little bit. Jesus Christ, are we crying."

Maria and her new husband, who held her hand and led the way, approached their car. The Mercedes was festooned with toilet paper. As he climbed into the driver's side Danny yelled to the crowd, "I love the car. 'Bye, you guys." Maria waved through a soap-covered window as they drove out of the driveway, away on their honeymoon, dragging a large wire garbage can behind them that clanged loudly as it flew from side to side on the asphalt.

As I stood in the driveway, which was strewn with rose petals, it seemed to me that my daughter and I were always saying good-bye to each other. At Maria's graduation from St. Mary's Catholic School in Greenwich, I had stood as I did now, watching as she left with her father. And I remembered waving to her at the airport terminal as she disappeared into the plane that carried her east to college. Now, on this happy night, I watched her drive off to begin her new, married life 3,000 miles away from me. It was a bittersweet moment.

In an attempt to reconnect with my mother, I had promised that I would fix dinner for her on Mother's Day. My brother Peter went with me. When we turned onto Ambassador Avenue my mother's house was dark, but as I turned the key in the lock and opened the back door leading into the kitchen I smelled food cooking.

"What's that I smell?" Peter was behind me, his arms full of grocery bags.

"I don't know, Pete. Maybe Mom forgot that I was going to cook dinner for her. I haven't spoken to her in a while." I lifted the lid of a pot simmering on the stove to find oxtails, a favorite dish of my mother's. Another held potatoes cooking away. *Odd,* I thought. *Why would someone be preparing dinner when the plan was for me to cook on Mother's Day?*

The house was silent. Peter glanced at me. "What's going on?" he asked.

"I don't know, Pete. While I'm taking some of these groceries out, why don't you let Mom know we're here?"

A little later I walked up the curved staircase and down the hall into my mother's dressing room. It was twilight, and the shadows inside the room lent an eerie cast to everything. Peter seemed to have disappeared, and my mother wasn't in her dressing room.

I moved into the adjoining sitting room. Floor-to-ceiling mirrored closet doors reflected the room. I had expected to find her there at the round table. It was a favorite retreat where she would sit and sew for hours, but the room was dark in the twilight, everything still and quiet.

"Mom?" I called out.

She appeared in the doorway leading to her bedroom. She was wearing a Moroccan caftan, and as she came toward me she offered her cheek for a kiss.

"Happy Mother's Day," I said, kissing first one cheek and then the other as she turned her head.

"The same to you," she said. I hadn't seen her since I returned from Maria's wedding, and our greeting felt stiff and formal.

"What's dinner on the stove for? Did you forget I was cooking tonight?"

"I wasn't sure you remembered." Her tone of voice was distracted, distant, as if she were thinking of something else.

"Of course I did. I just brought all the groceries in a few minutes ago. Did you see Peter?"

She stared at me. "Yes. He's in visiting Mary."

"How's she doing?"

"She rests most of the time. The chemotherapy treatments make her very sick. But the doctor says that she's in remission."

"That's wonderful news," I replied. "It must be working." She was silent. "Is Mary strong enough to come join us for dinner tonight?"

"I think so. Sonya's here." Sonya Bertrand was a family friend. "She's staying in the guest room. She's taking care of Mary."

When Peter walked in, I thought that the two of them might want to talk privately, so I went downstairs to start dinner. Mom joined me shortly thereafter.

We were alone; my mother was arranging roses from the garden and I was chopping onions. The sharp snip of her scissors matched the rhythm of my knife blade as I brought it down on the board. The silence in the kitchen was all but suffocating. Her silence could still shut me out, as if I no longer existed. As a child I would do anything I had to to end that exclusion, go to any lengths to get back in her favor.

I knew something was definitely wrong with her tonight; she seemed very angry and she was taking it out on me. This was so familiar, and like a child, instead of talking and breaking the silence, I was becoming lost in it, not knowing how to end it or what had caused it.

Mercifully, the ring of the phone broke the deadly silence.

My mother answered. "Hello. . . . Just a minute. . . . It's for you." She held the phone out toward me. "Person-to-person, long distance." She was frowning.

"Happy Mother's Day, Mom," Maria chirped happily over the line.

"Thanks, honey." I took a deep breath; it was so good to hear her voice.

"That was Gaggy, wasn't it, Mom?" I glanced over at the sink.

My mother stood with her back to me, arranging the flowers in a tall crystal vase.

"Uh-huh!" I replied.

"I don't want to talk to her. That's why I called person-to-person. I'm still angry at her for not coming to my wedding."

The stiff set of my mother's shoulders told me that Maria's message had been received. "Okay." I changed the subject. "Thanks for the lovely flowers."

"I'm sending you a copy of the wedding video as soon as I can edit it. It's too long and boring. I'm also sending you another video of stills edited to music. I can't wait to see it."

I listened to Maria's enthusiastic voice talking about her new life and found I missed her even more than ever.

As we spoke, Mary Coney came into the kitchen and sat on the stool at the end of the counter. She looked thin and pale. I motioned that I was speaking to Maria. "Mary just came in." Mary threw her a kiss. "She sends you a kiss."

"How's she doing, Mom?"

"Fine, just fine," I exaggerated.

"I've got to run, Mom. I'm running up a huge bill. Tell Mary I send my love."

"I will."

" 'Bye. I love you, Mom."

"I love you, too, honey." And she was gone.

I turned to Mary as I put the phone back in its cradle. "Maria sends her love to you, Mary."

My mother whirled around and stood facing me, her eyes blazing.

"She sends her love to you, too, Mom," I quickly lied.

"She could have told me herself. Why did she call person-to-person?"

I could see that this was going to get out of hand if I wasn't careful. Mary just sat staring at the two of us. "I guess because she wasn't sure when I would be here. There's a three-hour time difference." Silence. She was waiting for more. "She had a lot of news she had to tell me. We had a lot to get caught up on. It was her nickel and she probably wanted to spend the time talking to me."

After a long pause she said, "You're right. She probably did." She turned, picked up the vase of flowers, and went out of the kitchen.

"How are you enjoying school, Judy?" Sonya Bertrand sat next to me at the long blue lacquered dining room table. The dinner was half over and the conversation was forced.

"It's very interesting, Sonya. There's a lot to absorb and the homework is pretty heavy, but I love it."

"You're going to school and working at the same time?"

"Yes. I do secretarial work, so I'm able to work around my school schedule." The dining room was quiet again, filled with tension. My mother had been silent for most of the meal.

"Who gave you the flowers, Mom?" The centerpiece was a generous arrangement of spring flowers.

"Tom sent them." It was highly unusual for Tom to send her flowers; they hadn't communicated in years. My mother's face was expressionless.

I don't remember who was talking or what the conversation was about, but I distinctly remember my mother's words to me; they stay in my memory to this day.

"You're a real survivor, aren't you?" My mother's voice cut through the conversation, leaving someone's sentence dangling in dead air.

I turned to see her glaring at me. The anger and fury in her look momentarily shocked me, taking my breath away. "Yes, Mom, I am. What's the matter? Don't you want me to survive?"

She sat rigidly in her chair, her hands in her lap, her body set for battle. "Well, so am I. And you're not going to take me down with you."

"I don't know what you mean by 'taking you down,' " I replied, "but if you don't know by now that I'm your friend, then you've missed the boat."

She stiffened. "You and Maria were talking about me. I heard you on the phone saying 'uh-huh' and 'uh-uh.' " Before I could answer she continued. "I know you were, and I know Maria didn't send me her love."

"No, she didn't, Mom."

"You lied, didn't you?" she challenged.

"Yes! I did. I didn't want you to feel bad and so I told you that she remembered you. The truth is that she's still angry with you for not coming to her wedding." I had kept my feelings inside for a month; it was time that she heard the truth. "Frankly, I don't understand either why you didn't come to her wedding. No explanation to Maria's in-laws could justify your absence. I tried and they were very polite. They said they understood, but I know they don't."

Her eyes flashed angrily. "I made it perfectly clear why I didn't go in the letter that I wrote to them. I wrote to Maria telling her I wouldn't attend." As if that put an end to it.

"You didn't even remember the day she was married, did you? You didn't call her to give her your best wishes. You never even sent a telegram. You just plain forgot, didn't you?"

She pushed her chair back from the table and spat out the words, "Yes! I did." Rising out of her chair and throwing her napkin down on the table, she yelled at me, "I want you to leave! I want you to get out of my house!" She left the dining room, pausing in the doorway. "Thank you for ruining my Mother's Day." Turning, she walked up the staircase and disappeared from view.

Peter stared at me across the table. After a few moments he pushed back his chair and went upstairs after her. No one spoke.

Mary finally broke the silence. "What brought that on?"

"I really don't know, Mary." My voice was shaking and tears were welling up. *Her Mother's Day,* I thought. *What about my Mother's Day?* I got up and started clearing away the dinner plates, the remains of my carefully prepared dinner.

I was in a daze as I filled the dessert cups with strawberry ice and placed fresh strawberries on top. *What do I do now? Do I leave the house in disgrace? What am I being punished for? For speaking my mind?* I put several cookies neatly around the plates, brought them out to the dining room, and served them to Sonya and Mary. Both women watched me in silence, neither knowing what to say.

After I cleared the rest of the table, I had reached a decision. The truth between my mother and myself was years overdue.

I kissed Mary. "I'm saying good-bye, Mary. The only time I will ever come back into this house again is to see you. I am finally cutting the umbilical cord." I left the dining room and headed up the stairs.

As I reached the top I heard voices within the darkened recesses of my mother's bedroom.

"She's just being used." It was my mother's voice coming from the open bathroom door.

I went in. "If you have something to say about me, you can say it to my face." I saw her reflection in the wall of mirrors above the double marble sinks. Tears were streaming down her cheeks. Peter was standing beside her. Her gaze flew from Peter to me. She hadn't expected me.

"You may leave, Peter." It was an order. She didn't want him as a witness.

But I did. "You don't have to, Peter. There isn't anything I have to say that you can't hear." My mother and I stood glaring at each other, neither flinching.

"I think I'll stay," Peter said, perching on the marble countertop.

"Then *I'm* leaving." My mother made a move toward me, but I blocked the door with my body.

"No!" Unknowingly I raised my right hand high on the doorjamb, my arm pressing with all its strength against the wood. I was an immovable object directly in her path. "We're going to have this out here and now, once and for all."

Her hand flew back, poised to strike me, stopping at the height of its swing. "I'll slap your face."

"I don't think that would be wise," I replied, standing my ground. Slowly she lowered her hand.

"You're blackmailing me." The tears were gone. Had I imagined them?

"How am I doing that?"

"If you write a book I'll sue you. You're sick." Finally it all began to make sense. She had never believed me when I told her that I wasn't writing a book. She had held on to her anger for almost two months.

"I already told you that I wasn't writing a book."

"I don't believe you," she replied. "You're sucking off of me." Her voice was choked with anger.

"Are you referring to my tuition for school? You write it off your income tax as a deduction. I'm a tax write-off."

"What about the apartment?" I knew that she was referring to the condominium that we had bought together.

"What about it?"

"You sublet it all the time that you were in New York and you paid me only five-hundred-dollars-a-month rent."

"That was our agreement. We split the cost of the down payment, leaving the title in your name. We agreed, at the time, that I would pay you five-hundred-dollars-a-month rent. You would get the tax write-off and we would both be building equity in a jointly owned apartment. I have no legal protection. If you died tomorrow the property would be part of your estate and I would lose my investment if I didn't have the cash to buy your half. I have paid you the agreed-upon rent for six years now."

"You received fifteen hundred dollars a month when you sublet it." She hadn't heard a word I'd said.

"All my furniture—everything I own was in it. Wasn't that worth something?"

"And who gave you that furniture?"

"Joe and I bought it from Grandma when we were married."

"I sent you most of your furniture from the set when the show ended." Where was all this coming from? I was having difficulty keeping my patience, but I persisted.

"Do you remember you called and told me that you didn't want to pay storage on the furniture, that it had already been amortized, and, if Joe and I wanted it, we would have to pay the freight from L.A. to New York, which we gladly did?"

Leaning forward, a few inches away from me, she suddenly lowered her voice. "I'll buy the apartment from you for ten thousand dollars."

"No!" I replied. "It's my home. I don't want to be in the streets." In a flash I knew she intended to sell.

"I'll sell it anyway." We were standing directly in front of each other, little or no separation between us.

"You do, and I'll call a press conference and tell the world that you are selling your daughter's home out from under her. Is that what you want? Is that the public image you want the world to see?" I challenged.

She stared at me. "I'll pay you ten thousand dollars for your half of the apartment."

"No," I answered. "I have an investment in it. It's my home, even though my name isn't on the deed. I won't sell it to you."

There we stood, mother and daughter arguing over possessions . . . things.

"These are material things we're talking about, Mom. Where's the love? You've never loved me, have you? You showed me a picture recently when you were six months pregnant with me and you told me that you were never so unhappy in all your life. That's not something you tell a child you love."

Her voice was cold. "And why shouldn't I be unhappy? Wouldn't you be if you were a movie star and the father of your child was a movie star and you couldn't have an abortion because it was a mortal sin?"

"Why did you keep me? I'll never understand that. You didn't want me. Why didn't you give me to a family who did?" This was the question I had always wanted to ask, one I dearly wanted an answer to.

"Leave this house. I never want to see you in my house again. Leave." She brushed past me in the doorway, pushing my arm out of the way as she did. I followed her into the dressing room. I refused to be dismissed that easily. There was a lifetime of things I wanted to say and she was going to hear me, whether she liked it or not.

It all came pouring out—all the years of hurt and abandonment, all the feelings of not belonging, of being an outsider in my own family, years of repressed emotions that couldn't be contained any longer. The floodgates were opened and the words flowed unchecked. There was no caution or even fear of retaliation, just that old familiar need to be acknowledged.

"I didn't ask to be born. All I ever wanted from you was to belong. To be accepted and loved. If you couldn't do that, why didn't you care enough about me to give me to a family that would have been good parents to me?"

She was pacing now, back and forth, between the dressing room and the bedroom. "You're using your psychology on me."

"Why don't you want me to learn something new, to be successful? I'm struggling to turn my life around and build a new career and future. Why aren't you pleased for me? Why don't you want to help me accomplish that?"

She paced even faster, enraged. Then she stopped. "I'm the only one that's been here for you. Your father wasn't and your stepfather wasn't."

Peter joined us. He had been standing in the shadows of the dressing room. I'd forgotten he was there. "She's right, Judy. She has been here for you."

"She gives that illusion," I replied. I turned toward my mother. "You kept me from knowing my father. Maybe we could have had a relationship. You didn't give me that chance. And as for my stepfather, you knew he was cruel to me and you detached yourself. You were never consistently there for me."

"How could you have known your father? We were both movie stars with careers to protect. It was a mortal sin."

It was as if something burst inside and I screamed at her. "I am not a mortal sin! I will not have you call me a mortal sin ever again!"

She looked surprised. "I never did."

"Yes! You did, in this very room, you once called my birth a mortal sin."

She pointed at me and said to Peter, who stood still and silent between us, "She's lying. I never said that."

"Yes, you did," I replied. "When you told me that you instructed Uncle Jack to change the wording in Grandma's will from 'issue' to 'child.' You didn't want it in the records that I was your issue."

She turned away and went into the bedroom, slamming the door after her.

Peter came over and put his arms around me, but I barely felt them. I was numb. Suddenly the door flew open and my mother came out, almost at a run. "Don't comfort her. You can do that outside. I want you out of my house."

I stood my ground. "Before I leave I want you to answer one question. Will you ever acknowledge to the world that I am your child, and that Clark Gable is my father?"

"No. I will never acknowledge what I consider a mortal sin—*my* mortal sin."

All hope vanished. My dream that one day my mother would stand beside me and publicly say "This is my child, she belongs to me. Her father was Clark Gable" would never become a reality. I knew that now.

I turned and started down the stairs toward the front door.

My mother followed close behind, still talking, taunting me. "I hope you do write the book so that I can sue you."

"You can't sue me for telling the truth," I retorted over my shoulder as I opened the front door. Outside the scent of night-blooming jasmine fulled my nostrils, bringing sudden tears to my eyes. That intoxicating smell always reminded me of my mother; she had planted jasmine at every house we had ever lived in.

Peter climbed into the front seat next to me, and as I drove away I took one last look in my rearview mirror. The lights on the iron gate and front door went off, leaving everything in darkness. That was the last time I was ever in my mother's home.

The year that followed was extremely busy. I was working full-time as a secretary for the vice-president of a computer company; financial aid was paying for my education and I had graduated with a bachelor of arts degree and was already well into my master's program at Antioch. I had also begun my internship at a clinic in Redondo Beach, seeing clients on Saturday. I had not spoken to my mother since Mother's Day 1986, so I was unaware that Mary Coney had left her home and was now living at Nazareth House, a Catholic retirement home.

In July 1987 I took Mary to lunch. I hadn't seen her since I had kissed her good-bye more than a year before, and I was shocked at how frail and sick she looked. She was painfully thin. The dark brown wig that hid the ravages of further chemotherapy treatments accentuated her pale white skin. I knew nothing about why she had left my mother's house and I waited for her to tell me herself.

"All I wanted to do with my life is work. I've worked for other people since I was nineteen years old. If I had thought I'd be where I am today at age seventy-four, I wouldn't have been able to go on." Her eyes filled with tears. "My worst crime was getting sick. I was fired because I was sick. I haven't told my family in Scotland. I've just told them I've retired. I didn't want to worry them."

I looked across the table at Mary and thought about her years with the family. She had cared for Peter and Christopher through their childhood and adolescence; she had cared for my mother faithfully and loyally for thirty-seven years. My mother's life was Mary's. Mary was always there when we needed her. She was the one who warned me not to lean on the doorbell when I was kissing Russ good-night; she "wouldn't want Mr. Lewis to come down." It was Mary who held Christopher's head while the doctor sewed his cut lip, and it was she to whom Peter came when he was in trouble. And when Grandma had had a long, hard day with a difficult client, it was Mary who massaged her neck to relax her, and Mary who nursed my mother when she was sick. It was to Mary that I entrusted my infant Maria when Joe and I vacationed in Mexico. She cleaned, ironed, shopped, cooked, answered fan mail; she was always there, dependable, steady, and reliable. "Mary will know," we would say. "Mary will take care of that. Just call Mary, she'll make all the arrangements."

"I was always a servant." Her words interrupted my thoughts. "I spent every holiday alone. I was never a part of your family." But she had been family to me.

Mary told me that her disease was no longer in remission. Her doctor had ordered additional treatment along with her regular chemotherapy sessions. When she arrived at my mother's house after the first treatment, she began to shake from head to foot. That was all she remembered.

Two weeks later she woke up to find a strange woman leaning over her, a nurse with the board of health. My mother had arranged for her to visit and take care of Mary, but she hadn't called Mary's doctor. In fact, he knew nothing about her condition. When she missed a scheduled appointment, he called the house and was told that Mary wasn't well and couldn't come to the phone.

When she finally saw her doctor, he discovered that she had fractured her ankle, possibly during a fall that she didn't remember. He diagnosed an allergic reaction to the new medication and told her if he had been notified immediately he could have treated her with no loss of memory or discomfort.

When I asked her to clarify what she meant when she said that she was fired, she told me she heard that my mother wanted her to leave her house. "It came to me through the grapevine," she said. "Mrs. Lewis wanted me to go to St. John of God's."

I thought she might have been exaggerating. I couldn't believe that my mother would be that heartless, that she would put Mary out of her home when she was so ill. My mother had taken such wonderful care of Grandma, and Mary had been so good to my mother it never occurred to me she wouldn't care for her. I know it hadn't occurred to Mary either. I know that Mary thought she would always have a home with her Mrs. Lewis.

"What is St. John of God's?" I had never heard of it.

"A retirement home for the sick and elderly," she answered.

She told me that she had confronted my mother, while her close friend, Rosemary Ashley, was present. "Do you know what you're doing to me, Mrs. Lewis?" she had asked. "Why do you want me to leave? Why do you want me to go to St. John of God's?"

"Because that's where Father Devlin and Mr. Belzer died," my mother replied.

"I got up from my chair and stood in front of her. 'I'm not dead and I'm not dying. I'm alive.' Your mother turned on her heel and left the room without another word spoken between us.

"Later that day, when we were alone, she was angry. 'How dare you embarrass me in front of people like that. I don't like that.' And I told her, 'I don't like being fired because I got sick.' I asked her again, 'Do you realize what you're doing? Why are you doing this to me?'

"Finally she answered my question. 'Because you're a burden. You've been a burden for a year.'" Tears were rolling down Mary's cheeks.

There was nothing left for Mary to do but leave. First, however, she had to find someplace that she could afford. Once she had gotten sick her salary had stopped, and although she had some disability insurance, those payments had already run out. Fortunately, she had been very frugal and she had some savings, so Rosemary and her husband, Bill Ashley, were able to arrange for her to live at Nazareth House, another Catholic retirement home. On the morning Mary left my mother's house, she paid the gardener to help her move her boxes and suitcases. My mother was asleep that morning, but she had left Mary a good-bye note outside her door. When I heard this, it reminded me of the many notes I had received in lieu of live expressions of emotion. Later, to her distress, Mary learned from friends that my mother had told people Mary had just sneaked out of the house. "I told them that was a damn lie. That's the first time I've ever used that word."

On the way back to the retirement home she said sardonically, "Thirty-seven years of service and not even a gold watch." We both laughed.

"Not even two weeks' severance pay?" I asked.

"Not even that. So much for the golden years."

"I guess we're both alike, aren't we?" I told her. "You were dismissed because you could no longer serve her. I was dismissed because she thought I was writing a book, telling truths she didn't want anyone to hear."

"Maybe she did us both a favor," Mary replied. "I don't think the story's over yet, but we can't be hurt anymore."

Sadly, Mary's physical suffering was also not yet over. When I heard that she had taken a turn for the worse and wasn't expected to live another forty-eight hours, I called Peter, who called our mother.

Later Peter told me, "When I told her, she said to me, 'Why are you bothering me with this? We all have to die.' I thought she'd want to know, or at least allow me my sad feelings about Mary."

He was confused by her behavior. I was not. I had seen this dispassionate detachment before.

Forty-eight hours came and went, and still Mary didn't die as the doctor had predicted. Something was keeping her spirit alive, fighting for survival. I sat with my face inches from hers, stroking her forehead and talking to her; she had moments of recognition but then she would slip away again. Mary Coney lived for two weeks in this condition. No one could understand how or why. The last few hours before she died she seemed to be struggling to tell me something—what, I will never know.

The funeral was at the Church of the Good Shepherd in Beverly Hills, where Mary had attended daily mass and received communion for the last twenty-some years. By the time Peter, his second wife, Corinne, and I arrived, Mom, Chris, and his wife, Linda, had already gone into the church.

As I listened to the pastor's eulogy about Mary's devotion to her Church and her God, I kept thinking that he didn't really know her or of her devotion to all of us, especially my mother. One of her last remarks to Rosemary was, "Mrs. Lewis owes me an apology." Perhaps she remained alive waiting for that apology, but it never came.

Sitting in the church that day, I realized I would also never get the apology I was waiting for from my mother. I would never hear her say "I'm sorry I kept you from your father." She had already admitted she would never publicly claim me as her real daughter, something I had been wishing for all my life. Yet I still held a childlike fantasy, way in the depths of my heart, that at the very end, if I were to become ill, even close to death, my mother would finally love me and take care of me just as she had done for her mother.

My fantasy died with Mary, and on her funeral day I finally realized that if my mother could be that heartless with Mary, she could be so with me, too. Never mind a deathbed reconciliation of any kind during our lifetime. If I wrote my book, as Mary had urged me to do ("You owe it to yourself," she said), and claimed my identity by claiming my father and mother, I would have no family of origin.

I was standing at the side door after the mass was over, waiting for Mary's casket, covered in a simple white cloth, to be carried to the hearse when my mother approached me.

"Hello, Judy," she said. Her voice was ice. I turned around and faced her. Her eyes bore into mine, but for the first time the intensity of her look held no power over me.

"Hello, Mom," I replied and returned her gaze. We stood there, silent, unmoving for what seemed a long time until the pallbearers lifted Mary's casket. I turned and followed it through the door and out into the bright California sunshine, leaving my mother behind me.

That was the last time we saw or spoke to each other.

EPILOGUE:
A HOUSE OF MY OWN

In May 1988, Tom Lewis died of cancer. When I went to Ojai for the rosary service and drove by our old house, which Tom had sold the previous year, I had mixed feelings, but mostly sadness. His name was still on the sign attached to the iron statue of a little boy that I remembered from my childhood. In the past I had fantasized that Tom might will the house to Peter, Christopher, and me, and we could then share it with our own families. But that had been a wishful, unfulfilled dream, which made me even sadder.

In September of that year I received my master's degree in clinical psychology. I continued my internship in an office suite where Joy Schary, Jill's younger sister, had her successful private practice. In June 1989 I signed the contract to write this book.

My greatest happiness came on March 22, 1991, when Maria gave birth to her son, Michael Joseph Dagit. When I saw my grandchild sleeping peacefully in his hospital bassinet I couldn't believe the joy I felt; my child's child was so perfect.

Later, sitting beside Maria while she slept, I thought of my own birth in hiding and fear, with no father present or ever to be known to me, and a mother who would leave me. I rejoiced that the pattern had been broken. Danny had stood by Maria's side throughout her labor and delivery and together they welcomed their son into the world.

I stayed with Maria and her family for the next three weeks, helping her recover her strength. As I watched Danny change Michael's first diaper I thought how natural an act of bonding for father and

The expression on my face shows how thrilled I was to finally achieve a lifelong desire—my Bachelor of Arts degree from Antioch University.
AUTHOR'S COLLECTION

son. When Maria gently guided her newborn to her breast or stroked his tiny hand I was reminded of my own forgotten feelings when she was newborn. We laughed together as we gave Michael his first bath, I holding his squirming, wet body and Maria sponging him with warm water as he loudly squalled his disapproval; I couldn't help but wonder who had held me for my first bath.

Three months later Maria and I took turns sleeping on a cot beside his hospital crib when he had surgery for pyloric stenosis. When

1991. My grandson Michael Joseph Dagit's christening day. Left to right: Joe Tinney, Maria Dagit, me, Michael Joseph, and Danny Dagit.

1992. Michael's first-birthday party. Michael with his maternal grandparents.

Michael cut his first teeth I took care of him, while Maria and Danny were on their sailboat having a much-needed vacation.

A year later, I recorded my grandson's first birthday, this time on video. His paternal and maternal grandparents were there, along with his parents, aunts and uncles, and young cousins. In January, ten months after his birth, his only great-grandmother, Loretta, had written saying that she had made a New Year's resolution to tell him that she loved him and that she had bought some stock in his name.

As I look back on the years that my mother and I have been estranged, I realize they have been the benchmark for my future. During those years I have been meticulously searching for and finding those missing parts of myself that had been lost or taken away. They have been forged into a solid and enduring foundation for a house of my own, an authentic self.

During the last three years writing this book and reconstructing my personal history, I've experienced many illuminating, often painful, and, at times, ultimately healing insights about my life. More often than not I was genuinely surprised, not only at my unresolved anger and ongoing grief, but at the intense repression of feelings and events that I thought I had resolved, only to discover there was much more work to be done. And my dreams were so rich and incisive, often clarifying with great humor and delicious puns what my conscious mind was unable to perceive. What my dreams and mind didn't reveal, my body did. While working on one particularly difficult chapter my right shoulder began to give me such intense pain that my doctor ordered me to stop writing, wear a sling, and keep my arm immobile. A week later, after an enlightening psychotherapy session, my arm returned to normal, the pain instantly released.

There are running throughout my family history themes and parallels that aren't so subtle, and my years of training as a therapist have enabled me to view my life now in a different way.

My grandmother Gladys was abandoned when her mother,

Fanny Royal, died. Almost simultaneously, her father left her, giving her and her two sisters to relatives because he couldn't care for them adequately. The fact that he came back to claim his children years later was inconsequential. Those early psychic traumas had a profound effect on little Gladys, leaving a lasting impression that children can be given to others and that fathers vanish.

When it came time for Gladys to marry, she chose a man like the father who had abandoned her, and when she was left alone with children to support, she did with the two youngest, Gretchen and Jack, what her father had done with her—she gave them to others, once again out of financial necessity.

Gretchen was four (a year younger than Gladys was when her mother died) when she went to live with Mae Murray and her husband. Gladys's sister Carlene also sent her daughter away with Gretchen. Gladys herself said, "This was a wonderful opportunity for a four-year-old to live in a beautiful home and be given lovely things, things that her mother wasn't able to provide for her. I was at the time financially embarrassed." She believed that Gretchen would be better off with the things that money and power could give than if she remained at home with her family.

When it came time for her son, Jack, to choose another family, taking that family's name for his own, Gladys was repeating the lessons she had been taught. She had already introduced her daughter to the lavish lifestyle of a movie star, which Gretchen would later adopt as her own. So, too, did her son adopt a mother and father because they gave him privileges he couldn't have had with his mother. He was heir to his father and grandfather's legacy of abandonment by leaving his mother, and to his mother's legacy of choosing wealth over filial love.

My birth was the inconvenient consequence of my mother's love affair with my father. Fear of scandal prevented her from claiming me; so, out of necessity, she gave me to the nuns in the orphanage. My mother abandoned me until she could, like a movie, rewrite her life script and choose a more appropriate time to bring me back into the picture as an adopted child.

When it was time for my daughter, Maria, to go to college, I couldn't compete with her father's offer of an expensive education at an eastern university. So, following the family pattern, I gave Maria to her father, believing he could provide her with substantially more privileges than if she stayed at home with me, not realizing the value of my own parental love.

In my family the one who had the most money always held the most power, and that was usually my mother, Grandma's "little money-maker." But my birth didn't follow my mother's tradition. I wasn't a "little money-maker" for my mother. Although my father was an extremely wealthy movie star, he did not offer any financial support for me, even though my mother discreetly arranged a way for him to contribute, which she must have naturally expected him to do. Instead, my father abandoned his daughter just as my grandfather had abandoned my mother, and she was left with the burden and financial responsibility of an illegitimate child to raise alone.

I can only imagine her shock and fury at my father's irresponsibility and I understand how she must have felt. She would only be human if her repressed feelings toward her own absent father were transferred on to my father. Once more a piece of history seemed to be repeating itself: The father she had wished for as a child, one who would "take care of her" (and by now she must have equated money with love), she hoped to recreate. Clark Gable could give their daughter what she never had. Again she was disappointed. He not only didn't take care of his daughter, but less than a year after her birth he began a love affair with Carole Lombard, whom he later married. I can understand how devastated she must have been, blaming not only him for his desertion of both of us, but also herself, feeling responsible. She herself told me that the greatest regret in her life was that she didn't get Clark Gable to marry her.

When my mother's father finally did return, twenty-two years after he had vanished, possibly to claim his family, as Gladys's father had done before him, he was kept away by his own mother and made to promise that he wouldn't embarrass them by his presence. It was he who needed care, and once again my mother paid. How she must have hated supporting the man who had caused such pain for her, her mother, and her siblings. It only reinforced her already strongly internalized image of a worthless man taking money from a woman and giving nothing in return.

My mother replaced her absent father with God, Who was everything he was not. He was omnipresent, omnipotent, and omniscient. It wasn't important that He didn't always answer her prayers because she knew all she had to do was submit to His will and He would take care of her as no man had ever done before. She believed that He would not fail her if she was true first to Him and then to herself. The more she tried to make decisions on her own, the less her Father would do. "Thy will, not mine, be done," she often said.

Instead of giving me my father, my mother replaced him with God. She baptized me in the Catholic Church and taught me how to be God's child just like her. Unlike my mother, I had never known my own father, but I was always aware of the presence of his absence. That never disappeared. When I missed my own father or when my stepfather was unkind and distant, it was only natural that I turned to God. On several occasions as a child, I stayed up all night waiting for Him to appear, as I was sure He would, so that we could discuss my problems. He was my idealized father. I, too, believed that if I was a good child, God would take care of me since my own father didn't.

It is said that one lives the life of one's birth. I am a firm believer in that premise, for my beginning fetal home within my mother's womb was one of tight restriction where I could not feel comfortable because I was not welcome. In order to disguise her pregnancy, my mother bound her clothing tightly around her. I must assume this was the case for at least five months, perhaps longer, while she was starring in *The Crusades*. This had a traumatizing effect on her fetus.

Then, at the moment of birth as I gasped for oxygen, my mother's hand stifled my cry, choking my voice back into my infant throat, suffocating life's breath with her palm. She meant to smother the reality of my existence because she feared discovery. From the moment of my birth I inherited the memory of her shame and guilt.

She left as soon as she was able, abandoning me to the care of strangers. It is believed that an infant bonds with the mother in the very first days of life, and even if the mother leaves and returns infrequently, as mine did, her familiarity still remains with the infant. This fact alone would explain the question that I have so often asked myself: When did I know that my mother was my real mother? I have now come to believe it was a truth that I always knew at a primitive level.

But it is impossible for me to know what kind of care I received during the first highly crucial nineteen months of my life. I am quite sure I made no cries for hunger or for attention; they would go unheeded. I believe I knew I mustn't make a mess or display anger for I'd displease, and I'm convinced that I lay very still asking for nothing, as I had in my womb, holding on to my feelings, not infringing upon my world, fearful of annihilation if I asserted myself. The mother who had carried me had vanished; there must be something missing and wrong with me if she left so abruptly.

When I was finally brought into her home as an adopted child, my sense of having a self, independent of others, was emerging; I needed reliable and positive mirroring from my mother to differentiate my true self. But my mother saw me as a mirror of herself. What better gratification object could she have than her own child upon whom she could impose her feelings and desires. I was at her disposal and dependent upon her for my very existence, and I would do anything I could to avoid losing her. She could see herself mirrored in my love and admiration, confirming for her what she had missed in her own childhood. When I became too difficult or demanding she could abandon me, as she had before, to another stranger. This doesn't preclude the fact that she loved me; she did, but always on the condition that I present my "false self."

Instead of developing the experience of my own feelings and emotions, I developed what my mother needed, adapting to her narcissistic needs instead of my own, mirroring her emotions and repressing mine. As my nurse Margaret so aptly put it, "You were always everyone's darling, just everyone's darling, doing what you were told." The only negative emotion she said I showed was fear.

When I did attempt to display my emotions, my anger, and pushed over the coffee table at age four, I was ignored. My true self remained noncommunicative and I learned instead to communicate indirectly with my mother, mirroring her communication with me. I carried that mode into my adult life.

That is why I never expressed how important her presence at the screening of "The Outlaws" was to me, hoping the invitation was sufficient, which of course it wasn't, for she had her own personal agenda. And again, when I wore the loose-fitting dress to announce my pregnancy, I hoped for some positive mirroring from my mother but received none, once again ignored.

I think my final effort came on the occasion of Maria's wedding. When my mother refused to attend, saying the trip was too expensive, it resonated those old and all too familiar feelings of abandonment, always because of money and out of necessity.

This time I didn't accept her excuse, nor did I believe her, for she had ample enough financial resources to make the trip. I most especially didn't want my daughter to suffer the same painful feelings that I had felt. When she persisted in her excuse and abandoned Maria anyway, leaving me helpless to prevent my daughter's embarrassment, I knew I had to end this pattern. I had to separate finally from my mother.

When my mother married Tom Lewis, she once more denied me a father by ignoring Tom's offer to adopt me; so another family pattern and genetic thread was woven into the fabric of my life. I was lent the surname of Lewis, as my grandfather was lent his surname of Young, without benefit of legality. This might have been convenient for others, but it offered no entitlement for me, and that legacy has persisted throughout my life.

When my half-brothers were born, I knew they were authentic and I was not; my tenuous relationship with my stepfather was fractured by their arrival. My place in my family system was now that of the intruder. My position was precarious and so I had to gather all my energies, giving those around me what they wanted, trying extra hard to be "everybody's darling" so that I wouldn't risk expulsion.

The Christmas that I sneaked downstairs to see the tree was so devastating to me, and remained in my memory for so long with such clarity, because I believed I had been "bad," that I had disappointed my mother and ruined her Christmas. In truth I wasn't responsible for the happiness or well-being of my family, and I wouldn't have been abandoned and sent away for the least little infraction. The fact that my mother *did* keep me when it would have been easier for her not to cannot be ignored. But because of my very early psychic traumas, my ability to order experience was damaged and my version of reality was unreal and distorted. My early responses at self-preservation kept me always feeling uneasy, helpless, and guilty.

When I *was* sent away to finishing school, I was a sexually emerging adolescent, and my mother viewed me as competition. It was advantageous to remove me from the family; her marriage was shaky and Tom's behavior toward me was disruptive.

In some ways my mother saw me as her echo. She viewed my relationship with Russ as similar to hers with Grant Withers (she was my age when she married him). Thus, my sexuality was hers; she did think then that I was pregnant, just as she had been with me.

By sending me away to school she confined me in an unwelcome environment and constricted my sexuality with Russ and my freedom in New York. After I accommodated my mother's needs, she didn't reciprocate as promised; she stalled our wedding plans. When I finally broke my engagement to Russ, she had symbolically achieved what her own mother was unable to do with her—annul a marriage. All this was done "because Russ wasn't good enough for me," just as Grant Withers hadn't been for my mother.

I realize now that when I married Joe I was once again accommodating my mother's needs more than my own. I didn't know what my authentic feelings and needs were then; they lay buried in my unconscious. All I knew was my mother's script, written for my enactment. When my true feelings bubbled to the surface on my wedding day, they were swiftly anesthetized so the "false self" could go on with the ceremony.

From the very moment of my birth and throughout my life my

mother has stifled my voice, feelings, sexuality, early efforts for an acting career, and all knowledge about my father. When Joe Tinney finally told me that I was Clark Gable's daughter, I didn't ask my mother for the truth because I knew she wouldn't tell me. Fearful of losing her love, I told myself that I couldn't really know who my father was until *she* told me willingly, until she gave him to me.

At a very deep level I believed that I could have only what my mother gave me, and that applied to many things throughout my life. I couldn't have my father, a husband, an acting career, or a second child unless she publicly legitimized me by being present to acknowledge me. No matter what I accomplished, her detachment lessened both the reality and my own personal sense of self-esteem. I was never quite sure whether I had achieved what I had on my own merits. Still attached to her, unable to separate, I remained vulnerable to her.

What was common knowledge to the world and to everyone who was even remotely connected with me was uncommon knowledge to me. My mother had successfully stifled everyone else's voice as well as my own. She kept that knowledge and the power it gave her to herself.

She must have seen the truth as a weapon to be used against her; she was, after all, a product of her early childhood environment. But the Hollywood of the fifties was no longer the Hollywood of the thirties and forties. Attitudes had changed over the decades. Many years later when she thought I was writing a book and claiming my identity, she accused me of blackmailing her. It never occurred to her to tell me the truth when there was still an opportunity to seek out my father and have the possibility of pursuing a relationship with him, something she had never had with her own father. Even though her sister Polly Ann begged her to tell me, and when she refused didn't speak to her for some time, she still kept the truth from me, rationalizing that if I knew, I'd call off my wedding.

In the Hollywood of today a child can be born to unmarried movie stars and the public accepts them for the human beings they are and lets the situation go at that. This is a far more realistic world than the one I was born into; in this world I could have known my father and he me, Maria could have had her grandfather, and there would have been no regrets.

Unfortunately there are regrets, too many of them. I regret the waste of parts of my life that I can never recapture and the losses I will never regain as the result of keeping my mother's secret and living her lie.

What I don't regret is giving birth to my daughter and recognizing and ending some of the familial patterns before I unwittingly passed them on to her. Divorce is a traumatic experience for any child, but Maria does have a loving mother and father in her life, and for that I'm very grateful. She also knows who her grandfather is — too late, unfortunately, to have known him, but the lie is no longer

1992. My daughter, Maria, with Michael.
AUTHOR'S COLLECTION

passed on to another generation. My grandsons will know about their great-grandfather; that's their right.

Cumulative latent feelings cannot stay repressed forever, and when the explosion between my mother and me finally happened on Mother's Day it marked our final separation. What should have taken place gradually, when I was very young, had built up and been delayed all those many years.

Finally, I had refused to accommodate her in the old way, that of the compliant daughter grateful to the benevolent mother who kept and took care of her. I had finally come to terms with my true self, no longer hidden in the unconscious, and I spoke my truths to my mother for the first and final time in my life.

When she thought she could no longer stifle me, she was furious that I was alive to tell the truth, and her true self raged at me for being a survivor. As she put it, "You're not going to take me down with you." In her narcissistic mirror the only way I was entitled to live and breathe was to keep her secret and live her lie.

This was no longer acceptable to me; her "mortal sin" is neither *my* shame nor *my* life. I had to claim what is mine, separate from my mother, and live my own life.

I have no way of knowing if my mother and I will ever reconcile; it seems unlikely now that I have told the truth about our relationship. Only time holds the answer. And only time can tell the consequences of my publicly revealing my story to the world and finally claiming my true identity. If there is to be a reunion at all, it will be between two women—I will never again be the compliant child. Perhaps I am, in the final analysis, true to my heritage; wishing for the perennial happy Hollywood ending when this is one story that can't be packaged so neatly. As I said before, only time will tell.

When people ask me, as they are bound to, why I wrote this book, and why now, while my mother is still alive, I will answer: because I *had* to; I had no other choice. Now that I have told my story, and my existence and the facts of my life are truly common knowledge, I can go on with my life a whole human being. For that I have no regrets.

July 13, 1993. Maria gave birth to Gregory Daniel Dagit. Top: The first time Michael saw his new brother, whom I am holding. Bottom: Michael giving Gregory his pacifier.

Summer 1993. With my fiancé, Andre Willieme, on the beach, with the beautiful Santa Barbara hills behind us.

INDEX